PRESENCING AND SPIRITUAL DIRECTION

UNCOVERING SACRED STILLNESS

Copyright © Chris Blakeley, 2025

Published 2025 by Waverley Abbey Trust, Waverley Abbey House, Waverley Lane, Farnham, Surrey GU9 8EP, UK. Registered Charity No. 294387. Registered limited company No. 1990308.

The right of Chris Blakeley to be identified as the author of this work has been asserted by him in accordance with the Copyright, Designs and Patents Act 1988, sections 77 and 78.

All rights reserved. No part of this publication may be reproduced, stored in a retrieval system, or transmitted, in any form or by any means, electronic, mechanical, photocopying, recording or otherwise, without the prior permission in writing of Waverley Abbey Trust.

Unless otherwise indicated, all Scripture references are from the NIV, New International Version® Anglicised, NIV® Copyright © 1979, 1984, 2011 by Biblica, Inc.® Used by permission. All rights reserved worldwide.

KJV: King James Version.

MSG: Scripture quotations marked MSG are taken from *THE MESSAGE*, copyright © 1993, 2002, 2018 by Eugene H. Peterson. Used by permission of NavPress. All rights reserved. Represented by Tyndale House Publishers, Inc.

NKJV: Scripture taken from the New King James Version®. Copyright © 1982 by Thomas Nelson. Used by permission. All rights reserved.

ESV: The ESV® Bible (The Holy Bible, English Standard Version®). ESV® Text Edition: 2016. Copyright © 2001 by Crossway, a publishing ministry of Good News Publishers. The ESV® text has been reproduced in cooperation with and by permission of Good News Publishers. Unauthorized reproduction of this publication is prohibited. All rights reserved.

VOICE: The Voice Bible Copyright © 2012 Thomas Nelson, Inc. The Voice™ translation © 2012 Ecclesia Bible Society All rights reserved.

NRSVACE: New Revised Standard Version Bible: Anglicised Catholic Edition, copyright © 1989, 1993, 1995 the Division of Christian Education of the National Council of the Churches of Christ in the United States of America. Used by permission. All rights reserved.

TLB: The Living Bible copyright © 1971 by Tyndale House Foundation. Used by permission of Tyndale House Publishers Inc., Carol Stream, Illinois 60188. All rights reserved.

WEB: World English Bible, public domain.

Every effort has been made to ensure that this book contains the correct permissions and references, but if anything has been inadvertently overlooked, the Publisher will be pleased to make the necessary arrangements at the first opportunity. Please contact the Publisher directly.

Concept development and editing by Waverley Abbey Trust.

Design and typesetting by Richard Lyall Design.

Printed and bound in the UK.

Paperback ISBN: 978-1-78951-539-8

To the late Dom Nicholas Seymour, former Spiritual Director and Guestmaster at the Abbey of Our Lady and St John in Alton, Hampshire, who showed me what a life of Love really means in practice.

Thank you, Father Nick!

...Destined to become a classic for spiritual directors. In our culture increasingly dominated by functional thinking, Chris' experience of leading others into a somatic knowing of the Divine presence is refreshing. This is a deep treatment of pausing, stilling, breathing and grounding ourselves, enabling a 'gathered' state of awake attention that better prepares us to listen, notice and receive more of God. Active surrender then enables us to trust, follow and abide in Christ, which is how we live 'life to the full'. Full of insights and helpful questions to use, this is a book that has emerged from many years of practice. As a former directee of Chris, I can heartily recommend his approach.

PAUL VALLER
Formerly Chair of The London Institute For Contemporary Christianity

---

I found this book profoundly helpful in reminding me how the practice of 'presencing' helps me return to God with all my heart, soul, mind and strength. It gently encourages us to notice our own tendency to strive and how 'presencing' helps us return to the humble posture of 'being', allowing God's presence to work in and through us. The book, like its author, is gentle, lyrical and authentic, full of practical 'how to' guidance and rich with Godly wisdom from the wellspring of life and love.

KAREN BROWN
Chair of The London Institute For Contemporary Christianity and formerly Director of Tearfund

Chris recalls us to some fundamentals of the spiritual life and distils what is essential if we are to align with God's good and beautiful purposes for our unique selves and be directed aright. Such fundamentals include for example pausing, breathing and noticing (and each reader will have their own list which particularly resonate); deceptively simple, strikingly communicated and wholly convincing – read, mark and inwardly digest!

MIKE HARRISON
Bishop of Exeter

Having listened to Chris Blakeley's stimulating lectures and class presentations for several years, I see this book as the prayerful culmination of a life's work in exploring the depths of the human soul and its connectivity to the Divine. *Presencing and Spiritual Direction* will aid spiritual formation and interior growth for any novice, student, seeker of truth, or spiritual director.

JENNIFER CAMPBELL
Programme Leader, Spiritual Formation, Waverley Abbey College

For the spiritually curious, this book offers a winsome invitation to explore one's internal landscape and discover pathways to deeper integration. For those who long for a deeper walk with, and dare I say union with Christ, Chris offers to pilot our soul boats, leading us to deep waters and encouraging us to surrender to the sea. For those who accompany the souls of others, Chris's lived insights into the fields of spiritual formation, depth psychology and somatic work offer us frameworks and tools to enable us to be used by God as a life-giving presence to others.

JILL WEBER
Head of House of Prayer, Waverley Abbey.

It has been a delight to see the transformative experience of so many who have journeyed spiritually with Chris Blakeley over the years through our retreat work at The Royal Foundation of St Katharine. This book opens up Chris's practice and work drawing on so many different dimensions of spiritual, psychological and practical wisdom. The art of presencing is a practical path of opening up an abundant life in the midst of the busyness that most of us experience day to day. I think this book will be a great help to all those involved in offering and receiving spiritual accompaniment in all its different forms.

ROGER PREECE
Master, The Royal Foundation For St Katherine

I have found this book profoundly helpful and insightful. Chris writes with a wonderfully accessible wisdom on how to deepen one's inner journey and experience flow in the midst of the demands of daily living. For anyone desiring a more contemplative approach to their faithful following, seeking the deep that calls to deep - this book could be just what is needed. There is a wonderful mix of the profound and poetic, drawn from an author who has clearly practiced what he is now putting to paper. This book addresses spiritual formation not simply from a conceptual, head-knowing approach but draws on the deeper understanding that emerges from our hearts, bodies and inner-attention. I hope the gift of Chris' writing helps many wake up and begin to find their way home to themselves and Christ within.

PAUL WENHAM
General Director, Ashburnham Christian Trust and Founder, Enneagram UK

How do I live life to the full? How do I become more Christ-like in character? As a spiritual director, how can I support others to be all that God has called them to be? If these questions engage you, then journey through this book, based on Chris' extensive experience. This is not so much a book to read, but a book to experience and relish. Let the practical guidelines and wisdom it contains transform you and your practice as a spiritual companion.

ANN LEITCH, OMS
Spiritual Director and formerly Strategic Programme Director, Suffolk Diocese.

ACKNOWLEDGEMENTS

ONE REASON THIS BOOK has been written is quite simply because my publisher, Joy, asked me to! I am so grateful for her invitation and patient support along the way. Written as a support to the work here at Waverley Abbey on spiritual formation, it has had me commit uncomfortably to paper what flows so freely in the rich experience, rawness, and reciprocity of learning in the group room. So, my gratitude therefore goes to the many, many people who, whether in a 1:1 or a group setting, have had the courage to open up their hearts to share the sacred mystery of what it really takes to live a life to the full. If you are reading this, you know who you are. Thank you!

Alongside this, particular thanks go to those who have in one way or another transferred their wisdom to me to inform what is shared here. All of us who work in this field know full well that we stand on the shoulders of giants and it is a great privilege to be able to use this space to acknowledge at least a few of those who have helped me do so. This must begin with all the Benedictine Brothers at Alton Abbey, who taught me so much over so many years, just by their constant lived example of what it takes to lead the spiritual life. And most of all to the late Dom Nicholas Seymour, who was my spiritual guide and mentor for the most formative years of my life.

Then there are all those in the Waverley Learning and Crossroads Retreats Community who have been with me on a constant journey of exploration and deep enquiry on our regular annual retreats – some of you for over 25 years! With special acknowledgement to Graham Bailey, John Lavers, Jeremy Clare, Mike Clargo, Elisabeth and Richard Toothill, Paul Lambert, Liz West, Jacqui Zanetti, Hilary Nickell, Jim Wright, Chris Spray, Daphne Clifton, Jeremy Cox, Karen West, Tony Woollett and the late, dearly missed, Richard Garnett and Zena Johnson.

A special thank you flows to those who have contributed directly to the formation in me of some of the wisdom practices that are described in this book. This includes Tim Jeffery, Jani Rubery, Calvin Germain, Paul Redwood, Corina Grace, Tim Richardson, Jennifer Campbell, David Wise, Virginia Luckett, and my current spiritual director, Julian Maddock. Thanks also to Elaine Delay for being my writing buddy in this work. Alongside this is all the learning I have received from the 'Inner Work' retreats led by Russ Hudson and Jason Stern and the tremendous blessing of the Ignatian exercises, led by Roger Dawson at St Beunos. My gratitude also flows to Aneurin Owen, Adrian Botwright, the Community of Ynys Enlli and my lifelong friend John Whitley for walking alongside me in my recent exploration of 'Heraith'.

Finally let me express the very deepest gratitude to three extraordinary people without whom nothing in this book could have come to be. To my former wife, Karen, who taught me how to think and write and teach and attend critically to what really matters in life. To Mary, who has stood unfailingly with me though all the struggle of recent years and has been a constant source of encouragement, deeply attentive feedback and grounded guidance in the writing of this. And last, but never least, to my other constant spiritual companion in all this work, Karen Stefanyszyn, for being alongside me all the way in the endless soul-deep learning that such a work as this entails. Thank you!

CONTENTS

INTRODUCTION — 11
Presencing and Spiritual Direction

CHAPTER ONE — 23
What is presencing?

CHAPTER TWO — 31
Why presencing and why does it matter so much?

CHAPTER THREE — 49
Why presencing matters in the Christian faith

CHAPTER FOUR — 59
How do we presence and where do we start?

CHAPTER FIVE — 79
Presencing and attention

CHAPTER SIX — 91
Inner transformation and renewing – the work of the heart

CHAPTER SEVEN — 113
Presencing and spiritual formation

CHAPTER EIGHT — 135
Presencing and our relationships

CHAPTER NINE — 149
Presencing and prayer – life as prayer

CHAPTER TEN — 167
Presencing and discernment

CHAPTER ELEVEN — 181
Sustaining presence in daily life

CHAPTER TWELVE — 201
The role and experience of the spiritual director

AFTERWORD — 229

BIBLIOGRAPHY AND FURTHER READING — 235

ENDNOTES — 239

APPENDIX A: COLLECTED STATE MEDITATION — 243

APPENDIX B: BODY SCAN MEDITATION — 247

INTRODUCTION

Presencing and Spiritual Direction

WELCOME. WELL COME. And thank you – for choosing to begin this book.

I sense this is a good place to start. With this gratitude. And a wish that you may in some way be blessed by what you read.

This is a book about presence, and it only has substance if I am present in my writing, just as you are present in your reading. And *as* I presence, sensing myself fully here in this very moment, the first thing I notice *is* gratitude – for the impulse in you to pick up this book and read. It is a very generous thing to read another person's words.

My hope for this book, and the challenge I want to embrace as I write it, is that we can somehow find a way to *stay* present – body, heart, soul, *and* mind – me as I write, you as you read, available to our true selves and to the greater Mystery that is always beyond. It may seem a strange thing to ask, until we allow that time maybe is just another dimension too, but I would welcome your prayer (whatever that word means for you) for me as I write, just as I find myself in prayer now for you as you read – and for the utterly unique encounter that you will have with the words I write. Words of course that will be received by you in ways I can never anticipate.

It is worth saying from the start that this book is a mining of my experience – of the journey of my own becoming and as an accompanier of others in theirs, in my role as a retreat guide, leadership coach, spiritual director, and friend. Whilst I will draw on relevant theory and frameworks, what you will be accessing is the product of a personal journey of 'listening people into growth'. Part of the gratitude I am feeling is to the very many others from whom I have learnt so much along the way.

So, the book will present what seems to have served me and others in this process. My main criterion for choosing what I write about here is that 'in my experience, it seems to be reliable and true' rather than 'it is fact'.

So, why this book?

There is an ancient piece of wisdom from the prophet Jeremiah that I sense best captures what this book is all about, and speaks to the choices we make in life and where they lead us...

> *Stand at the crossroads and look;*
> *   ask for the ancient paths,*
> *ask where the good way is, and walk in it,*
> *   and you will find rest for your souls.*
>
> JEREMIAH 6:16

This verse has been part of my life for over 25 years, since I first stumbled across it as the inspiration for our Crossroads Retreats programme. Now it seems to have found me once more to help me introduce this book and its rather unimaginative title, 'Presencing and Spiritual Direction'.

'Presencing' at its simplest is all about 'standing and looking' – 'just' being wholly aware of where you truly are, who you are, and all that is present there with you. I put 'just' in inverted commas, which I will do throughout this book because a truth that I have encountered as a spiritual director is that, whenever the word 'just' arises, something immense seems to follow! So, I have learned to prick up my ears when it pops up.

'Spiritual Direction' is exactly what it says on the tin – finding your true 'spiritual direction', i.e. the 'way' that is 'good' and brings 'rest for your soul'. Gradually we learn to use that greatest gift of all, our own free will, to choose that particular 'way' – because it is our soul's way, and no one else can find it for us. We know we are on it by the 'rest' and peace it brings, however challenging the path might be.

After all, our soul is the only thing we will take with us as we leave this life. One might even say that care for our soul is our greatest responsibility. We can help others care for theirs, and create conditions to support their soul journeys, but we cannot carry the responsibility for them. One common misunderstanding is that a spiritual director is someone who 'directs' others on their path. The contrary is true; our job is 'just' to 'stand' there with them and help them discern their own 'good way'.

The 'good way' has an important double meaning. It relates both to our unique path and pilgrimage in this life (which is often what purpose-driven people like me come to spiritual directors for help with!), but also to our 'way of being' on the journey and our 'way of being with' those we encounter along the way.

As a spiritual director, I have found there are two consistent questions with which most people come to me. One is a desire to find more peace in life (within, not without). The other, usually but not always for people with a faith, is 'how can I get closer to God' (whatever they may mean by that word).

As I write, you may notice how you respond to these thoughts – whether they are or are not pertinent to the questions you are bringing with you as you pick up this book. Indeed, whether it is these questions or something different, now may be a good time to pause and give your responses fuller attention. *'What do you want?'* is the first question Christ asks the disciples in John's Gospel. It's not a bad place to start.

> *What are the questions you are bringing to this book? There may be clear questions, expressed as thoughts or words. You may also, if you can feel inwards a little, notice your questions more as an impulse – a wish or even a yearning in your heart – an inarticulate sense of wanting something to be different...*
>
> *If so, whether this desire is fierce/urgent or gentle/subtle, maybe allow yourself a little time to feel it, sit with it, welcome it, and let it be what it is... If you can to some extent remember this and have it available to you as you read on, it may enrich your reading . You might notice how this book is speaking to you at that level – at the level of being – as well as notice the thoughts and ideas it contains.*

Concerning the two questions above, if you find any resonance with them, the good news is that experience shows me unequivocally that you can find both – peace and God. That the presence of the Divine and of peace are here just waiting to be 'found' – each of us in our own 'good way' – and that these do provide a different, clearer, firmer base from which to lead our lives, and to which we can keep returning. This is my primary reason for writing this book, my foundational hope, and deepest wish for you.

Experience has also shown me that there are practical ways in which to help people find peace and God – and that these seem to 'work'. By 'practical ways', I do not really mean techniques. It is not a clever book in that sense. It is more a book about remembering, in that all of us know how to do this, probably from before the moment we were born. But we have just forgotten. So, there is a kind of 'back to basics' quality about it. That does not mean it is easy, because we may find ourselves having to change our habits and that is always hard. But it does mean that we are working with the grain, that what we need is here, even if we have to strip off a few layers to find it again!

This book is an attempt to share these practical ways, as much as is possible via the written word. So, as well as being a book for those who want to 'find' God and/or peace in life, it is also a book for those who want, in whatever way, to be able to support others in this. I have put 'find' in inverted commas because, as this book will address, this is not something we can 'attain' through our own effort. There is always an element of mystery and grace at work. It is more accurate to say that there are things we can do, and help others do, to cultivate a disposition of life that enables these mysteries to 'find us'. Indeed, as we cultivate this disposition, we may even come to realise that the things we are most looking for such as 'peace' and 'God', do not need finding at all, *they are already here*, present. It is just that we are not! That is why I call this disposition of life 'presencing'.

Wendell Berry expresses this simple truth poetically for us this in his nature lyric *The Wild Geese*:

> *Horseback on Sunday morning,*
> *harvest over, we taste persimmon*
> *and wild grape, sharp sweet*
> *of summer's end. In time's maze*
> *over fall fields, we name names*

that went west from here, names
that rest on graves. We open
a persimmon seed to find the tree
that stands in promise,
pale, in the seed's marrow.
Geese appear high over us,
pass, and the sky closes. Abandon,
as in love or sleep, holds
them to their way, clear,
in the ancient faith: what we need
is here. And we pray, not
for new earth or heaven, but to be
quiet in heart, and in eye
clear. What we need is here.[1]

When I say above 'we are not present', I should actually put the 'we' in inverted commas because it refers not to our fullest selves, but rather to the smaller part of ourselves that right now is the 'I' that is determining our experience. Part of not being present is also being disconnected from our own true, whole, selves. The poet above is describing a moment of fuller awareness of who he is and what is in flow within him and around him – a fuller state of being.

I remember years ago being on an 'outward bound' team-building experience. Part of it involved locating vital information using an avalanche rescue tracker. This involved a transmitter, sewn into the little bag containing the clue, and a responder which bleeped faster and faster the closer one got. In the melee and over-excitement of the task, one person, Tommy, picked up the responder and set off to find the necessary clue. He was to spend over an hour in the task. Everywhere he went the bleeper got faster and faster and then, just when he thought he had found it, slower and slower. He seemed to be right upon it and then it just slipped away. He found several possible hiding places, all to no avail. He set it to maximum sensitivity, and it just got worse. But he kept going on – seemingly finding it then losing it.

The rest of the team were getting more and more frustrated. In the end someone grabbed the responder from him and said, 'Let me have a go!' (You can imagine the scene; this was a very 'high achieving' business!) When Tommy miserably gave her the instructions envelope from his pocket, she opened it to find not only the instructions for the responder but also the tiny clue bag with the transmitter sewn into it. It had been put back in the envelope for safe keeping after someone had already solved the exercise a while back and gone off to do something else – failing, unfortunately to let anyone know!

The hapless Tommy had spent the last hour literally going round in circles looking everywhere for a clue that was tucked up in his own pocket, like a dog chasing its own tail! 'Tommy truly found himself on this programme' became the running joke of the event.

This is the central comedy and tragedy that this book will explore. Is it just possible that the most significant, fundamental things that we are seeking in life are already here? Within us? All around us? Including God?

You may find yourself reacting to my statement 'what we most fundamentally want', as though I am assuming it is 'peace' or 'God' for you... You could probably put other words there, such as 'joy' or 'happiness' or 'love' or 'equanimity' or 'trust' or 'courage' or 'kindness' or 'excitement' or 'beauty' or 'creativity' or 'freedom'... and I will be bold enough to hope that the premise above would still hold true.

Or you may react against the question itself: *'What I want is irrelevant, it's what God wants and others need of me that matters...'* Yet, in a way, that is still what you want – to be of service. And the same proposition may still apply; the best way to be of service, to God or others, is to be wholly present with them.

But, of course, there is only one way to find out...

I am conscious that already, with this focus on 'soul' or 'spiritual formation', the book may come across as individualistic in focus. My trust is that a focus on 'what is good for your soul' will have the exact opposite effect. What is for another's 'good' is what is for my 'good'. I am reminded of the Ubuntu principle: 'I am because we are. We are because I am.'

Returning to the Jeremiah verse, we can note that Christianity in its earliest practice was known as 'The Way' and that Christ's whole ministry is embodied in a simple human being, Jesus, living wholly and truly in His own 'good way' – apparently wandering, yet always so clear about who He was and what was needed in each day and each encounter of His short life. It is the 'being' of Christ, more than His teaching, which is the great gift to humanity.

This is echoed in a central parable in Jesus' teaching, that of the Prodigal Son, which is about a young person who, exuberant for life, sets off blindly into it and loses his way. When he eventually 'wakes up' to his situation, in the pig pen, his choice is to find his way back home.

The prodigal is no doubt all of us, in one way or another, and the story helps us acknowledge that we are all going to wander. Some of us will wander at the impulse of our own misplaced desires. Some, less fortunate, will be pulled off the path by the abuse and deceptions of others. However, whenever and wherever we 'come to our senses' and 'stand and look', our 'good way' is calling us back home. Or it may be that we just allow ourselves to be brought back... with much rejoicing by a heaven that really, really cares.

Then, as St Benedict reminds us in his rule of life, 'Always, we begin again...'

So, whilst my intention in writing is to share practical approaches that I hope will be helpful, this book will be more about 'being' than 'teaching'. My life as a spiritual director and leadership coach has given me the immense privilege of being alongside so many people from so many different walks of life at a level of depth that is rarely possible in the normal patterning of things. Everything I share here has been given to me by and through those I have worked with in their honest, open, and beautiful shared struggle to find their 'way'. I am deeply grateful for each and every one of them. My hope for this book is that it may honour what has been so freely shared and transmit this onwards to others.

It is written for anyone who is taking seriously their own journey of becoming – literally 'coming into being', a fuller way of being than you may be inhabiting right now. It assumes that sooner or later growth into 'fuller being' will involve a spiritual dimension to your life – a living connection with a Being beyond your 'own'. Although my attempts to address this spiritual dimension will draw from my travels in the highways and byways of Christian mysticism, I hope this will not be a barrier to those whose paths have taken them elsewhere. I trust that whatever true wisdom it contains will be beyond doctrine and accessible to all.

It is also a book for anyone who in one way or another, whether as a conscious 'work' or 'just' as a friend, seeks to support and hold for others in their journeys. It will present the learning that has 'stuck' with me and seems to have served in this process. It will involve drawing on my own lived encounters with people in this work, and the stories and examples I bring will reflect this, although anonymised to respect confidentiality.

From this perspective, anything that may be a helpful insight for you can only arise when what I share here in some way touches your own experience. Please do use your own reference points to assess the validity of what I write here and please let that be your guide. If I make statements that in any way come across as an assertion of some kind of 'truth', please mentally add to it, 'In Chris' limited experience...'!

As with the established, and possibly deeply irritating, trait of anyone who works in my profession, the book will probably raise more questions than answers. If so, I hope that these will be fruitful too, because questions that really capture our attention open to us the possibility of finding our own way into answers that are there waiting for us. The book may also on occasion create confusion by embracing contradictory truths or things that are contrary to your own understanding. If so, and if the confusion is 'good' – an invitation to explore something more fully or in a different way – I hope you can trust it and stay with it until it yields its fruit. If it is 'bad' or seems just plain 'wrong', please lay it aside, or, even better, write to me and tell me so!

The phrase 'spiritual formation' may be familiar or alien to you. 'Becoming' or 'unfolding' may be simpler ways of putting it. To be alive is to travel, individually and collectively – quite literally on a planet whirling through space and time – through experience and growth, beginnings and endings, history and evolution. We each play our part in this mysterious unfolding of something way vaster than ourselves. Some may call this 'the will of God', others the 'infinite universe', others 'unfathomable chaos'.

To be alive is also to make choices about how we play our part – choices to act, to wait, to speak, to be silent, to give, to take, to offer, to withhold, to engage, to hide, to build, to break. In all this, all that we do and that is done unto us, we are 'formed' – into this person I call 'I', this society I call 'we' (sometimes 'they'). The question this poses for all of us is, 'What do I want or hope to become?' And the corollary immediately follows, 'And what am I actually becoming?' Then we 'mind the gap'. That can often be the start point for spiritual direction.

To add the word 'spiritual' to qualify this process of 'formation' is to bring a particular perspective to it. It implies formation with a purpose – to grow, maybe, in certain qualities that may be deemed of spiritual 'worth' or 'maturity', such as love, compassion, humility, conscience, honesty, courage, patience, kindness, gentleness, generosity, wisdom, selflessness... Or to contribute to a 'higher purpose', to something bigger, a 'greater good', beyond our limited understanding. But it also implies that we are not on our own, that there is a source of help, a 'greater good' that wants us and indeed wills us on to play our part to the full.

I find myself writing now in quite an abstract, conceptual way. And as I notice and re-gather, I become aware of this deep conviction in my own heart that this is more than abstract, that our becoming – yours and mine – matters... It *really does* matter – even if it doesn't always feel like it at those times when we find ourselves asking, 'What's the point?' It matters not just for us, but for everyone. It matters because our world today needs a different quality of being to address the challenges of our age. But more than all that, it matters because maybe it is just, simply, what life is...

Christ's simple statement of His own intention comes to mind: 'I have come that they may have life, and have it to the full' (John 10:10). I wonder if it is possible to hear these words spoken with gentle, heartfelt sincerity and wishfulness – almost as a kind of a promise that this really is what God, life, love, the universe really wants for us...

Christ may want it for us, but do we? What is our part to play in this? There is always a choice: we can participate wholly in the process of our own becoming, even when this, as we shall see, may often simply be a conscious act of receiving, or we can fall asleep at the wheel. 'Red pill or blue pill?' for those who have watched *The Matrix*.

My proposition here is that 'presencing' is both the core quality and the core resource that we have available to us to play our part in the conscious process of our own becoming – of 'living life to the full'. It is also possibly the very opposite of how we have been taught to learn and 'develop' in our modern educational systems.

The intent is also to provide something of practical value to those who, whether one-to-one or in groups, seek to support others in their journey of formation. This may include coaches, counsellors, pastors, retreat leaders, facilitators, mediators. I believe there is a kernel in this which is foundational to all of us in this work and that each reader will arrive with their own level of knowing. This will mean parts of it may seem obvious, even platitudinous to some, whilst parts of it will seem obscure and impenetrable to others. I hope you can feel free to skim read when you deem it necessary.

Before I close this introduction, let me say something about the structure of the book. Like many books, it has chapters and, if I may, I would encourage you to treat each chapter as if you were coming into a new day – so with an opportunity to pause, ground, breathe, and presence before you enter it. In the words of an old Anglican prayer, 'The day [chapter] lies open before us... may the light of Your Presence set our hearts on fire with love for You.'

The chapters fall into five sections as follows:

Section 1 – *What is presencing and why does it matter?*
This lays the foundations for the ensuing sections. Chapter One will *define* what we mean by 'presencing' and will do so in a fairly classic cognitive way. Chapter Two will look at *why presencing matters* in our lives today and will have more of a personal, experiential style. The third chapter, again more cognitive in approach, will look at the 'why' question from an explicitly *Christian perspective*. It will draw on some of the core teachings of the Christian Bible for those who are familiar with these, and I hope it will give Christian readers a sense that there are some solid biblical foundations beneath it – solid enough at least to continue reading into the chapters ahead. (Some readers may be familiar with these foundational concepts and, if so, may want to skim read or skip onto the next section.)

Section 2 – *How we 'do' presencing – the 'inner work'*
This section will go into the *practice* of presencing – how we do it. It will take us into the essential 'work' of personal transformation – in all aspects of our 'inner being', soul, heart, body, and mind. This will build from basic aspects of presencing to more advanced and 'deeper' ones. In Chapter Four we will look at how we *'gather ourselves'* into a fuller, more aware state of being. This is the foundation of all we cover here and I would invite you to use the short presencing practice described there before you start each chapter thereafter. In Chapter Five we will look at the crucial role of our *attention*. In Chapter Six we will look at how we work in the *depths of the heart* to release into greater fullness and freedom.

Section 3 – *How we embody this in our 'life and work'*
This section will look at how our work of presencing contributes to our capacity to 'live life to the full'. In Chapter Seven, again a more conceptual, positioning chapter, we will look at the *'soul journey'* from cradle to grave as a

process of 'formation' and how presencing helps us in this. In Chapter Eight we will look at what it means to be more conscious in our *relationships*. In Chapter Nine we will look at how this plays out in the life of *prayer*, which we treat as an intention to 'be with' the Divine, whatever that means for us. In Chapter Ten we will look at how it all comes into focus in our *decision making and discernment*.

Section 4 – *Sustaining our practice in daily life*
In Chapter Eleven, we come back to the 'how to' of presencing, but this time from the perspective of how we sustain it in the pattern of our lives so it is more available in the multiplicity of choices, large and small, that we make on a daily basis.

Section 5 – *The role and experience of the spiritual director*
In this final section, Chapter Twelve, we will look specifically at what it means to accompany others in the processes described in the preceding chapters. If you are already an experienced spiritual director you can , if you want, choose to look ahead to this section at the end of every chapter, to be with its contents from this perspective too. Or you may just read this at the end as a summation of all we have covered from the perspective of accompanier, rather than recipient.

Finally, I am just so conscious in writing a book like this of Christ's words about the Pharisees: 'They tie up heavy, cumbersome loads and put them on other people's shoulders' (Matthew 23:4). It is so easy to write a book like this and for the reader to infer that this is simple Christian practice. Nothing could be further from the truth. Everything in this book is hard! But so as not to put you off reading it, let me also reassure you that none of it is actually hard to *do,* nor are the concepts in it hard to grasp or *remember*. They are just hard to *remember to do*! We can approach this work of presencing humbly and with the absolute clarity that we will never be any good it. But we won't let that stop us. We don't need to be good at it. We just try – and hope and pray that we remember to presence when we can, and (a sincere, heartfelt prayer) when we are most in need of it. Presencing is, as they say, a percentage game, and we will all have good days and bad days. That, I suspect, is the way it is meant to be – lest we take ourselves too seriously!

Therefore, I begin this book with a plea that everything written it you hold *lightly* – and anything you do pick up and hold in your intentions, please do so with a prayer that it may be shared with a greater power that so longs to hold it with you.

CHAPTER ONE

What is presencing?

BEFORE WE GO INTO MORE DEPTH in subsequent chapters, I thought it would be helpful in this short chapter to begin by defining what I actually mean and intend by the use of this word 'presencing'.
It is not an everyday word in English. It has the feel of a familiar noun, 'presence', being forced into a verb. So it is valid to ask from the start, 'Is this something that we can actually "do" or is it a state of being, a quality, that just "is"?' This question of grammar points us to something that will become more important as we go through the book: how much agency do we really have in 'presencing' and, indeed, can the very act of striving to do it result in diminishing what we are seeking to achieve?

An interesting exercise here may be to consider the words 'grace' or 'wisdom' or 'peace' as we are considering 'presence'. I cannot 'grace' myself or 'wisdom' myself or 'peace' myself. These are qualities that emerge in a more elusive, mysterious way. But what I *can* practice are certain things that increase the likelihood of grace and wisdom and peace manifesting themselves in my life. In other words, how I look after the 'vessel' of this body, heart, mind, soul can lead to these higher qualities flowing in and through me. For example, stilling, praying, reflecting, acts of kindness, creativity, and, yes, 'presencing'.

The *Macmillan Dictionary* definition of 'presencing' is 'The act of bringing yourself into the present moment', which seems a good place to start. From this we can extrapolate:

1. It is an intentional act. It involves us consciously and intentionally doing something
2. This act is one of 'bringing ourselves'. This raises a couple of things we may want to hold in awareness:
    a. It is an act of attention and focus, of 'bringing' our awareness consciously to bear on something
    b. It involves our 'selves' and therefore the mystery of this – 'who am I?' Who is my real, true, whole self? Or, more relevant maybe, how much of my real, true, whole self am 'I' able to bring?
3. We are bringing ourselves into 'the present moment'. This also raises some curious challenges and possibilities:
    a. Where are we really bringing ourselves to? The present moment is notoriously difficult to identify – because as soon as I have 'arrived', it has gone. It defies measurement and boundaries. It contains everything that is – including my act of perceiving it. To think on it is to miss it
    b. How do I 'bring' myself into the present – aren't I already here? I can bring myself to a meeting because that is somewhere or sometime else. But how do I bring myself to where I already am?
    c. And then, who is the me that is doing the bringing and who is the me who is being brought?

Here is an invitation to boundless philosophical enquiry! However, all these questions are resolved in the word 'experience' – that mysterious blending of subjective and objective, of 'I' and 'it', of the inner and outer, the transmitting and receiving that is present in the miraculous 'flow' of consciousness – which still remains a mystery to science. This includes sensation, perception, thought, emotion and desire, energy, 'spirit', intention and will. To be presenced is to be present and awake to all these things – 'fully alive' in the consciousness of my full experience.

The dictionary definition refers not only to the 'present moment' but also to an indefinable energetic 'quality of being' that we often pick up intuitively.

We 'sense' presence. We talk about someone, or sometimes a place, having 'presence'. We feel something and it affects us. In business you can find training programmes on 'presence and impact', implying the cultivation of a certain natural authority or charisma. We talk about 'making our presence felt', implying that we are bringing something of the full power of our being to bear on a situation. Also, of course, there is a whole body of literature on the 'Presence of God', or the 'Divine Presence', which seems to have a profound, lasting transformational effect on those who experience it.

This somewhat philosophical detour helps, I hope, to emphasise the mysterious quality of this activity. We will never 'know' entirely how to grasp it. A bit like great jazz or art, we sort of lose ourselves in it – and occasionally, unpredictably, something amazing or transformational occurs and we grow. Then, when we think we have grasped it, we lose it again... and then, again, we grow! Finding and losing are perhaps core aspects of the dance.

But let's get more concrete. When I am 'presencing', what is it that I am actually doing?

The image that immediately pops up as I ask myself that question is a memory of a walk on a beautiful summer's day in the Clwyd Valley in North Wales. On a little path by a small mill stream, I come across a red admiral butterfly basking on a nettle leaf, wings spread wide in the late afternoon sun, seemingly still, poised, vibrant. But actually, on closer examination, it is gently moving and pulsing in its own ambience.

The presence of the butterfly is captivating – hypnotic almost. So still and bright, wings wide open, soaking in the sun, with an occasional rhythmic folding and re-opening. There are tiny subtle movements of its feet, almost a slow-motion dance on the leaf. Scientifically, we know that the insect is soaking up the sun to re-energise itself and that the closing of its wings helps with its digestion and the subtle movements of its feet are to 'taste' the plant it is on and sense where there is food. But, like everything in the natural world, what is striking is its 'is-ness': just going about its business, oblivious to anything beyond its own necessary experience, soaking in the substance of the day.

Then there is also what it is transmitting – life, colour, peace, beauty – and the necessary business of spreading pollen and sustaining the fabric of wider ecosystems including, in this instance, the nourishing effect on my own being as I pause to soak in the wonder of the moment. And it is doing all this merely by 'being' – being 'just' who and what it is.

My own journey of presencing has taken the form of a gradual shedding of my own self-consciousness – the part of me that is always trying to figure out how I am meant to be – and slowly learning what it means 'just' to be. I track the roots of it back to my childhood, growing up between the mountains and the sea in North Wales, in those lovely moments of awe when I found myself swept up in the beauty and wildness of the landscape, and in the poetry of Wordsworth, Coleridge, and Keats as I studied Literature at college. I also find its roots in my spiritual life, in learning the power of silence and stillness in prayer and contemplation. But perhaps the biggest breakthrough for me was when a dear friend taught me how to notice and experience the 'intelligence' of my body – the constant flow of energy, sensation, feeling, and thought that it contains. Suddenly a whole new world of experience opened up for me as I learned to notice that presence was more present than I thought – not just restricted to moments in nature, poetry, and prayer. I began to find the amazing sensitivity of my body – the tingling aliveness of my skin, the sensitivity to light, sound, taste, scent, touch, the beating of my heart, the flow of blood in my veins, the quality of breath as it flowed and energised and cleansed. I also learned to tune into subtle sensations deep inside me – for example, a tension in the chest and shoulders, a tightening sensation in the tummy, a deep, dark, warm strength in the base of the gut. I realised also that all these things were communicating to me – information about the deep and subtle flow of life within and around me.

These things are often taught in meditation classes (but less so, interestingly, in most forms of Christian prayer) and gradually, as I learned simply to notice and 'be present' with what was flowing within me, a new expansion and inner freedom started to open up. I could choose to notice when my body was telling me something, place my awareness inside this and something would happen. Most obviously, my mind would still and quieten, especially if I was worrying about something. Then new insights and perspectives would emerge. These began to feel more like 'wisdom' than knowledge – a different kind of knowing.

As I experiment now and come out of my head and pause and breathe, I find my awareness drawn to my solar plexus. Immediately, as I settle here, I am aware that in my mind there is a constant background anxiety about writing:

'How will I explain this stuff? Who would be interested in it? It's already been widely written about. What's different or new or interesting about what I am writing? How will it land with a Christian readership… a non-Christian readership?' I can feel the energy of this – a kind of buzzy, bright, hot shrillness around my head and upper torso – and I can feel its power to captivate and distort my thinking – the tightness that comes and the striving it induces. I recognise my need to be clever, to be 'right'. As I presence my awareness in it and 'feel into it', I notice the tightness begins to settle, as though it is grateful for being noticed. It calms, almost apologetically: 'I am just making you aware, that's all.' 'Thank you, I've got it,' I respond. It relaxes, but I can feel it poised, waiting, ready to spring up again.

Then, as I return my awareness to my solar plexus, I feel a fullness, a clear, almost liquid energy: 'presence' is the word that pops up. It feels strong, nourishing, substantive, almost like the substance of life itself. As I give it attention, it seems to expand and flow gently, powerfully upwards through my back. Words form in the lower centre of my mind: 'You are fine just as you are… You really are…' Then, after a little pause, 'Notice the simplicity of this… Let it come… Enjoy it…'

There is a peaceful quality to the words. I trust them enough to print them here, just as they are. I wonder if they are not only for me.

So often in my work as a coach and spiritual director, some of the most helpful words and 'interventions' for my clients would just 'come' in this kind of way. Gradually, I learned how to trust them, and to begin to spot my own deceptions too, mainly by noticing the quality of the energy, and/or the texture of 'presence'. I began to realise that this mind that is so used to running the show, and indeed is probably the one writing at the moment, is not really the best one to be in charge. It thinks it is, because it sees its job as keeping me, and others, safe. But actually, it is here to *serve*, to follow and not to lead – to discern and surrender to a deeper flow, a richer wisdom, a bigger Presence – if I can but notice, let go and trust…

What began to happen for me, slowly, imperceptibly, in fits and starts, was a kind of growing expansion of awareness – I just began to notice more, and then to experience more, and then to 'allow' more of this wider experience into my life, work, and relationships – and it was good. I felt, I feel, more alive. I also found I was closer and more available to the mystery of the Divine Presence – in myself and others.

Nowhere has this helped me more than in my work as a spiritual director, where I have learned more and more to settle into a mutual 'field of Presence', which is often tangible in the atmosphere around and within us, and let truth, love, wisdom, beauty, strength, courage, hope arise and flow – through absolutely no agency of my own.

So, whatever exactly it is, this indefinable quality that partly I am writing the book to understand better myself, it has *really helped* me – both in my own journey and in my work as a spiritual director and retreat host.

I hope it will help you too. It's that simple.

I will of course go on to explore and expand upon these assertions more fully and in more depth later in the book. But for now, staying with the introductory purpose of this opening chapter, let me return to a more rational framework, for those who may find the above a little too subjective. This I hope will help provide a more precise, cognitive grounding for what I will go on to cover in more depth in the rest of the book.

'Presencing', as I will work with it here, comprises some or all of the following elements:

- A capacity to observe, and choose to focus attention on, the nuances and subtleties of both inner and outer experience
- The deliberate placing of one's attention and experiential awareness in parts of one's being beyond its habitual location in the head (e.g. body, heart, 'soul', 'spirit')
- A quality of curious and compassionate self-observation that has us able to attend to whatever is flowing within us – comfortable or uncomfortable
- A sensing into and discerning the deeper energy that is really moving one's thoughts, words, and actions
- A sensing into and being receptive to the distinctive substance, wisdom, and intelligence of a greater 'Presence' – both within us and around us in others, including the Divine
- An assumption that this substantive 'Presence' is 'knowable' – from the point of view that we can at the very least sense and feel it – and notice its invitations to respond

One thing I see already in writing this is the different meanings that I intend when I use the word 'presence' in different contexts. So here are three of the most common different uses, which should bring some clarity to this as we move forward:

1. As an active verb: to consciously place or focus my full awareness in an aspect of my experience. E.g. 'to presence in my fear' – meaning to fully experience the emotional and physical sensation of it and enquire into it, rather than avoid or downplay it.
2. As a reflexive process: 'to come into presence', or 'to become present', meaning to come into a particular state that is conducive to the expanded awareness, sensitivity, and atunement to the present moment as described above.
3. As a noun or quality: to experience 'Presence' – as something embodied or in some other way sensed as the power and substance of pure being – whether one's own, another person's, a group who are present together, nature, the Divine, or something else mysteriously 'beyond'.

These should be clearly and easily distinguishable by the context in which they are used.

Finally, in this opening chapter, I want to say just a few words, at least as a conceptual start point, about what this work of presencing can contribute to our lives. This will be explored in more depth, practicality and subtlety, as we go through the book, but here are four fundamental propositions to get us started.

1. If we take the view that human beings are constantly growing, and that it is our *experience* that is the primary 'food' or 'daily bread' for that growth, I want to suggest that presencing is the art of processing that food. It involves us fully and consciously attending to our experience, of whatever nature, and allowing it to be *transformed* within us into a growth in wisdom and maturity.
2. Presencing is also about opening our *full being* to growth and becoming. We probably all know of people who are very developed intellectually but very underdeveloped emotionally – or vice versa. If we do not open ourselves up to growth in all aspects of our being, we miss it. To grow in wholeness, we need to learn to be present to emotion and not fear discomfort, to be curious and

alert in our thinking, not lazy-minded, to be conscious in our will and choices, not reactive. Those familiar with the 'Waverley Integrative Framework'[1] or other 'Integral' models will be familiar with this.

3. Presencing is also about recognising and living in our fundamental *interconnectedness* with all life around us – the mystery of the Life that we all share. The quality of our being affects the quality of being of those around us. At its simplest, if we are in a bad mood and acting it out, it is not long before we 'infect' others with it too. If we have an insecurity that has us hoard and grab resources for ourselves, then of course we deprive others of these. If we have a blindness to the fact that our life is utterly dependent on the integrity of the ecosystem of which we are a part, then we will degrade it without a care. If we love only that which makes us feel good, then we will fail to give love where love is most needed and it will leave us in an increasingly loveless world. Presencing helps us sense into what is really needed in the mutuality of life and to let it flow. You may remember, for example, a time when you noticed somebody neglected or struggling in some way and your heart moved within you and you just did what was natural and helped them. Because you were present enough to notice.

4. From a spiritual or religious perspective, presencing also helps us be aware of our interconnection to the mysterious Presence of the Divine, or indeed the very essence of 'Life' itself, which is always 'now', both within us and around us. For those with a religious faith, this is about becoming *present to, with, and in God*, and therefore more available to the unfolding of God's will in and for our lives. For those without a specific faith, it helps us sense into something indefinably bigger and less limited than ourselves. Again, why not take a minute to remember just one time when you experienced yourself in some way closer to the presence of the Divine, or the awe, wonder, and beauty of nature/life in some way...

When we are presenced, quite simply, we are bigger, better, kinder, gentler, clearer, stronger. We are more whole, more aware, more connected, more available to the powerful forces that transform our world for the better – love, joy, peace, compassion, patience, perseverance, hope, creativity, wisdom, beauty, truth, grace. And, most importantly, we are free. We get to choose – to become who we are drawn to be, not driven to be.

CHAPTER TWO

Why presencing and why does it matter so much?

Having defined 'presencing' in the previous chapter, these next two chapters will attempt to 'make the case' for its significance i.e. why it is so important a facet of our lives – this chapter from a secular perspective and the next from a Christian one. In doing so I am conscious I will be on well-travelled ground and it may be that you are coming to this book already well versed in the arguments around the 'why' of presencing. If so, you may wish to skim read these chapters or move onto Chapter 5 where we start to address the core purpose of the book – the 'how' of presencing (rather than the 'why').

I have already mentioned the small charity I work with, Crossroads Retreats, which offers time and space to explore the 'where next?' moments in life. As part of this, we recently asked our supporters and volunteers to do a bit of informal research – just to ask people they came across, from all walks of life and backgrounds, faiths, origins, a simple question: 'If you had to name the one fundamental thing you most wanted in life, what would it be?'

There was one word that absolutely dominated the responses. That word was 'peace'.

It left me wondering what these answers tell us about our human experience today. I wonder how other generations may have answered the question? Why peace? Peace from what? For what?

This desire for 'peace' seems to come across as a real *cri de coeur* in this day and age, with all that now bombards us, internally and externally. To explore why, I will borrow from the medieval tradition and paint an 'everyman' picture. 'Every(wo)man' is a composite – everyone and no one – in which we can hopefully recognise characteristics of our shared experience of life today. I apologise in advance if you do not recognise yourself in this, because it will inevitably make a set of assumptions about context, class, gender, and social milieu which can never be wholly representative. But I hope you can enter this world imaginatively, even if it is not your own.

Jo and Joe are in a relationship. They have some worries. Jo's job is not paying brilliantly and is demanding more and more time and energy. So is Joe's. Joe switched jobs a year ago, and the new job looked to be better, but it hasn't really changed. It's just as busy, but at least it's closer to home. Their jobs are important to them both. They want to do something worthwhile in the world and have found jobs they 'kind of' believe in. At least something they can commit to. They juggle childcare between them, with Joe probably doing a bit more, along with help from extended family. Their son has just been accused of bullying at school, which is just so not him. Their daughter is in a highly competitive friendship group which is spilling over noisily in all sorts of ways into the family setting. Jo wants to move into a new neighbourhood and get the kids out of their current school. Joe is vehemently opposed because of his own experiences of moving school as a child. Joe's parents have separated and retired and his dad is lonely, a bit lost and not in great health.

Jo earns more than Joe and feels she carries the burden of the finances, which is something she is OK with because her father brought her up to be self-sufficient and to get things done in life. Joe, if he's honest, feels a bit inadequate about that but would feel even more inadequate raising it with her. So, he keeps busy and shows he is contributing in other ways. But his energy gets a bit flat sometimes. The quality of their interaction is pretty functional a lot of the time. They do get out to enjoy themselves in the evening with friends, although this is rarely relaxing: there is a 'comparative' edge to the conversations and the journey home afterwards is often spattered with 'why did they say that?' and 'what on earth made you bring that up?' – and a slightly uneasy dissatisfaction as they go to bed. Then, next morning, up and into it again – always plenty to do.

Joe's main thing is organising the holidays, on a budget, which he loves. He's already planning this year's in Scotland. Jo goes along with it because the kids love it, but secretly would love just to flop on a beach. Jo's thing is the church – always an active part of her life, though she is often frustrated she is the one always doing all the work. She also secretly feels she is failing spiritually because she doesn't 'hear from God' like others do. Recently the children stopped coming which she is embarrassed by, though she claims not. Still, at least she *serves*, 'which is more than many do'. Joe goes along and enjoys the company of a few people but finds the whole thing a bit of a ritual, especially now the kids have stopped going. He does wonder though whether there is something wrong with him. He can't quite see the point of it all – and rarely gets satisfactory answers to his questions about inconsistencies in the 'teaching'. But there are some good, kind, well-intentioned people there, which seems a bit of a rarity nowadays.

And then there is the problem with the boiler, and the car, the friend whose marriage is splitting up, the note from the form teacher, the environmental crisis, the fairtrade weekend in church, the appeal against the closing of the local hospital, the weekend break they promised themselves, the war in Ukraine and the local refugee work, the need to re-mortgage, the dream of setting up their own business, the opportunity to go to the World Cup with some friends in the autumn if... And of course, the need to prioritise oneself in all this, find a fitness regime, prayer time, meditation/yoga, plus some downtime. Then all that church teaching, to help the poor and suffering, listen to God, be 'salt and light' in the world, be kind, thoughtful, caring, loving. And then, parenting, 'where/how did we get that all so wrong? Why can't they at least *look* well-behaved like most the other kids do...? Still at least they haven't had any mental health issues... or have they, and we have not noticed...?'

There is hopefully no need to go on.

Let's just imagine the mental whirring and self-talk generated by this kind of snapshot...

- 'I wish we hadn't bought that wretched car. I told her they were rubbish...'

- 'Right, we are going to impose a "no devices" rule this Sunday – or at least try...'
- 'That presentation for the funding bid, I just remembered I haven't included Peter'
- 'I noticed Keith was a bit off with me the other day, what's that about?'
- 'I must get up earlier to pray. Why can't I? I'm such a useless Christian'
- 'Oh, my goodness, the Americans are on about China invading Taiwan... what next?'
- 'I'm so looking forward to getting away in May – make sure we make the most of it this time. I'll take the day off before... maybe half a day'
- 'Why are we even staying in this country? I could get a job anywhere in the world. Brexit makes me so angry. What have we done?'
- 'So much to do with the new education campaign – and no one's really interested. Feels like pushing water uphill'
- 'I am so sick of my boss; he just doesn't listen – or respect anything I say. He's always interrupting, taking over. Then yesterday when he took all the credit for what I had done... it makes me sick'
- 'I should love this job, it's everything I wanted, so why is it such a struggle?'
- 'I haven't seen my best friend for two years now... must get in touch'
- 'Am I happy? How do I even answer that? Are the kids happy?'
- 'I'm bored... where has the fun gone?'

We could continue. We could do similar versions for the kids, for Joe's dad, for the friend whose marriage is splitting up, for the local vicar, the newly-arrived refugee, the local GP, MP, care worker, and so on.

Who *wouldn't* want peace from all that?

Whatever your context, I hope this sketch conveys something of the truth of our lives today. Almost irrespective of how 'busy' we are on the outside, on the inside our minds are crowded with a barrage of thoughts – practical matters, worries, self-doubts, speculations, dreams, fantasies, interpreting and re-interpreting of others' behaviour, imagining scenarios, conversations, what-ifs, yes-buts, if-onlys and oh-noes. All these problems, things and people to look after, tasks to get right, people to make happy... all to make us feel better about ourselves. Even fitting in and enjoying some fun things becomes just another problem to be solved.

We tell ourselves that we'll just get through this/solve that and then we'll be fine, but of course there's always something else... It's never finished. And even if it was, we will find something else to think about/worry about/seek to have. And on top of this are all the expectations, of and from others – employers, customers, colleagues, the media, our friends, priests, community, parents, siblings, children. And finally, of course, what we expect of ourselves. And even if we got past all that, there's still the matter of saving the planet, loving the poor and needy, and let's not forget doing the will of God.

And then, when we try to force our mind to stop, or think of something else, or pray, or anything else, within minutes we find ourselves back there, thinking the thoughts again, but now with the added frustration and powerlessness: 'Why can't I just stop thinking about this stuff?' 'Why can't I even be in control of my own mind?' 'Why doesn't prayer even work?'

You can almost hear the soul-cry: *'Let me be! Please, just for a moment... LET... ME...BE...'*

You may recognise aspects of this. Whatever your context, this is the constant chatter at best, overwhelm at worst, of a mind that is never still. We react, we tighten, close, contain. Then we can find ourselves caught in a cycle of 'containment, with leaks'. For example, a melee of anxious or angry thoughts which feed negative feelings in our hearts; which then feed more negative thoughts, which cause us, say, to snap at the kids – a perfect self-reinforcing cycle which can become the very pattern of our life.

Who *wouldn't* want to be free from that?

What happens when we listen to the soul-cry? Interesting, isn't it, that we *have* one?

'All I want is a moment's peace...'

When you pause and think about it, it's pretty obvious why 'peace' topped our poll.

So, why 'presencing'? Let us start to explore the relevance of this and, if you are willing, explore it in and through your own *experience* too, rather than just fictitious others. To do this I will pose a few questions for your reflection. May I invite you, after this bombardment of an opening, to read the rest of this chapter more slowly, with pauses? I will indicate where. I hope it might be more helpful.

One way to begin to get perspective on this can be to recognise, as I suggested in the opening, that life often presents itself to us as a series of questions. For example:

- What should I do... with my life? In this situation? To help, serve, win, build...?
- How should I do it...?
- How do I relate to you, or get along with you...?
- What do I (really) want...?
- Where is God, how do I find Him/Her...?
- How do I become a better person...?
- What's the point...?

> Let's allow a pause here to notice...
>
> What are the questions that keep you up at night at the moment? You might jot down what pops up.
>
> Then, another pause...
>
> No, *really*, what are the questions that are truly challenging you right now? What happens if you just let them be questions... no need to answer them?

When faced with a question, what is the human response? We naturally bring it into our minds and try to solve it, to find the answer. Our distinctive, beautiful gift of problem-solving. I remember with joy a stint in life writing IT programmes – wrestling with the problem, the trial and error and then, wow! It worked! The thrill of getting it right. A toast with a teacup, and then on to the next problem, and the next...

Our inner problem-solver loves to find answers, and hates it when it can't! I would lie awake for hours wrestling in my mind with a programme and where the bug might be. But life has the knack of throwing up more questions than answers, and some, possibly many, that have no answers, like how to understand another human being or even ourselves.

Welcome to the 'worrying mind' – in a neutral sense of the word. Like a dog with a bone, it won't leave a problem alone. It is actually a beautiful thing, in its proper place. I will call it the 'functional mind' in this book. It sorts things out for us. Unfortunately, though, it tends to hog centre stage. Instead of being an aspect of 'I', it rapidly becomes 'I' as a whole. It takes over. 'I' become my thoughts – 'I think therefore I am', as Descartes put it.

When that happens, I am identified with my functional mind and lost to other aspects of my being, such as heart, soul, body. James Joyce captures this beautifully in his pen picture in *Dubliners*: 'Mr Duffy always lived at some distance from his own body.'[1] This takeover may happen because the 'functional mind' is largely fed by our early education, is triggered by our primary survival drives, and is the natural mechanism for much of our day-to-day practical living and decision-making.

If we are not careful, life becomes a series of problems to be solved, most of which are unsolvable. Why? Because they are not problems, they are just questions – invitations, adventures, explorations, learnings. To paraphrase Kierkegaard: life is something we are invited to *experience*, not a problem to be solved. But we forget that. Paying attention to experiencing life is something that gets in the way of us solving our problems – the 'I' that is our functional mind is much too busy for that.

The risk is that, in our preoccupation, we miss most of our actual *experience*; what is really present and flowing in our being, including those very things that I referenced right at the start: peace, wisdom, grace, and even God…

Kierkegaard's wisdom points us to a central premise of this book: that our experience is the primary 'food' for our maturation and spiritual growth, our 'becoming'. Being present is attending to what we are really experiencing, not just thinking. We may indeed be given our 'daily bread' of meaningful experience, but if we are not present to it and the questions it poses for us, how can we grow?

I am conscious that I am writing from and speaking to the functional mind. It is one of the paradoxes of this work that we have to logically convince the functional mind to give up its grip and allow us to experience life in a different way. Maybe we can take another pause here for you to notice what you are experiencing as you are reading this?

> So, let's do that. Let's take a breath and pause and sit in quiet for a minute or so, just to notice what else we may be experiencing – not just thoughts, but sensations: the feeling of breath maybe, or taste in the mouth, or the sounds and atmosphere around you. What happens as you do this? Maybe close your eyes for a minute and rest and notice whatever you notice.

What have you become aware of – sensations or feelings maybe? The atmosphere of the room or the presence of others around you? Or people and things this book has brought to mind? Your questions from earlier? Or the whirring of your thoughts? Or time passing? Maybe an irritation at wasting this time when you could be getting on with reading or doing something else.

Whatever we notice, we can notice what it is telling us. What in this brief pause seems significant? Worth remembering? Or worthy of more attention?

We can choose...

This, simply, is the beginning of presencing. We will go a lot further with it but, at its core, it is about fully and consciously attending to our experience, of whatever nature – 'positive' or 'negative' – and allowing it to be received and transformed within us into growth in wisdom, maturity, and love.

As I write this, I find myself remembering a pilgrimage walk I made with a group of friends, including a man who had not long before lost his 20-year-old son. We didn't say much, we just walked, in the unspoken presence of the pain and grief and all the unanswerable, agonising questions that the experience had left him with. It was evident from his whole demeanour that he had met with the full horror of what had happened – he had allowed the pain to blow right through him. There was no anger, no denial, no self-judgement, no blame, no pretence of strength, nor faith, nor even acceptance. There was only sadness, sorrow, surrender, and so much heartbroken love. It was like the experience had emptied him, swept him clean of anything he had once held and left him there 'on the dirt-floor basement of the heart', as Barbara Brown Taylor once expressed it.[2] Yet here he was, wholly present, with everyone – and he was simply, purely, blessing them 'just' by being there. He almost certainly did not realise it, but what he was transmitting was a love and a solidity of being that was palpable around him, as well as honesty, humility, wisdom, grace, and more beside. People were drawn to his presence, whether or not they knew his story. It became an extraordinary time for everyone involved – we all came back changed in ways we will probably never understand.

This is an extreme example, but I hope we can receive it. The point is that it is not the just the experience, of whatever nature, it is the extent to which we can be with it.

If we can, we come to develop profound sustainable qualities or virtues in the process such as courage, serenity, compassion, humility, love, resilience, and, yes, peace. This is possibly the most fundamental task we face as human beings, and we will explore this more in the book as we explore the process of 'soul formation'.

If we cannot, then our experience can shape us in ways that diminish the capacity of our humanity – cynicism, defensiveness, bitterness, despair, to name a few. Unprocessed experience leaves us in a place of 'dis-ease' and reactivity. Unfortunately, we can then push this out into our world and relationships and 'infect' others with it. As Richard Rohr puts it in his book *Falling Upward*, 'What we don't transform, we transmit.'[3]

You may remember Christ's words that I quoted earlier: 'I have come that they may have life, and have it to the full' (John 10:10). To live life to the full, we must dare to experience it. The real question is: 'How do we "do experience"?' How 'awake' are we to what is going on?

But then that becomes another problem to solve! How do I do that? How do I live life to the full (if indeed I want to)?

What if we just let the questions be questions and leave it at that – let go of trying to solve them and just inhabit them? And breathe. And live. Just letting our questions be questions. The poet Rainer Maria Rilke has the wisdom for us here in his *Letter to a Young Poet*:

> *'I beg you sir, be patient toward all that is unsolved in your heart and try to love the questions themselves, like locked rooms and like books that are now written in a very foreign tongue. Do not now seek the answers, which cannot be given you because you would not be able to live them. And that is the*

> *whole point – live everything. Live the questions now. Perhaps you will then gradually, without noticing it, live along some distant day into the answer.*[4]

What does it mean to 'live' some of your biggest questions? Perhaps the simplest thing right now is just to take one of them and see…

> I invite you again to pause and notice some of the biggest questions that life right now is posing you. The ones that just won't go away.
>
> Just take one of them and spend a bit of time with it.
>
> If you can, let it come to mind as fully as you can and, as you do so, try to feel into the energy that comes up with it (rather than get sucked into a pattern of thoughts).

As you do so, I imagine you will find that the energy that arises is more than just a natural, clean, curious problem-solving energy. I imagine you may find a stronger driving emotional force, or passion.

It could have an urgency to it: 'I have to get this done'; 'I can't let her down'; 'What if I fail?'; 'What if it doesn't work?'; 'What will they think of me?'; 'Don't miss the boat on this!'; 'God's told me to…'; 'I'd love to, but…'

Or it could have a calmer, clearer quality: 'This matters…'; 'I really want to…'; 'I come alive when…'; 'I'm up for that…'; 'I love this…'

As we progress, we will look with more and more subtlety at the 'energy' that underlies our thoughts and intentions. Where is it flowing from? What is its nature? In many ways it is the fundamental task of spiritual direction – what is it that we are allowing to drive and energise our decisions and choices? At this stage, we can notice a very basic distinction between:

- A compulsive, harsher, harder energy that 'grabs us' and takes over our thinking
- A wholesome, gentle, life-giving energy that inspires us and 'lights us up'

Richard Rohr, again in *Falling Upward*, refers our being 'drawn, not driven' in how we go about our lives.[5]

These different qualities are both powerful and necessary – there is nothing intrinsically wrong with either. But the former, if we are not careful, can catch and consume our attention. It is demanding and can harden the heart. The latter is inviting. It leaves us free to choose, with the heart open and online.

Our 'driven' energy can be a wonderful thing that helps us get so much done. But you may start to notice and become curious about its consuming nature. Possibly it wants what it wants just a bit too much, a bit too quickly. Or it may flip you the other way: 'This is impossible, so what's the point?' As you come to recognise it, you may also notice that, even when its demands are met, it is rarely satisfied. For example, this energy can be seen in the 'overachiever', whose every success tastes a bit hollow, and so he or she moves quickly onto the next challenge. Or in the 'people-pleaser', who can never rest, nor ever please the one person who matters most – themself! These energies are commonly referred to as 'ego-drives'. You may know some of your own well by now. Again, there is nothing wrong with them. They contain underlying positive energies – to grow, to deliver, to serve, to love. You may notice these in yourself, too. It is just that they can get overdone, mainly when they hook the 'striver' or the 'worrier' in each of us – the self that is so valiantly trying to perfect itself, to prove and improve itself by what it does.

This is the process of 'identification' – I become something I want or need from the outside world, or I become something I think I need to be. In doing so, I can forget how 'just' to be. One of our greatest acts of freedom is to choose what is driving us – what I make my 'I', the energy and focus of my will, and why.

Our questions and problems in life will never go away. We know that. The more we solve, the more we will find. Our 'driven' selves, if we have them, will never go away: they will always tend to be hungry to do the best they can. Nor will our fearful selves, our rebellious selves, our people-pleasing or pleasure-seeking selves. They are all fine and here for a reason. They just don't need to be running the show. We have a choice. It is all about where we presence our awareness.

I began this book by inviting you to reflect on what you want in life. How would it be if what you wanted was nothing, not one thing at all? How would it be if your greatest and simplest wish in life was simply 'just' to be?

PRESENCING AND SPIRITUAL DIRECTION

'Presencing' is to shift the centre of our gravity from the 'I' that's striving (or fearing or rebelling) to the 'I' that 'just' is – my being. Then I am free. I can say a warm 'hello' when my inner striver or worrier takes over my problem-solver, give them a hug and acknowledge them, but stay in the unresolved adventure of 'living my questions'. I can learn more and more to trust that, in the fullness of time and with the help forthcoming, I will 'live my way into the answers'.

I know your eye will pass rapidly over the big blank space I have left here, but why not stay there for a while? Just look at the blank page and keep looking at it. Notice what comes up in your head, any thoughts that are popping up. Feel your way into the emotions that are arising. Notice what it feels like physically in your body, the sensations that are flowing. Notice that you can notice. And what it is like 'just' to notice all this. Just notice. Right now, in the presence of a blank page, this is what my experience is…

This is awareness.

This is where our work of presencing begins, by starting to become aware of all the objects of our consciousness, not just our thoughts. These include:

- Our senses and sensations: what we are experiencing both outside and inside in the body
- Our thoughts and imaginings
- Our feelings, desires
- Our energy and intentionality
- Our deeper soul prompting, such as conscience and even the indwelling presence of the Divine

This, I will suggest in what follows, is what it means to be fully present – to be consciously in touch with all these things without being 'triggered' by them into reactivity.

And the more we notice, the more choice we have. Then we are free.

Shall we just try a simple form of 'presencing' together for a few moments? To shift from our striving 'I' to our being 'I' and see what comes?

What we do is shift our awareness from whatever it is currently identified with, usually our thoughts, and place it as wholly as we can into 'just being'. What is being? It is simply the life that is flowing. Where is it flowing? In our own bodies, so we begin there. (It is also flowing in every living thing around us, and we can use the natural world in a similar way.)

I will share a short practice with you, which is foundational for all this work, whether with groups or individuals. It can take one minute or twenty minutes, as you wish. It may already be familiar to you, in which case you can just follow your own practice.

It may also, I hope, be something you can choose to do every once in a while as you consciously pause and presence to notice your experience in the reading of this book.

Presencing in breath

This is by far the easiest place to begin. Most of the world's religions use breath in some way as a practice. In the Christian tradition, life itself begins with God breathing into dust. So, to presence in breath is to presence in that primacy of being.

Find a comfortable chair to sit on, feet planted on the ground shoulder-width apart, back well supported by the chair, so that the spine is upright and your head is just resting on your occipital joint, not tilted in any way. Let your arms rest in your lap or by your side.

When you are comfortable, close your eyes and bring all your awareness into your breath, drawing the air consciously down into your belly, noticing the expansion and release as you do so. Begin with four or five deeper breaths – breathing in through the nose (counting slowly to three on the in-breath), pausing, and then releasing out through your mouth (counting to five or more on the out-breath). Then let your breathing return to its natural rhythm and keep all your awareness focused on the experience – feel the sensation of your tummy and chest rising and falling with each breath. Feel the air coming in through your nose and out through your mouth and over your lips. Feel the experience of the air coming into your lungs; notice how your body receives the goodness of the air and returns what it no longer needs; notice the subtle refreshing flow of energy from the air as it spreads out through your body and down your limbs. Just stay noticing. If you find your mind wandering, bring it back to the experience of the breath, the simple breath of life. Just be in it. Stay for as long as you like.

When you return to your habitual state, do it really slowly. Feel into the experience of opening your eyes and letting light reach

> you. Feel into the sensation of slowly moving your hands, bending to pick up this book.

If you want to go a bit further, the other simple thing you can do as an extension of this practice is to consciously release the striving self, which will have implanted itself at a cellular level in your body – usually in the form of 'tightness' or 'hardness'. You can do this by a body scan with an intention to invite each part of your body to relax and 'let go'.

> Begin with your eyes – really feeling into them and noticing any subtle tightness or squinting or squeezing or focusing. Then up into your brow – any furrowing or frowning, however subtle. Then let your whole face just soften – cheeks, jaw, mouth, lips, nose, ears, scalp – just by feeling into each in turn and letting go. Take as long as you need.
>
> Then scan down the whole body, doing the same. Where you find any signs of stored striving – whether tightness in your muscles or stiffness in your spine and joints or clenching in your belly – just breathe into it and let go. Scan all the way down your body until you end up with your attention fully in your feet and let these soften too and almost melt into the earth, the clay, beneath you. You may notice you are almost breathing with your feet, down into the energy of the earth beneath.
>
> Then just rest, noticing possibly a new freedom and expansiveness of awareness; perhaps you can feel your face, your feet, your belly, your heart, your mind all just softly, gently rising and falling in the timeless rhythm of breath shared by every living creature on this planet. Breathing in the miracle of the air, planted on the miracle of the earth.

> And then just enjoy inhabiting your own being, feeling into the life that is flowing:
>
> - in your own skin, in every tiny nerve ending
> - within you, deep in your veins, bones, body
> - through you and around you, the flow of sensation in your skin and the feel of the atmosphere around body, face
> - about you, the sounds and substance of life everywhere
> - all just here, now, flowing.
>
> And breathe...

Welcome back! As you pick up this book again, just take a minute to notice your state, maybe any subtle differences from before. How are you feeling? What is it like in your body, your mind, your heart?

Oh, and just one more thing before we close this chapter: see if after doing this you can locate anywhere within you a sense of calm or quiet or stillness... without trying to make anything happen. It can often be experienced as a kind of absence, a feeling of nothing, emptiness, a pure space within that you can just breathe into. If you do discern a little bit of calm, however small, simply notice it and gently locate where you are experiencing it within your body. It may be in your chest, your heart, your gut, your head – all or none of these. Find that place or those places if you can. As you do, and if you sense any feeling of calm or quietening within you, drop your awareness down into it. You do this by feeling into it and noticing the physical quality of it – does it have a temperature (warm or cool), a substance (solid, air, liquid), a colour or a feel, a middle, an edge – and feel what it is like in there, as though immersing in the sensations. Try not to let the mind start trying to classify or analyse it, just relax and breathe and sink into it. Notice what happens as you do. Does it fill, expand, flow, move in any way... what starts to happen as it does?

If you have found anything, just stay there for as long as you like and enjoy it – and breathe – and rest. And simply notice.

Is it possible you have just found your peace?

Our peace. As I said at the start, what if it was here all along? What if it has never left us? What if we have just forgotten it, or become blind to it? Or, more accurately, forgotten how to inhabit it, maybe by seeking to possess it. How does this happen? How do we come to lose, or forget, our peace?

Here are a few answers that come to me straightaway:

- Maybe it is because being peaceful doesn't get you to the top of the class, or help you win at sport, or get you noticed by the girls or boys, or the adults, or teachers, or bosses or all the other 'people who matter'
- Maybe it is because being peaceful is not exactly what you think your parents wanted for you in life
- Maybe it is because being peaceful is not very profitable – it does tend to decrease consumption rather than engender it
- Maybe it is not very ambitious, or clever, or influential
- In fact, maybe it's rather 'boring'
- Maybe it is that no one ever told you how beautiful and simple and precious it was, so you focussed your attention on other things
- Maybe you never really appreciated it when you had it... until you lost it... and then you couldn't remember how to get it back
- Maybe you don't ever 'get it back', maybe you just presence back into it...

However, let us at least notice one thing about you and your peace: it sure makes you nice to be around!

In his letter to the Romans, all those years ago, St Paul wrote to his followers, with much subtlety and with a heartfelt plea, not to 'conform to the pattern of this world' (Romans 12:2). Christ expresses it more bluntly: 'What good will it be for someone to gain the whole world, yet forfeit their soul?' (Matthew 16:26).

We forget, or rather we fail to remember, because we conform to an alien patterning, something that is not 'us'. This idea will form the substance of Chapter Four: how to be wholly in the world, but not 'conformed to the world'.

Before we get to that, however, I am conscious that this book is in part written for a Christian audience, for whom this opening may have stirred some significant theological and spiritual questions. Therefore, next I will address, in relation to Christian teaching, the question, 'Why presencing?' If you do not share the Christian faith, or find this approach and language somewhat alien, you can pass straight on to Chapter Four, to explore how we break free from the conformance of our 'patterning'.

CHAPTER THREE

Why presencing matters in the Christian faith

IN THIS CHAPTER, we will explore presencing from the standpoint of the Christian faith and what it teaches about living life to the full (see John 10:10). It will be something of a biblical exposition and therefore quite different in style from my other chapters, and I come to it conscious of my own shortcomings as a theological thinker.

I will start with the basic tenets of the 'The Way' that Christ points us to, and from here connect into the significance of presencing in the process of our formation. This process is often referred to as 'becoming more Christlike'. I will invite the same approach as I have previously, of letting questions arise and seeking to 'live them' rather than answer them.

If we choose to take Christ at His word, that He is 'the way the truth and the life' (John 14:6), then we can do no better than go to His clearest guidance about this 'Way' – His direction in how to connect with God in prayer. This is possibly the cornerstone of the Christian faith, alongside Jesus' two 'commandments', which we will come to shortly.

At the heart of the Lord's Prayer are these two lines: 'Thy kingdom come,/ Thy will be done in earth, as it is in heaven' (Matthew 6:9–13, KJV). ('Thy' is the intimate 'Thou', a distinction we have lost in our modern English.)

I remember when I first encountered the Christian faith, the question that immediately arose for me was, 'How do I know what Your will is, Lord?' (rather than my own will or some manipulation of psycho-social conditioning). Eventually, after many years, I noticed the passive language in the Lord's Prayer: 'Thy will *be done*'. Perhaps I don't have to figure out God's will and strive to do it (or 'plan for my life', as I hear so many people express it). Maybe I just need to be receptive and available, and let God's will flow in and through me.

Christ's example clearly embodies this idea. So many times, He points us directly to this truth, for example in John 14:10: 'The words I say to you I do not speak on my own authority. Rather, it is the Father, living in me, who is doing his work.'

But this then replaces one 'how to' question with another: how do we become available to God's will? And how do we stay in this will once we start doing it? As soon as I give it thought, the functional mind takes over and it quickly becomes *my* will or my interpretation of God's will, and when I open my mouth to speak, they are my words, not God's.

Christ says, '[Father,] I gave them the words you gave me and they accepted them. They knew with certainty that I came from you, and they believed that you sent me' (John 17:8). There is also the powerful passage in Isaiah which speaks of the power of God's words:

> *'As the rain and the snow*
>   *come down from heaven,*
> *and do not return to it*
>   *without watering the earth*
> *and making it bud and flourish,*
>   *so that it yields seed for the sower and bread for the eater,*
> *so is my word that goes out from my mouth:*
>   *it will not return to me empty,*
> *but will accomplish what I desire*
>   *and achieve the purpose for which I sent it.'*
>
> ISAIAH 55:10-11

So how, Lord, do we know what comes from You? How do we hear and embody this 'living Word'? This is perhaps the key question for this book.

Christ's words in John 15 seem to point the way: 'Remain in me... remain in my love.' In this passage, Jesus uses the metaphor of the vine and its branches. Jesus is the true vine and we are His branches, bearing fruit for the kingdom, or not. All that is not in the true vine is cut off, withers, and is burnt. It is useless and ephemeral, because it has no reality in the life of God, and ultimately therefore no true existence.

This gives rise to a further question: how do we 'remain'? Or, in the lovely King James translation, how do we 'abide'?

We can pose the same 'how' question to Christ's other foundational precept: '"Love the Lord your God with all your heart and with all your soul and with all your mind… Love your neighbour as yourself." All the Law and the Prophets hang on these two commandments' (Matthew 22:37–40).

How can we drum up a love for a God whom we never get to see face to face? It is hard enough to love ourselves, let alone our neighbours. At least we get to meet them… We all know that we cannot love someone until they start to open up to us. Who are You, God, and how do we get to know You, so we can learn to love You? How do I do love if I don't feel it?

We will explore love much more fully elsewhere in this book but perhaps we can notice one facet here as a start. Can you maybe remember a time when you truly loved someone? If you can, may I ask you to take yourself back there? What was it like? Where was the love coming from?

Like many things in this work of presencing, we enter mystery. Love seems to arise within us. We can certainly block love or reject it, but can we will it into being? Maybe we do not have the agency in love; maybe love has the agency in us. Maybe that is why we talk about *'being* in Love'. Just as we talk about will *'being* done'.

The use of the word 'I' is also interesting in relation to love. Who is 'doing the loving'? When Paul talks in Ephesians 3 about being 'rooted and established in love', he seems to be pointing us to a 'together love', a power, together with all the Lord's holy people, to grasp how wide and long and high and deep is the love of Christ, and to know this love that surpasses knowledge – that you may be filled to the measure of all the fullness of God' (Ephesians 3:17–19).

I noticed, as I was writing the paragraph above, how I felt a weight growing on my heart – a feeling of heartbreak, of sensing the pain, the burden, of centuries of striving – of people in the Christian faith working, sacrificing, struggling, spending themselves to do works of love from hearts so under-resourced to do so. I certainly feel the inadequacy of my own love and the sense of self-judgement at 'not trying hard enough'. But it is not just that. I wonder if this is something of Christ's heart for the suffering of His people – so beautifully intentioned in all they are seeking to do for Him, but so burdened when disconnected from the source, 'a spring of water welling up to eternal life' (John 4:14). The heaviness of expending limited resources of love without replenishing. 'Dry' is the word so often used to describe this state.

'Follow me' is perhaps Christ's other fundamental command. But again, how, Lord? You know the Way, You are the Way. I may know and believe that, but where are You? How do I know I am following You? How do I know I am with You?

How do I know, how do I follow, how do I abide, how do I love, how do I do God's will? How?

These 'how' questions, to which we will keep returning, are, it seems to me, the big questions of the Christian life.

> Before we move on, I wonder whether you may want to pause and notice some of your own 'How do I?' questions? Whatever they may be, large or small. And, as in the previous chapter, notice the energy or feelings that arise within as you sit with them for a few moments. And just let these be. (Maybe note them in your journal if you want to.)
>
> And, my same invitation: let these questions be available to you as you carry on reading. It may be that, now presenced more consciously in these, reading this book may become a somewhat different experience for you.

Some of these 'how' questions can be painful. Following my own 'conversion experience', the question that immediately leapt up in me, alongside the 'will' one, was 'How do I help others know You, Lord, in the way I know You?' It literally burned in my heart. We so *want* to do these things, but how? St Paul, in his own deep frustration, poses the same question: 'I do not understand what I do. For what I want to do I do not do, but what I hate I do' (Romans 7:15). Paul describes a struggle with what he calls the 'sinful nature' or the 'body of death' (Romans 7:24). And it seems this 'body of death' has the capacity to keep hijacking our best intentions and running the show.

It is at this point that I would like to return to our word 'presencing'. It is a strange word – my spellcheck screams at me in red as I write it. However, I hope it will serve as a helpful portal through which to enter our enquiry into the questions above.

Let us return to the Way. In Luke's Gospel, Christ says to his friend, 'Martha, Martha... you are worried and upset about many things...', and you can hear His tender heart for her as He says, 'but few things are needed – or indeed only one. Mary has chosen what is better, and it will not be taken from her' (Luke 10:41–42).

This well-known passage is a good pointer for our 'how' questions. What exactly is it that Mary is doing? Sitting, resting, listening. Is that it? Is that all we need to do? But what happens if we ask, 'How is she being?' We can never know of course. But, as I ponder it, the following words arise. Present, attentive, still, quiet, receptive, loving and beloved... Maybe, in contrast to Martha, she has shifted from her striving 'I' to her being 'I'.

> You may want to pause now and take a few moments to inhabit the scene yourself in your mind's eye and pay attention to Mary as you imagine her sat with her Lord and friend and teacher. Look at her closely, and maybe even sense into what is going on within her, what it feels like to be there, experiencing things as she is.
>
> What do you notice? What arises for you? I imagine some different and richer words may come up for you than those I found above.

You may also look again at Martha and her beautiful heart for service and care, probably expressions of her true being too. Let's remember she was the one who brought Christ to Lazarus. Christ is quite explicit and careful in His words. It was not *what* Martha was doing – serving – that was the issue, it was *how* she was doing it. She was worrying (and complaining about her sister). Maybe it was her 'striving' energy, not her actions, that Christ was inviting her to notice. Too often we conflate 'being present' with stillness or inactivity.

We can be fully presenced in activity too – our work as an expression of our being – even though it is a challenge to remain there when our functional mind kicks in, as Martha found.

What then do we mean by this word 'presencing' in a Christian context? One definition is 'being *fully* present, in our *whole* being'. When I first wrote this, the wisdom of the first commandment hit me in an entirely new way. It is very specific. It does not say 'Love God', as many people often reduce it. It says very explicitly to love God with *'all your heart, soul, mind, and strength'* – with every aspect of our being. Its explicitness directs us to be attentive in *all* these faculties, each of which, as we shall see later, has its own distinctive way of 'knowing'. My head 'knows' in a certain way – it sees what is true. My heart 'knows' in a certain way – it feels what is true. My body, or 'gut', 'knows' in a certain way – it senses what is true. My soul 'knows' in a certain way – it is drawn to what is true. To be presenced is to be attuned in all these faculties – fully aware, fully awake, fully attuned, fully alive.

And then, is it possible that when we are present, we are present to the Lord? How can it not be? Because the Lord is always present. 'When two or three gather in my name, there I am with them' (Matthew 18:20) and 'I am with you always...' (Matthew 28:20). Paul expresses this idea with absolute clarity:

> *The God who made the world and everything in it is the Lord of heaven and earth and does not live in temples built by human hands... Rather, he himself gives everyone life and breath... so that they would seek him and perhaps reach out for him and find him, though he is not far from any one of us. 'For in him we live and move and have our being.' As some of your own poets have said, 'We are his offspring.'*
>
> ACTS 17:24 (MY ITALICS)

This can be our reality if we are present, not hijacked by 'the body of death'.

Joshua Luke Smith composed for Tearfund a fabulous rap 'I am a temple'.[1] In it is the line, 'When I am present, His presence permeates the present.' When we are present, the opening words of the first commandment start to become true: the Lord our God *is* One; we *are* one, in Him, in whom we live and move and have our being – our presence and His presence are inseparable. Like the prodigal, we have come 'home' to our true being. As Paul puts it, nothing can 'separate us from the love of God that is in Christ Jesus our Lord' (Romans 8:39).

When we are present, what Christ calls 'the kingdom' can come, can be 'now'. Here, there is a chance that His will *will* be done. The great joy, purpose, and fulfilment of our lives – His will at work in and through our being. All we have to do is be 'gathered'... available... present. 'Here I am, Lord, ready to do your will' (see Psalm 40:7–8).

From this perspective, via the foundational 'commands' of the faith, this 'work' of presencing sits at the very core of how to be in the Christian life. We presence 'just' to *be* with God. Then, His good, pleasing, and perfect will may *be* done... in the 'perfect imperfection' of this human *being*.

Scripture points us to another aspect of presencing that it is worth noticing. It is the connection between presence and rest, or Sabbath. In the book of Exodus, the Lord says to Moses: 'My Presence will go with you, and I will give you rest' (Exodus 33:14). Christians talk about 'resting in the Presence of God'. In Psalm 62:1: 'Truly my soul finds rest in God.' In Isaiah 30:15 (NKJV): 'In returning and rest you shall be saved; In quietness and confidence shall be your strength.' And in Jeremiah 6:16: 'Ask where the good way is, and walk in it, and you will find rest for your souls.'

Here we come to our final 'how to'. How do I 'presence' in order to love You, Lord, and rest in You and let Your will be done?

The good news, as we began to explore in the last chapter, is that presencing is actually something that we can do, or at least initiate. It is something that, in the lovely language of Brother Lawrence, we can 'practise'. There is such a wholesome wisdom to 'practising' – to do it as best we can, over and over again, without any illusions about getting it right, but just learning as we go.

As the Bible passages above imply, our work of presencing is little more than consciously and attentively making ourselves available to the greater Presence. It involves cultivating an essentially *receptive* state.

This is a paradox. If we are seeking actively to do God's will, how do we combine the *activity* of doing will with this essentially *passive* receptiveness? Christ's other great command, or rather invitation, comes to the fore here. It is to follow. In John's Gospel we read of the disciples asking Christ, 'Where are you staying?' His answer: 'Come, and you will see' (John 1:38–39). But if we follow the logic of this, where actually *is* Christ staying? Paul in Ephesians is unequivocal – Christ is 'dwelling in our hearts'. His Spirit finds His home in the 'temple' of our bodies. To follow Christ is to follow Him within, through His indwelling presence, as well as without, in His 'living Word', His teaching, and His presence in and through others. Thomas Merton captures this powerfully: 'God speaks me into being in every moment. If I can be true to the voice that utters me, then I will be everywhere in Him and Him in me.'[2]

So, we 'come and see'. We presence – and that is both active (come) as well as receptive (see). Christ describes it clearly in Matthew 11:29–30: 'Take my yoke upon you and learn from me, for I am gentle and humble in heart, and you will find rest for your souls. For my yoke is easy and my burden is light.' Eugene Peterson paraphrases this verse using the phrase, 'Learn the unforced rhythms of grace' (MSG). It is not our place to seek to make anything happen. We are utterly dependent on grace for that. But we can do our bit to be as present as possible, to be ready, 'yoked', available and awake to grace as and when it is moving. 'Few things are needed – indeed, only one.' Is this, I wonder, the 'good way' that Christ is pointing us to?

Finally, let us notice how easy it is for us to say 'no' to any of the qualities we have been enquiring into here. No to love, to will, to grace, to mystery, to Christ. So, we are most certainly capable of *not* being ready and available to grace, of being well and truly 'not present', sound asleep in our own distractions. This is the stony or weed-choked ground of the Parable of the Sower, the 'body of death' that Paul describes in Romans. It is the action of constantly 'seeking', of living in the question, that has us open to the possibility of receiving. I imagine that when Christ urges us to 'stay awake', to 'seek', to 'ask in my name', this is what He is pointing us to.

So, this book is all about how we learn to play our part. How do we become present and remain as present as we can – recognising the bulk of the work still lies with the grace of a power well beyond our own? Viewed in this way, we could begin to see presencing as maybe the greatest, and only, 'work' needed in the Christian faith.

The reference to Brother Lawrence above is a reminder that this book follows in a long and rich line of much greater works, dating back to the Desert Fathers and Mothers and many other early monastic texts such as *The Cloud of Unknowing*.[3] I will not seek to reiterate what these others have written but what I can realistically attempt is to draw from their wisdom and bring it as best I can into a practical understanding of what 'presencing' may mean in our lives today.

One consistent principle in the works of those mentioned above is the importance of *attention*. So much of this 'work' of presencing seems to be about how we deploy our attention – what we choose to focus on and allow into awareness. In Christ's words, this might be about having the 'eyes to see' and the 'ears to hear' (see Mark 8:18). 'Listen' is the first word of the rule of St Benedict, drawing from Proverbs 3: 'Incline the ear of your heart.' Mary's 'better way' has her listening and gazing at Christ. Brother Lawrence and more recently the missionary Frank Laubach invite us to be constantly thinking of God: 'We must know before we can love. In order to know God, we must often think of Him; and when we come to love Him, we shall then also think of Him often, for our heart will be with our treasure.' Laubach even set himself the task of thinking of God once a minute throughout each day. The author of *The Cloud Of Unknowing* invites us to feel into our deepest desire and constantly 'Beat with a sharp dart of longing love upon this cloud of unknowing which is between you and your God'.[4] The many different forms of prayer all invite us to do something specific with our attention, either to direct it towards God (however and wherever we conceive God to be) or to come into stillness and silence and 'no-thingness' so that we are freed from distraction and therefore wholly available to God. 'Be still, and know that I am God' (Psalm 46:10).

One key aspect of our attention is its tendency to be 'caught' – an attaching of our thoughts, emotions, or desires to something. Where our attention goes, our energy flows, often unconsciously – and ultimately where our energy flows, our life goes. A common challenge I have already highlighted is being caught in the 'head churn' of 'worrying about many things'. This can literally take us over, and the Bible often talks about this as a type of slavery. Paul highlights the inverse of the 'yoke' of Christ that we referenced earlier: 'It is for freedom that Christ has set us free. Stand firm, then, and do not let yourselves be burdened again by a yoke of slavery' (Galatians 5:1).

I mentioned earlier in the chapter that Paul spoke freely of his own struggle with the yoke of slavery: 'It is no longer I who do it, but it is sin living in me that does it' (Romans 7:20). And so, we come to the 'sin' word. It is such a problematic word because it immediately conjures up emotions of shame, guilt, and unworthiness on one hand and anger, judgement, and hypocrisy on the other. It is almost therefore impossible to use it 'cleanly' in a book of this nature, whether with a Christian or secular readership. I am going to take the broadest possible definition of 'sin' for the purposes of our enquiry here – based in Christ's teaching about the vine that we referenced earlier. What if we view sin as everything that is not originating from the will of God... the stuff that must wither on the vine and be burned? From this perspective, everyone sins (see Romans 3:23). And the more presenced we become, the more conscious we become of the scale of our sin. To be fully human is to sin but, as Julian of Norwich famously put it, 'Sin is necessary.'[5] It humbles us and brings us into redemption. The ultimate folly, the apex of the striving 'I', is to strive to perfect ourselves not to sin – and its corollary, to feel worthless and ashamed when we fail. In the face of this, Christ gently directs us to the wisdom of the prodigal. We stray, we come to our senses 'in the pig pen' (Luke 15:17), we repent, return, begin again. 'In returning and rest you shall be saved' (Isaiah 30:15, NKJV).

Paul, later in Romans, has perhaps a more helpful way of shining a light into pretty much everything we have covered in this chapter. We will use what he said as the foundational scripture to inform our enquiry in our next three chapters into *how* we actually do this 'work' of presencing.

> *Therefore, I urge you, brothers and sisters, in view of God's mercy, to offer your bodies as a living sacrifice, holy and pleasing to God – this is your true and proper worship. Do not conform to the pattern of this world, but be transformed by the renewing of your mind. Then you will be able to test and approve what God's will is – his good, pleasing and perfect will.*
>
> ROMANS 12:1-2

CHAPTER FOUR

How do we presence and where do we start?

You become what you understand.
SOREN KIERKEGAARD

THIS CHAPTER and the next two provide a step-by-step description of how the work of presencing may be undertaken. For precision, I will focus on presencing as conscious, set aside 'inner work'. But I must emphasise from the start that, once we have become familiar with presencing, we can practice it at any time and for any duration – from a few breaths to a lengthy retreat. It is a 'work' that at first may seem complex, but the complexity is more in the explaining than the practice. In section 3 we will look at practising presence in a more fluid way in the context of daily life.

In this chapter we will look at how to enter a 'state' of presenced awareness – what I call the 'gathered self'. This concerns how to come in contact with the full resources and intelligence of our being, expanding the capacity of awareness by coming into a fully 'recollected' state.

In the next chapter we will look at what becomes possible to us in this recollected state. This will focus on the role of attention in (i) 'enquiring' into what is truly present – including the Divine and subtle spiritual qualities such as peace and (ii) transforming our experience into the substance of our growth.

In Chapter Six we will look at how, with this expanded, presenced, awareness available to us, we can participate in the deeper work of transformation in the life of the heart and the soul.

Bringing ourselves online – the gathered self

As I suggested in the previous chapter, the cornerstone of this work of presencing is accessing a fuller, more aware and resourceful state of being. In the Judaeo-Christian tradition, this is what the first commandment is referring to when it reminds us to love the Lord 'with *all* your heart and with *all* your soul and with *all* your mind and *all* your strength' (Deuteronomy 6:5, my italics).

Unfortunately, as I have already described, that is not the 'normal', 'habitual' or what I term the 'functional' self with which we go about our daily lives. If we are not awake to this fundamental truth (which is probably why it is the first commandment!) then we 'forget' our fuller being and spend our lives inhabiting this functional self, which is ruled and driven by an essentially 'mechanistic' mind. Let me say a bit more about this before we then explore the process of how we 'gather' ourselves into our fuller being.

Our functional self is the mind that St Paul refers to as open to 'the pattern of this world' (Romans 12:2). Our functional self is amazing! There is absolutely nothing 'wrong' with it (except maybe its tendency to be always judging itself). It is here to serve and is constantly evaluating its performance. This mind is highly effective at enabling us to live our lives based on constructs and reliable 'patterns' that we do not need to keep reviewing. The extract below from a paper on the 'hierarchically mechanistic mind' describes this idea with a clinical precision:

> *The HMM describes the brain as a complex adaptive system that actively minimises the decay of our sensory and physical states by producing self-fulfilling action-perception cycles via dynamical interactions between hierarchically organised neurocognitive mechanisms...*[1]

The functional mind is extraordinarily capable, but it is only a representation of reality, the map not the territory. It serves us until, one day, it does not.

The problem arises when we 'lean on our own understanding' as the proverb says (see Proverbs 3:5–6) and allow our representation of reality to become reality. Modern psychology has long understood that the mind has an inherent tendency to 'laziness', to lean on the patterns of our habitual associations. Daniel Kahneman distinguishes between two 'systems' of thought. System 1 is reactive, associative, and relatively ungoverned by consciousness and will. System 2 is aware, awake, curious, questioning and reflective – but slow and hard work. 'The operations of System 1 are fast, effortless, associative, and often emotionally charged; they're also governed by habit, so they're difficult either to modify or to control.' This reluctance to question the underlying patterns of associations leads us into an increasingly disconnected, self-reinforcing state which starts to shape our experience of reality as we act it out. As postmodernism has highlighted, we end up making our own narratives the 'truth'.

You can see these patterns most obviously in relationships. When my children were young, I always related to them on a level about two years behind where they actually were (though they may say twenty years behind!). I suspect that I, like many parents, succumbed to 'managing' my children and forgot to simply *be* with them – with that sense of wonder, curiosity, and amazement about what they would come up with next. This is what happens when we treat our representation of reality as 'truth'. We limit what is possible. We do the same in our attitude to God. We even do it to ourselves: the patterned mind holds our self-concept, the 'I' that I think I am or that I strive to be – the story that I construct about myself. This is likewise limited, usually formed from clusters of associations and identifications from *past* experience and therefore not really *present* at all. I become the memory of myself.

In this state, the resources of our true being – heart, soul, strength – are either offline or severely constrained. As the first commandment indicates, these aspects of our being are not offline to God. It is likely that Divine wisdom and presence is being shared with us throughout our being – in body, heart, soul, and our higher mind. The first commandment speaks of '*all* your mind'. Sadly, we rarely switch it 'all' on. In over-relying on the 'functional mind',

('System 1'), we miss the dynamic intelligence available in what I will refer to as the 'the higher mind' ('System 2').

The Divine, which is always present, will be speaking to us in the higher mind, which is open and present, rather than the functional mind, which is a representation of the past. (As you develop your somatic noticing, you may actually experience this as a physical constriction – a subtle pressure around the inside of the skull, like a kind of hood, or cloak on the mind.) Iain McGilchrist refers to the former as the 'Master', which perceives the Greater Intelligence at work and which he locates on the 'right side of the brain'. The latter he terms the 'Emissary', which carries it out – which he locates on the 'left'. When the power balance between these two becomes reversed, we become blinded by functionality (and fear). For those of you familiar with the book trilogy *Lord of the Rings*, this is dramatically displayed in the third instalment of the series, *Return of the King*, when the steward Denethor usurps King Aragorn.[2]

Otto Scharmer, the leadership writer, describes presencing as 'learning from the future as it is emerging' in contrast to 'cognition' which he calls 'learning from the past'.[3] He views this as essential to our capacity as a species to embrace change and evolve in conditions of ever-increasing complexity. The Bible, particularly Proverbs, teaches us that understanding needs to be constantly illuminated by 'wisdom', an aspect of the Divine that we can intuit, receive, and participate in, which, from a spiritual perspective is the necessary lifeblood of Kahneman's 'System 2'.

> *Blessed are those who find wisdom, those who gain understanding, for she is more profitable than silver and yields better returns than gold... Her ways are pleasant ways, and all her paths are peace. She is a tree of life to those who take hold of her; those who hold her fast will be blessed... My son, do not let wisdom and understanding out of your sight, preserve sound judgment and discretion; they will be life for you, an ornament to grace your neck. Then you will go on your way in safety, and your foot will not stumble. When you lie down, you will not be afraid; when you lie down, your sleep will be sweet.*
>
> (PROVERBS 3:13-14, 17-18, 21-24)

As we lean less on the understanding and learn to trust the flow of wisdom, the understanding can be transformed, enabling us 'not to stumble' but find fresh, timely, relevant responses beyond our pre-existing patterning and indeed to reset our patterning to enable new 'wise habits' to be formed.

This requires us to be available to the emanations of the Divine, which are always now – the greater wisdom that enables us to discern true Will. The mental state required is what we might call an 'open mind', available for the 'renewing of our minds' that Paul talks about in the Romans 12 passage I quoted at the end of the last chapter. This way of being can, however, be scary because it involves a profound feeling of loss of control. It requires a high degree of trust. You might see this trust displayed in a young child, who is both fascinated and terrified by their first encounter with, say a pet dog. Fearful wariness and excited curiosity are flip sides of the same response. When these appear, something unpredictable is happening. But the side of the coin we choose creates the 'reality' of our encounter. For the mind to open, the heart has to be online, not shut down by fear. For the heart to be online, the body has to feel grounded and secure. That, as we shall see, is foundational to the practice of presencing that I describe below.

So, if presencing is essential for the 'renewing' of our minds, whether for the purpose of embracing complexity or Divine wisdom, or both, how, then, do we go about it?

I am going to suggest a six-step process here as a fundamental basis for our 'work' of presencing. I am putting 'work' in inverted commas so that we can remember that presence is not something we can make happen solely in our own strength, it is always dependent on an element of grace, the help of something mysterious beyond our own agency. But we can 'work at being present' such that when grace is at 'Work' we are available to receive it and collaborate with it. As we proceed you will see this combined 'work/Work' is a subtle dance between the active and the passive, the initiating and the receptive.

The basic process I am outlining here has usually to be initiated from the functional mind. This comprises six conscious steps which I will now go on to describe in more detail in the rest of this chapter:

1. Voluntarily releases its grip on our being by...
2. Consciously presencing awareness in the body and releasing

tension so that we can come into a more settled, expanded state in which we can...
3. Presence awareness in the life of the body, the flow of sensation and...
4. In the life of the mind, the flow of thought and...
5. In the life of the heart, the flow of feeling and desire and then finally...
6. In all these aspects simultaneously, i.e. in the awareness of the totality of our being

In this book, I am calling this process 'gathering' ourselves into a 'recollected state', in which we are fully awake, alive, and, most importantly, from a spiritual perspective, available to the immanent Presence, Wisdom and Will of the Divine. As I describe this, I will go into some detail and indicate how or why these different steps are important or useful to our work going forwards. It may therefore seem somewhat long, or complex. However, the basic steps are very simple, and I will highlight these in boxes as I go. The most important thing, which I will keep emphasising, is that we do this with *no other agenda than just to 'notice' what is present.* We are not trying to make anything happen, simply expanding awareness into all our facets of being so these are available to us. How we respond to what emerges we will cover in later chapters.

Step 1: Coming out of the functional mind

The first step, perhaps the greatest challenge, is to free ourselves, however fleetingly, from the grip of the 'functional mind'. We do not need to silence or stop this mind, but we can learn to 'disidentify' with it, to leave it happily working in the background, and put our awareness in our other faculties – heart, soul, higher mind, and body. If the functional mind is too dominant, these faculties become buried and resort to acting in a reactive, subversive way, often subconsciously. This can, in turn, be experienced as disorder and dissonance in the functional mind, further exacerbating its tightening.

The functional mind is paradoxically essential to our work of presencing because it must notice and learn that presencing is needed. The simplest way to ensure this is by creating some kind of practice or rule of life, which includes, say, prayer, stillness, or creativity, and to embed this in the functional mind as a habit. To do this, however, the functional mind must perceive the practice as 'functional' – i.e. worth doing.

It can take a while for this realisation to land with sufficient force to overcome the more reactive drivers. (For example, have you ever tried pausing in the middle of a work meeting for midday prayer?) Gradually, however, we come to recognise that our lives are more productive and peaceful and that we are better people on the days we have our time of quiet than on the days we don't. Once the functional mind has accepted this as a practical truth, it is more likely to find the will to prioritise it. So, the functional mind is not the 'enemy', it is our friend in this work. But it needs training. We will say more on this in Chapter Eleven.

Outside of a daily discipline, the functional mind can also develop a capacity to self-observe and recognise when presencing is needed. In many ways this is what this book is all about. By self-observe, I mean the mind coming to recognise that it is 'stuck' or that something (e.g. wisdom) is required from it that is beyond its cognitive patterning. It may be realising that something is not working out as it expected, or recognising being caught in an unproductive pattern, such as getting impatient, anxious, or over-controlling. At such a point, the functional mind may have learned the awareness to say to itself, 'pause', 'breathe', or 'pray' (rather than panic or tighten). Through these actions we surrender the illusion of control to access a fuller state of being, one which may have the resources necessary better to handle what is going on – including, of course, access to the wisdom and grace of the Divine.

I often imagine Jesus doing this in the Gospel accounts, just pausing and waiting for wisdom to emerge, for the right words to come. A good example might be when, with the crowd poised to stone the woman caught in adultery, Jesus pauses, looks down at the ground and writes in the dust with his finger. I imagine Him breathing and calming and grounding Himself amidst all the frenzy and turmoil of the situation, and His own horror, anger, and sadness. Then, as He accesses something deeper, more stable, His inner peace, presence, and wisdom can flow: 'Let any one of you who is without sin be the first to throw a stone at her' are the words that arise – and the situation diffuses (John 8:7). These words clearly came from a different place than the functional mind. Later, Jesus describes where His wisdom comes from: 'These words you hear are not my own; they belong to the Father who sent me' (John 14:24).

> The presencing process is thus initiated by the functional mind, which, recognising its own limits, voluntarily chooses to surrender its dominant vigilance and control, and then steps back to play more of a 'gatekeeper' role (see John 10 – 'the gatekeeper opens the gate').

Step 2: Becoming present in the body

To 'surrender control' in this sense is to release our habitual identification with the functional mind and its triggers, reactions, and associations – recognising that 'I am not my thoughts.' The simplest way to do this is to locate our awareness elsewhere by 'grounding' it in the body and breath. The power of the body and breath are that they are present *experiences* of being, not ideas or memories of being. Grounding in the body and breath is an increasingly accepted element of life nowadays, as it is found in many meditation and prayer practices, such as mindfulness, yoga, or centering prayer. Breath is massively significant, as we shall see later, and this is reinforced by its primary place in the Bible: 'And the LORD God formed man of the dust of the ground, and breathed into his nostrils the breath of life; and man became a living soul' (Genesis 2:7–9, KJV).

Whilst we cannot think our way to presence, to an expanded state of being, we can sense our way there, as we do when walking in the dark, with all our senses fully alert. Our sensory knowing is the most present, because it is the fastest – as we witness in our instinctive reactions, which way outpace our emotional (next fastest) and our cognitive ones.

On a retreat recently at Worth Abbey, Fr Martin McGee introduced me to an extraordinary passage about this power of 'sensing beyond seeing', recorded in the book *And Then There Was Light*, written by Jacques Lusseyran. As the result of an accident, Jacques became blind at the age of seven. He writes that his blindness turned out to be a blessing because it enabled him to tune in more and more to his inner light, which he describes as 'life and love', and how, in this light, everything in his life fell into place:

> *It was a great surprise to me to find myself blind, and being blind was not at all as I imagined it. Nor was it as the people around me seemed to think it. They told me to be blind meant not to see. Yet how was I to believe them when I saw? ...*
>
> *I still wanted to use my eyes. Finally, one day... I realised that I was looking in the wrong way... I was looking too far off, and too much on the surface of things... At this point some instinct made me change course. I began to look more closely, not at things but at a world closer to myself, looking from an inner place to one further within...*
>
> *I was aware of a radiance coming from a place I knew nothing about, a place which might as well have been outside me as within. But radiance was there, or, to put it more precisely, light. It was a fact, for light was there. I saw light and went on seeing it though I was blind...*
>
> *Still there were times when the light faded almost to the point of disappearing. It happened every time I was afraid. If, instead of letting myself be carried by confidence and throwing myself into things, I hesitated, calculated, then without exception I hit or wounded myself. What the loss of my eyes had not accomplished was brought about by fear. It made me blind.*[4]

There is so much power and subtlety in Jacques' experience and it is the fruit of profound and prayerful inner work. But he makes the point, which we shall explore further, that there is much more resourcefulness available to us than we 'think' – if we can get past our fear and our need to control our experience.

We will look more at the power of attention later, but presencing awareness in the body and senses is one of the most simple and effective ways of enriching this crucial aspect of consciousness. In the Gospels, Christ is constantly referring us to it: 'Those who have ears to hear and eyes to see'.

For our purposes in this chapter, the main reason for bringing awareness into breath, body, and the senses is that it takes us directly into the flow of Life within us, the same miraculous flow that permeates all living things – river, breeze, ocean, trees, sap, blood, and breath. I will suggest a simple body presencing practice in a minute, to help us notice what it is like to be awake to this flow (if you like, our own 'inner light'). We learn to rest awareness in the miracle of our physical being, with its pulses of energy, its strength, its subtle substance, and delicate sensibility. As we do so, we begin to recognise that

'Life has us' rather than the other way round. It brings us out of our fantasises of control and reactive associations and into a place of pure being.

Having developed this capacity for self-observation in the body, we can then do the same in the head and enjoy the inner experience of the flow and 'substance' of our thoughts, and the miracle of the vast field of intelligence which produces them – we can 'see our thoughts' without being caught in them. The mind can breathe. We can do the same in the heart and notice the presence and 'substance' of our emotions, desires, and deepest yearnings and again just allow them to be here, without any need to act them out. The heart can open and relax and reveal its many treasures. More on this later.

If you are approaching this as a spiritual practice, we can note that this is again what St Paul refers to in Romans 12. We are making our bodies a 'living sacrifice', fully alive, fully offered. As we do so, we may experience gratitude for the miracle of our creation – our 'true act of worship'. As we will see later, this step of 'living sacrifice' becomes the starting point for 'transforming' and 'renewing'.

To sacrifice something is simply, consciously, and deliberately to offer it up. So that is what we do – as systematically and thoroughly as we can, scanning through the body, relaxing and 'letting go' – sensing into anywhere or anyhow we are 'taut', or clenched, trying to retain control. If we were to take this completely literally, that means releasing every single cell of our body from our own tight grasp and offering it up – coming into a place of pure receptivity for the breath of God, the true, constant Life force within us. Fully alive, fully receptive.

As we presence in the body, we begin to realise we are not present in something static, but in something flowing, constantly alive and moving, like the flow of a river, the wind in the trees, or the pulse of the ocean. The most obvious is the pulse of our own heart and blood, but we may also notice tingling on the skin, taste in the mouth, subtle pressure around the face, cheeks, eyes, temples and gradually we learn to tune into the intelligence of the body, the senses. It is the fastest intelligence we have, the instinctive. The body knows what to do to live. From the minute it was born, it knew how to suckle, to clasp, to breathe, to eat, to touch, and to make connection, long before the conscious mind started trying to instruct it to do the things it wants.

So, how do we do this? Let's have a go at presencing in the body as you may already have done briefly in Chapter 3. We will then follow this by presencing more actively in the senses.

> The simplest way of presencing in the body is with a complete, head to toe body scan. You can find a recording of a guided body scan in... **chrisblakeley.uk/meditations**.
>
> Start with breath – three or four deep breaths into the belly, breathing in through the nose and out through the mouth, and really feeling it. Let your centre of gravity drop and, if you can, when you return your breath to normal, leave a tiny bit of awareness in the belly, feeling it rising and falling in the endless rhythm of breath.
>
> Then, beginning with the face, relax the muscles – coarse muscles, fine muscles – eyes, brow, forehead, cheeks, jaw, mouth, lips and tongue.
>
> Do the same with the rest of your body, scanning all the way down to your feet, relaxing muscles, tendons, joints, releasing any tightness.
>
> Go deeper, bones and fascia and organs.
>
> Pay particular attention to places where we store our striving – small of back, tummy, shoulders, chest, feet, and hands. The parts of us that are always clinging on, not wanting to lose control, loosen their grip. Bring your awareness into these and breathe into them with a relaxing, softening breath.
>
> If you have time and space, you can breathe into every part of the body, aerating it. In the words of the old hymn, 'Breathe on me breath of God, fill me with life anew'. Just enjoy it and let go. You may notice how your body gratefully receives the invitation

to rest, to come back into its natural form, its God-given shape. You can be in this fully, sensing into fingertips, toes, tongue, kneecaps, eyes and forehead, just letting them relax and breathe. Literally coming to rest – not a sleepy rest, but a fully awake state of equilibrium, poised, ready to move again when willed. You can do it in silence, seated in a meditation pose, or lying down, or even when walking – just let the body be.

To consciously place your attention in your body is like dropping your mind down into the place you are focusing on, say your feet, and feeling into it – noticing what it feels like there, any sensations or feelings of flow, temperature, substance. This is the beginning of noticing the amazing 'somatic intelligence' of the body, which is communicating to us all the time, though most of the time we filter it out. As you practice with this, your freedom and scope of attention can expand considerably also. You can place your awareness anywhere and can be aware that you are aware – that you are more than your thoughts, feelings, and sensations. You are free to experience them all, not just the ones that crowd in on you. You may also begin to notice your state is shifting too – a more relaxed, spacious feel to body and mind. As you notice, let be, just enjoy it. Try not to let the brain engage and start trying to make sense of it or 'capture' it.

Step 3: Presencing in sense and sensation – our 'somatic intelligence'

The next step is presencing in this awareness of flow, the life of the body. The easiest place to start is with sensation, the tingling aliveness of your skin, maybe beginning with your feet and hands, and then just let it fill up your limbs and around the body and face. You may notice the sensitivity to touch, temperature, texture. You might also be able to feel the energy just above your skin and the atmosphere around you.

Feel breath, drawing it deep into the belly and then spreading sensation, warmth, temperature within the body. This can be done as a simple conscious offering. The easiest form for this is gratitude for the miracle of this body and all it does for you – acknowledging it as gift – as St Ignatius does in his *Suscipe* prayer: 'You gave it to me Lord, to you I return it.' As you experiment with shifting your awareness into different locations within the torso and head and noticing what it is like to sense inwards, you might also choose to do so with a conscious acknowledging that your body is a 'temple of the Holy Spirit', as St Paul puts it.

You can also presence your awareness in your other senses: the experience of scent(s) in the nose, of taste(s) in the mouth, of sounds in the ears, near and far, and, as you open them, of sight in the eyes, just allowing the experience of light and colour to land in a broad peripheral vision, and not worrying about focusing or classifying perception.

A helpful way to locate a sustained practice of this inward sensing is to bring awareness and breath into a point a couple of inches below the navel (known in some eastern traditions as the 'Kath' point, or 'Dantien' or 'Hara'). As you learn to feel down into it, you gradually start to become familiar with it as a sense, as a place of stability or inner equilibrium – like the core or centre of your physical presence – a place of groundedness and rootedness.

If you want to get into a regular practice of 'stilling prayer', this is a helpful location to focus awareness on and breath into. I often encourage people in the Christian faith to breathe into this place using the words from Psalm 46:10: 'Be still, and know that I am.' It can also be very helpful in the day-to-day when you encounter

> stressful or challenging or distracting situations – couple of deep breaths down here can ground you and restore your equilibrium and presence.

We can presence our awareness in any other areas within the body we wish. If we just experiment with this over time, we will get to notice some of the subtle flows and energy of this 'inner life'. Other places to sense into may include the legs and feet, the base of the spine, and the flow of energy up and down the spine from the coccyx to the brainstem. We can feel into different layers of energy and sensation in the belly and gut, right the way down into the groin and up to the tummy. We can also sense into the solar plexus and the heart (the wide oval of the emotional centre contained within the chest from the solar plexus to the top of the sternum). We may feel into the throat, a place of expression but also of containment and choking back. We can also notice different areas within the head – the back of the head, the cerebellum, near the base of the skull, the centre of the head, the front of the head, and the top of the head. As we do this we may start to discern subtly difference qualities of experience in these, each with its own intelligence and 'knowing'.

As we go about this, we can also allow ourselves to notice different *sensations* – of energy, temperature, or flow, or of blockage, disturbance, or constriction. This is developing awareness. There is no need to 'do' anything, we are simply noticing and offering up everything within us, just as it is – our extraordinary body, fully alive, fully at rest, a 'living sacrifice' – with an attitude of reverence or 'worship', as Paul expresses it. We are not worshipping the body, but have an attitude of worship in the body – 'loving the Lord with all our strength'. We are not trying to make anything happen or change anything, we are simply acknowledging the gift that is the life within us and, in the acknowledging, bringing it into conscious surrender or offering back to God. (The Hebrew word *rafa* in Psalm 46, which is often translated 'Be still', is more accurately translated, 'surrender'.)

As we surrender, we expand our capacity to be more and more aware of the subtle movements of life and energy – and Presence – within and around us. This is foundational in the 'work' of presencing – sensing into the wisdom of our embodied experience, our somatic intelligence.

Once we have cultivated this somatic awareness, we can use it to inform our *enquiry* into what is flowing within us – in times of discernment, for example, or the process Paul alludes to in Romans of 'being transformed'. In this process, which I will cover in more depth later, we start to enquire into what is 'at Work' within us, processing our inner experience in a way that brings us into wisdom and wholeness.

Step 4: Presencing awareness in thought

As the body relaxes and softens, especially if supported by prayer and an attitude of gratitude, we begin to feel safe. The parasympathetic nervous system comes more online, and we relax out of the (sometimes deeply engrained) 'fight/flight/freeze' patterns that inhibit our openness and natural curiosity. This enables us, as we let go of our self-protective wariness and the need to be in control, to presence and relax in the mind and in the heart. With the body in this state of 'living sacrifice', fully at rest, fully awake, and our somatic awareness expanded and free, we are then able to bring this awareness back into the inner life, the world of thought and feeling.

> A first step is simply to bring attention to the centre of the head, just between the ears and behind the eyes – this is a kind of resting place in the mind where it is possible simply to relax and experience what it is like to be in the flow of thought. In my meditations, I often use the analogy of sitting in a meadow and watching thoughts blow gently through, like the wind in the grass. The aim here is to enjoy the sensation of thought and just letting it come and go, with no need to attach to it or give any particular thought any attention – just to enjoy the experience of being a thinking being, in this vast field of endless intelligence.
>
> As we do so, we can become aware how far this field stretches – way beyond the limits of the head. How far can we see, where do thoughts come from and where do they go? We may also do this with an increasing reverence for the miracle and

> mystery and vastness of the gift of intelligence, of 'mind' and of 'consciousness'. Just simply being here, enjoying it and letting these gifts be present.

Psalm 139:17 comes to mind: 'How precious to me are your thoughts, God! How vast is the sum of them! Were I to count them, they would outnumber the grains of sand.' We may also allow ourselves to be aware of how the energy of thought in the mind mingles and collaborates with the energy of sensation in the body to create the awareness of our being, and we may experience this expanding as we do so.

Step 5: Then in emotion...

> From here, you can allow this expanding awareness to descend gently to a similar place of stillness right in the centre of your chest, just behind the sternum, about halfway down the rib cage. You can put your hand there to help locate it, if that helps. Let your awareness gradually settle here, right in the centre of the vast area of your heart, which in this inner sensing into the emotional life, can be experienced as a huge oval stretching from the base of your throat down to the solar plexus. As you rest your awareness here, you can just allow your heart to breathe and rest and relax too, like your body. You may even feel it open as you do this.
>
> As you do so, you can become aware of the substance of your heart, most obviously your feelings and emotions, but also desires and hopes and fears and of course deeper feelings such as love and care – and the things you most value and treasure in life which you 'guard in your heart'. Again, as in your mind, your only agenda is to experience these, just letting them all be. There is no need to do anything with them or pick anything up

> and start 'worrying it'; you can just 'welcome' them all – they all belong and are here for a reason.

In this basic 'gathering' of ourselves, we do not attach to anything. We can however allow ourselves to experience a certain gratitude that we can feel this much, care this much, that we are this alive on the inside as well as the outside. As we relax in the heart, as in the mind, we may feel it soften and open and become aware of its vastness too – the depth of the heart, our deepest yearnings and knowings and, of course, Love. We may also sense the breadth of the heart. As it softens, we may experience the warm energy of the heart coming out through the chest, mingling with the energy of sensation, to reach out and embrace the world and the flow of life around us. If we do, again, we can just enjoy the experience. There is no need to do anything with it.

Step 6: Fully presenced in the 'gathered self'

> As you do this conscious work of presencing in sensation in the body, thought in the mind, and feeling in the heart, you can come finally to a point where you are conscious of all three simultaneously. In this state, you are fully aware of, and available to, all the objects of consciousness – thoughts, sensations, feelings. This means they have no need to 'hijack' you – you can give them the conscious attention that you need and choose. As you do so, you may begin to notice what an expanded and peaceful state this is. It is sometimes called a state of 'self-recollection', literally a 'collecting' of our scattered self, brought back together into a whole. You may want to actively notice this as a state of expanded awareness, what it is like to be present in the fullness of your being – all its aspects – rather than being 'caught' or identified with one. Try to stay for a while in this, staying aware simultaneously of thought in the mind, feeling in the heart, and sensation in the body. If you find yourself getting

> attached to a particular object of your experience, just bring awareness back into breath, maybe using the deep belly as an anchor point, as I suggested earlier. The more familiar you become with this recollected state, the easier and quicker it is to gather yourself back into it.

As we practice this, we will begin to notice a change in our sense of being. It can feel a little uncomfortable at first, even a little giddy, as the functional mind releases control and we are just present, as we are, with no need to identify the mind with any of the objects of consciousness. We are free 'just' to 'be', from where we can begin to make more conscious, clearer choices about *how* we 'be'.

One of the most powerful things we can do in this state is also to notice the part of us that is aware – the one who is doing the noticing – and locate that capacity in ourselves. As we do so, we may experience a strange expansion or opening of consciousness – pure awareness – and begin to realise the freedom we have to place our attention anywhere and experience everything, including something beyond the realm of our immediate experience, something enduring... a greater Presence, in and through and beyond our own.

I have chosen the word 'gathering' to describe this process of self-recollection as a deliberate echo of Christ words when He says, 'Where two or three gather in my name, there am I with them' (Matthew 18:20). From this perspective, 'Gathering in my name' is simultaneously a process of gathering ourselves inwardly, even as we come together outwardly. It is only as we 'gather' with *all* these aspects of our being fully online that we can begin to be wholly present – heart, soul, mind, and strength – and if we are present, how can Christ not be, who is with us 'to the very end of the age' (Matthew 28:20).

In this recollected state, therefore, we can begin to remember who we truly are in Christ. We can become available to both Divine healing and leading. That is what we will look at in subsequent chapters. But let me close this chapter by re-emphasising that this recollected state is the absolute foundation of everything we go on to explore in this book. It is therefore something to keep on practising, whenever and however, as we remember to do it.

> We just bring awareness into breath, feel our feet on the ground, attend to the sensitivity of touch and sensation in the body and of other senses, become aware of the flow of thoughts in the head and the presence of feelings in the heart.

We can do this in a minute waiting for a train, or we can do it in an hour-long meditation – either is valid. As we do so, we develop the capacity to disidentify from our reactivity and free up our attention – and it is this, the faculty of a free attention, the main fruit of this self-gathering, that we will look at next.

But before you turn the page and 'enter' the next chapter, why not take a break to let this one seep in. Then, possibly, before you do begin the next chapter, and before every chapter hereafter, practise what we have covered here – a short time of stilling and presencing, even if only a couple of minutes, to gather yourself into the recollected state.

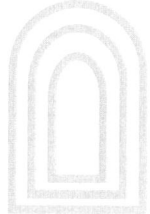

CHAPTER FIVE

Presencing and attention

*Surely I have stilled and quieted my soul,
Like a weaned child with his mother...*

PSALM 131:2 (NKJV)

THE PROCESS OUTLINED in the last chapter of 'gathering' ourselves into a recollected state of awareness in heart, mind, and body is the foundational step of presencing – and any significant transformational or spiritual work that may then follow. This may be to do with our own healing, our own 'call', or our capacity to be available to the second commandment. We will look at these 'fruits' of presence more in later chapters, but in this one we can begin to notice what becomes possible to us when we are thus 'gathered' – specifically how we use the full scope of our expanded attention.

In the recollected state, one of the first things we will begin to see and therefore find freedom from is the pattern of our 'identifications'. When I can just be, I don't have to be a something else, even if that something else is a narrative for my own identity. I don't have to make myself an object of my own consciousness. This is one of the fundamental distortions of the functional mind which needs to project its identity onto self-narratives, or other particular objects of consciousness, in order to acquire and sustain its sense of self. In short, the functional mind has to make itself an 'object' in order to have an existence.

These narratives could be external (e.g. roles/relationships) or internal (qualities, norms, values, religious beliefs). For example, 'I am a teacher', 'I am British', 'I am uneducated', 'I am angry'. These can become dense clusters of emotionally charged associations that fundamentally impact our self-concept and leave us vulnerable to 'comparative' distortions in our sense of identity and consequent behaviour. This was rather harshly referred to as 'envy' in early Christian teaching, for example, 'I am not good looking/clever/rich, etc, and therefore not worthy' or 'I am a Christian, therefore I must be a kind person. But I am not always kind, sometimes unkind and often pretend-kind, therefore I am ashamed and not worthy of God.'

Releasing ourselves from identification, including the carping voice of the inner critic, is one of the first major freedoms of the presenced life. As I gather myself into the recollected state, I can just be 'I' – pure awareness. In this state, I am free to notice everything that is present without having to react. This is the spaciousness of a free attention. With that freedom and curiosity available to us, we can now start to open up into a work of gentle, 'prayerful' enquiry. Freed from our 'patterning', we can begin to allow the 'transforming' that Paul speaks of in Romans 12. (I have put prayerful in inverted commas because I am conscious the word will mean so many different things to so many different people. I will cover prayer much more fully later, but I am using it here as a way of indicating a continuation of the same 'surrendered' principle we spoke about earlier – a release of control and a trusting in a larger presence, power, wisdom, or grace, necessarily beyond our understanding. This may or may not be a religious concept – and if it is, we have to be careful that we are not limiting God to our 'understanding' of God.)

'Enquiry' is an important term in this work. It refers to a process of examining what is happening in our inner state. It is the start point of opening ourselves to the possibility of healing, transformation, and growth, as well as to the movement of a greater Will within us.

> Enquiry begins with an honest, open, curious noticing. Having come into the recollected state with a balanced awareness in head, heart, and body, we can begin to notice what seems to be presenting itself to our attention – possibly at the instigation of the Divine presence or the Holy Spirit's 'nudging'. Expecting nothing, hoping for nothing, just simply noticing, what is present? What is actually being experienced? What seems to be wanting to make itself known to me?

When I am working with people who are happy with the language and prayer of the Christian faith, I will often encourage a prayer for the grace of protection over this practice. It can be as direct as the kind of prayer often used in the Ignatian tradition:

> 'Lord, may all my thoughts, words, actions, and intentions in this time of quiet be directed purely to serving You and glorifying Your holy name, and, Holy Spirit, please protect and guide me in my work.'

Or I might use the opening of Psalm 139 to locate the entire process of presencing into a power greater than our own. It is true prayer of 'living sacrifice':

> *You have searched me, Lord, and you know me. You know when I sit and when I rise; you perceive my thoughts from afar. You discern my going out and my lying down; you are familiar with all my ways. Before a word is on my tongue you, Lord, know it completely. You hem me in behind and before, and you lay your hand upon me. Such knowledge is too wonderful for me, too lofty for me to attain.*
>
> PSALM 139:1-6

> A simple prayer based on this might be, 'Give me the grace, Lord, to surrender to Your gaze, knowing that You search me with eyes of pure love and truth. Let me be 'hemmed in', that Your enfolding Presence may surround and hold me safe in all that arises.'

We then are in a position to 'follow', to enquire into whatever makes itself known to our attention. This may be anything – a need for some inner healing, a crucial relationship, a feeling we had not noticed before, a movement of our soul or deeper nature or even some kind of intimation of Presence from the Divine. Building on the practice outlined in the previous chapter, I always suggest beginning our process of enquiry with our somatic noticing. This is tangible, substantial, present, and therefore relatively undistorted by our cognitive patterning. Otherwise, if we are not careful, the functional mind quickly gets involved and starts anticipating and interpreting what we are experiencing.

> We may for example notice as we still, beneath all the more urgent things that are always clamouring for attention, the sensation of a previously unnoticed quietness, or calm, or even an emptiness in the heart. If we do, we can sense into this. What is the texture, substance, temperature etc? Where does it begin and end, what is its shape? We can notice what happens if we feel around it or into it, noticing how it feels on the outside, or what it is like to drop inside it. As we give it attention, it may well evolve and fill and spread and shift. 'What is this?' we can gently ask, and let it answer and yield its secrets.

If it is something we want to give fuller attention to, we can drop our awareness more deeply into it and consciously, actively, receive it in our being. If it is peace, we may notice how it flows, what it is like in the body, arms, legs, the feeling on our skin and the texture of the atmosphere around us. We may notice what it is like deep inside the belly or the head – gradually you become more and more 'peace-full'. As we do so, we may also begin to notice what happens to the quality of our thinking, our sense of presence and identity, our connection with the beyond – we may even enquire where and how the Divine is present in this, and see what happens. We may begin to sense an intelligence, a knowing in the peace, that is more than our habitual knowing.

Or we may discover something else, maybe a strange, warm or cool, bubbly feeling somewhere down in the gut, like a spring within – and as we sense down into it, it may reveal itself to be 'joy' and, again, as we allow it and welcome it and receive it more fully, we can experience its flow within, the energy flowing upwards, like liquid light, out of the top of the body, into the mind, and beyond, or an enlivening/quickening in the body, or we may drop down into the flow and notice where it is flowing from, a deep mysterious source way down within, beyond even. And again, we may notice an intelligence, a wisdom, 'truth and life' in the joy. I say all these things as a 'may' – we each will experience our inner qualities in different ways. We need just to allow this and not go looking for what we expect to find.

We may also choose to presence in more disturbing, darker, painful feelings and sensations – what are these too revealing to us? This can be more challenging and we may instinctively avoid it, or experience fear at what will be revealed. This is often the first step of inner transformation, sometimes referred to as 'embracing the shadow'. We will look at this in more depth in the next chapter on the heart.

It is quite common in my experience as a spiritual director for people to notice an emotion that is present – for example fear, or sadness, or joy – and then quickly move back into the thoughts this triggers in their minds to try to figure out what it means. But a powerful practice is to ask them to stay and be with the sensation of the emotion. 'Where are you feeling it in the body? What does it feel like? Does it have a texture, temperature, substance (hard, cold, warm, soft, tight, fluid, hard etc)? As people give attention to how the emotion actually is alive within the body and literally 'feel' it by sensing into it, they are able to unlock the true intelligence and wisdom contained within it – where it has come from, what is the wisdom it is revealing to them. We will look at this also in the next chapter.

Similarly, in spiritual direction, people may talk to me about having a sense of the presence of God, and I will often ask them to bring their somatic intelligence to this: 'How are you sensing God? Where in your body, or around you? What is the actual experience (warm, soft, strong, cool, light, colour etc)? What starts to happen as you fully receive the experience?' As they start to sense into the tangible, direct sensation of the Divine Presence within them or around them, it will invariably start to fill or flow, changing their inner experience, often doing some deep work of healing or transformation within the heart. It will also have an intelligence to it that will communicate itself to us, though not always in words, and invite us fully to receive. It is worth noting right from the start that the Divine seems always to work within us in a spirit of invitation, out of respect for our sovereign will. As in Jesus' question, 'Do you want to be well?', the Divine will always seek our assent before doing any work within us. Again, we will look at this more later, but in my experience it is a constant and immutable principle of how the Divine works within: 'May I?'; 'Do you want this?'; 'Come...'; 'Follow...'; 'Shall we...?'

The transforming quality of (prayerful) attention – how attention 'feeds' the processing of experience

It is important to say at this stage that often the best thing we can do is simply restrict ourselves to presencing and enquiry. We do not seek to force anything; we 'let flow', or consciously and choicefully 'follow'. The principle I try to work with is always to trust what is emerging, what is making itself known, and simply presence awareness into it as I described above. If it needs our conscious attention, it will make that known. The temptation is, as we become aware of things we may be containing, or that are stirring within us, to immediately start to work with them. The functional mind can quickly take over. 'What is this? What does it mean? What should I do with it?'

We try to stay as much as possible with the direct experience rather than our thoughts about it. Giving attention to something in our inner experience has a quality of 'feeding' it, so it can then do its work within us. We can view attention as being to experience what breath is to food. Just as the daily bread of food is converted into energy in the process of cellular respiration, so the daily bread of our lived experience is transformed into wisdom and growth in the process of attentive enquiry. What we give clear, clean attention to, if it is there for our transformation and growth, will flow within, releasing its wisdom – especially if we are doing this with a stance of prayerful surrender (i.e. 'Your will be done, Lord, not mine').

One big deception is to be side-tracked or distracted and fail to notice what is really at work within – often the 'still, small voice' amidst the earthquake, wind, and fire (see 1 Kings 19). That is why a *'surrendered attention'* is so important – that we allow ourselves to notice what we are meant to be noticing, what is revealing itself to us, rather than what we think we should be. This is where a spiritual director can be of help. Once we have brought things to consciousness, they will unfold in their own timing. In my experience, anything substantial at work within us will come forth in its own season and at its own pace – as long as we are able to trust and allow this – in the Presence of the Divine, who we know wants only our good. We learn to 'Trust in the LORD with all our heart and lean not on our own understanding', as Proverbs 3:5 puts it.

The next step, having noticed, is consciously to remember what we have noticed and fully receive any wisdom that has resulted from it. The functional mind, once it restores its control (as it must), will have a tendency to forget, or skip over, things that do not fit its current patterning. Journalling, as we will see later, can be a helpful way of consciously remembering. We simply notice anything that seems to be significant, that has an energy within it and, if we feel no prompt to open up into it more, we just note down that it is there. Then we need not be surprised if it pops up again, and can explore it further when the time is ripe. This is particularly true for more painful, or 'darker', feelings within, which may need to be given more time and space.

An attitude of constant prayer and dependency on the greater Presence can be most helpful. For Christians, this can be an active looking for Christ – 'Lord, where and how are you present in this? What are you showing me?' – being careful, though, not to manufacture an encounter or an answer from our own understanding. As we notice these things and give them our attention, transformation becomes possible. We will discuss this more in later chapters, but as a close to this one, I will say a few words about spiritual aspects of our experience that may warrant feeding with a bit more attention, still in this spirit of open, unconditional enquiry.

Giving attention to the spiritual aspect of our experience

As we bring the full resources of our 'gathered self' online and develop our capacity for expanded awareness, we are able to notice so much more and *with* so much more – not just with the awareness of mind, but also body, heart, and soul. This makes us more capable of sensing and connecting with deeper spiritual and subconscious flows that are present. We will come to the latter in the next chapter. Here, I want to focus on our capacity to sense and attend to the spiritual, which is so often 'hidden' or 'buried' in the coarseness of our more usual everyday experience – the still, small voice, I referred to earlier. The same principle applies – what we give our attention to grows. We can do this in relation to our outer or our inner experience.

In our outer experience, as we get more accustomed to presencing, we can develop our spiritual noticing and our sensitivity to our deeper connection with all things. One of the most immediate and obvious ways of doing this is in nature. Many retreats will feature what we call an 'awareness' walk, where we gather ourselves into the recollected state and then go for a walk in nature. With our capacity to notice increased, we can become sensitive to the flow of life around us in ways we had never noticed before. The Wendell Berry poem I quoted at the beginning of the book is a good example of this.

It is not uncommon on this kind of awareness walk for profound insights to emerge – often, nature has ways of speaking into our questions, which from a spiritual perspective is perhaps no surprise if we accept the premise that the Divine is present in the whole of creation, which God has literally spoken into being. It is a principle in many traditions, particularly Ignatian spirituality, that God is speaking to us in all of creation, if we can but find the 'ears to hear'.

I remember a recent pilgrimage, walking up a chalky down. The meditation we were in was on 'heritage', conscious of all the tiny sea creatures that had given their lives to become the chalk that we were walking upon. One of the questions I had brought to the pilgrimage was my state of 'spiritual homelessness' now that Alton Abbey, the Benedictine Abbey where I am in the oblature, was being forced to close its doors for the last time. As I was climbing, my eyes were drawn to the flint stones that made up the path I was walking. I felt them crunching and springing beneath my feet – so hard and strong. Suddenly I remembered that the Alton Abbey Church was build out of flint. The thought arose: 'The Abbey is always here. It is forever part of you, and it is your path. It is time to live your heritage. Walk it out into the world and into the rest of your life. Let it be the flint path beneath your feet... guiding and supporting.' Psalm 84 then came to mind with its beautiful juxtaposition of 'home' and 'pilgrimage': 'Blessed are those who dwell in your house; they are ever praising you. Blessed are those whose strength is in you, whose hearts are set on pilgrimage. As they pass through the Valley of [Sorrow], they make it a place of springs' (verses 4–6). It has proven a surprisingly transformational experience. I feel alive within me all I have received from my time with the Community in a way I have never felt before – like something that I thought of as 'theirs' had now become 'mine', and a sense of both gratitude and responsibility that comes with that: 'Own this.' 'Just' some flint stones – that is how nature can speak when we are ready and available.

If this is true in our outer experience, it is equally true in our inner experience. One of the best activities I know to demonstrate this is an exercise drawn from the Catholic tradition known as 'Memoria Dei'. It can be used to explore any experience of 'something beyond' and is not restricted to the Christian faith. You might want to try it with a friend.

Memoria Dei

After stilling and coming into the 'gathered self', you simply ask each other to remember a time when you had a close or memorable experience with 'something beyond', some kind of intimation of the transcendent or Divine – whether this was in prayer, in nature, in daily life, in adversity, it doesn't matter. You take it in turns to invite each other to relive the experience by going back there and talking about it. As you do so, help each other to remember the details and the fullness of the experience – what you were seeing, doing, thinking, sensing, feeling, and how the encounter progressed and the effect it was having within you and around you.

Having done this sharing for twenty minutes or so (ten minutes each), which is usually an engrossing and enlivening experience, you then just pause and still and notice what is present right now within you and between you. What has it been like just to be in this conversation, what are you aware of, what are your feelings as you notice?

I have run this activity so many times in groups and as people share, it is extraordinary what fills the atmosphere in the room – literally the tangible presence of love, joy, awe, peace, care, and compassion. I remember running a clergy retreat at St George's House, Windsor, and doing this as an exercise at the end of the day. Afterwards, we all left for supper, but I had forgotten something and had to pop back into the room we had been using. It was like walking into a bath of pure, soft, warm, bright, clear light. 'Truly the Lord is in this place,' I found myself saying – and I was filled with unforgettable awe.

The psalmist describes the power of this re-membering of the Divine quite explicitly in Psalm 42: 'My soul is downcast... therefore, I will remember you' (verse 6). Aware of his state of disconnection, he consciously remembers his encounters with the Divine on Hermon and Mount Mizar. As he does so, he finds himself once more in the living presence of God within him, which he describes as waves, and which awakens him to the flow of love and the beauty of the 'music' of creation and the one who sings it into being.

Re-cognition: 'deep calls to deep'

It is interesting to note that in many languages, including Hebrew, 'remembering' has no past tense. What we remember (rather than memorise) is here now. This brings us to one of the most important principles in the spiritual life – recognition, literally re-cognition. In any 'spiritual encounter', where in some way we recognise the presence of God, or Love, or Transcendence, or Truth, it is only possible for us to recognise it *if we have 'known' it already*. It must therefore be alive and present somewhere within us to be triggered into recognition – 'deep calling to deep'. When we encounter love, which we often think of receiving, it is also the love present within us being re-awakened. It is the same with peace or hope or faith or truth. If we allow ourselves to fully experience the moment, or the memory, of the recognition, we discover that these very qualities that we are so often seeking out there are in here, already within us – we have just forgotten.

As we feed them with our attention, these qualities can fill and grow within us and change us. As our state changes, we find ourselves thinking and acting in a very different way – more whole, alive, wise, present to the fullness of our being and the Divine indwelling. I suspect this is what St Paul is referring to as he continues in the passage from Romans 12 I quoted earlier:

'be[ing] transformed by the renewing of your mind' (re-newing of mind, literally re-cognition). In this state we see our lives and the world in a radically different way – possibly what he later refers to as 'the mind of Christ'.

Interestingly, this same principle can be applied to the imagination as well as the memory, as it is most famously in the Ignatian prayer exercises, where we are encouraged to place ourselves wholly in biblical scenes and 'experience' them as they play out for us – imaginatively feeling, sensing, tasting, touching what is happening. This is a powerful way of sidestepping the control of the functional mind and allowing our gathered being to come online in the presence of the 'Divine Help'.

In doing this kind of presencing, in our inner or outer experience, we become more aware of our spiritual as well as our human nature. With this activated, we can live a much more 'awake' life going forwards, more available to ourselves, to others and to the mysterious activity of the Divine. For many people, the encounters they experience in the four weeks of the Ignatian exercises become a reservoir of presence, perspective, and wisdom within their being – indeed a core part of who they are becoming. This serves as a reference point for many years to come if they can 'remember to remember' by conscious presencing.

The challenge then becomes how do we stay remembered, keeping this expanded state of being available to us? This is something we will explore in Chapter Eleven.

CHAPTER SIX

*Inner transformation and renewing –
the work of the heart*

*Behold, you delight in truth in the inward being,
and you teach me wisdom in the secret heart.*

PSALM 51:6 (ESV)

IN CHAPTER FOUR we looked at coming into the 'gathered self', which begins by stilling, presencing in breath and body. Our sensory awareness comes online, releasing the grip of the functional mind, enabling us to presence in mind and heart, letting these too breathe, relax, and open. It thus brings us into a state of pure receptivity – fully at rest, fully awake, alive, present – a 'living sacrifice', using the language of St Paul. In Chapter Four, we looked at how, when we are present in this state, we can be more attentive to the deeper energy of our being and what is really flowing within us.

We also saw how this offers the freedom to be who we truly are and to live 'life to the full'. Again, in the language of St Paul, we no longer 'conform to the pattern of this world' but are 'transformed by the renewing of [our] mind' (Romans 12:2). It is this process of deeper transformation and renewal that I am going to look at in this chapter, after which we will look at how this serves our lifelong journey of formation.

In the journey of our becoming, human and spiritual, there is an ongoing drama: to what extent does the way we have been 'patterned' by life so far enable, inhibit, or distort the true life force within each of us? Parker J. Palmer expresses this in the probing question he asks us all to consider: 'Is the life I am living the life that wants to live in me?'[1]

The clue to this lies in the challenging questions that life is posing us – to which I alluded in Chapter One – in which lies the invitation to transformation. Otherwise, we stay stuck and, worse, project our patterning onto the world, and the people, around us. 'What we don't transform, we transmit.'[2]

The question we will address in this chapter, again, is how? How does this 'work' of transformation happen? And how do we accept it? It is more a work of grace than our own agency, though our capacity to collaborate with it is crucial.

I have already referred to the heart's role as the seat of the emotional life and the place of inner integration. It is likely, therefore, that it is in the heart particularly where this work of transformation can take place, eventually flowing through into the re-newing of the mind. It is not for nothing that the Bible so often laments our 'hard hearts' and promises to restore in us a 'heart of flesh and not of stone' (see Ezekiel 36:26). Hard hearts lead to many of the problems of our world today. Christian spirituality often refers to this work as the 'purification of the heart'.

If the heart is the place of inner transformation, then this transformation is a tender and sacred work, because the heart is the most intimate and precious part of our being. It is probably the part of us that we guard most closely and the place we feel most vulnerable to deep hurt. It is also, potentially, the part that has the most intimate connection with the Divine: 'You will seek me and find me when you seek me with all your heart' (Jeremiah 29:13). It is also a place of a very different kind of 'knowing' to that of the head. The words of the disciples, 'Were not our hearts burning within us while he talked with us on the road' (Luke 24:32) point us to how their hearts recognised something that their heads had not. This highlights the heart's crucial role in awakening us to spiritual truths rather than cognitive ones.

The functions of the heart

Before we go on to look at how we practice presencing in the heart, let's look more at the function of the heart in our spiritual life. Clearly we are not talking here about the actual physical organ, but the centre of knowing and inner experience, which extends in a large oval from the solar plexus to the top of the sternum as the seat of our emotional life. Generally (though not always), if we want to notice and work with what is happening in the heart, we bring our awareness into this region. If you want, you may test this. Just ask yourself, 'How am I feeling?' about something or someone, and notice where your attention goes. Or you may put your hand onto your chest and presence your awareness there and just notice the quality of what you are sensing. That may give you a feel for the distinctive content of your heart. This is something you can keep practising if you want to be more present to your heart. When you have a decision to make, place your hand on your chest and ask 'how am I feeling' as well as 'what am I thinking' about this.

The obvious content of our heart experience is emotion. In this we learn the same principle as with our thoughts – to be with our feelings, but not to be caught into them. With our awareness online and awake, we are able to notice our emotions, to feel them fully but not to be triggered by them into 'acting them out'. This gives us the freedom to choose our responses rather than being hijacked. This is the basis of emotional intelligence.

However, the heart is the seat of more than emotion. It is also the seat of desire, including our deepest longings. These can often be felt as an 'ache' or a 'thirst' within. The heart holds the 'virtues' – as qualities of being rather than concepts. Courage is the most obvious, as its derivation from the French word *coeur* implies. There is also patience, humility, kindness, compassion, perseverance and temperance – as well as the three 'infused virtues' of the spiritual life: faith, hope, and love. These are all aspects of our human knowing that are beyond cognition – they are 'felt-known' or 'apprehended' rather than 'thought-known' or 'comprehended'.

Andrew Bennett's famous dictum that 'The longest journey you will ever take is the eighteen inches from your head to your heart'[3] points to the truth that access to the capacity of our heart is a such a huge step in human development. It is also self-evidently so to any spirituality rooted in love as well as truth, as the author of *The Cloud Of Unknowing* expresses: 'The universes which are amenable to the intellect can never satisfy the instincts of the heart.' This can, however, be experienced as excruciating vulnerability, or hopeless inefficiency, in the 'pattern of this world' where functional materialism is such a dominant driver.

One way of viewing the heart is as a container. It is a treasure trove of our emotional memories, the ones that are most alive within us, and the place where we store the things that are most sacred, precious and intimate. 'Where your treasure is, there your heart will be also' (Matthew 6:21). People often place their hands on their chest to indicate that something is important or 'heartfelt'. It is also the place of our deepest authenticity and the part that is most vulnerable to wounding or rejection. It is therefore also where we store the unresolved and unprocessed experience in our lives, often referred to as 'wounding', sometimes deeply buried, sometimes more available. In the Bible, we are told how Mary pondered what had happened to her in being chosen to bear God's Son, and that she 'treasured up all these things... in her heart' (Luke 2:19), aware that there was a bigger mystery at work in her Son's life than anything she could resolve in her own motherhood.

As Parker J. Palmer highlights, this work of integration is where the inner life 'that wants to live in us'[4] meets the outer life of the world flooding in as the raw, unresolved impact of our experience. No wonder so much of our time is spent trying to shield ourselves from experiences we do not want to feel. Our inner dramas about surviving, belonging, love, fairness, honesty, being valued/seen/heard/included all take place in the domain of heart. If they are not resolved, they are 'contained', and if they are contained, they are easily triggered and acted out. We all know people who are 'prickly' or 'sensitive' because of unresolved experience in their past.

I am going to suggest that, just as the body absorbs food, processes it, and transforms it into physical life and growth, so the heart absorbs, processes, and transforms our most moving experiences into soul-growth. This sets the foundation for our next chapter where we look at our 'soul-journey' into mature beings capable of wisdom, creativity, generativity, and love. It is a growth that happens in its own time and season, just as it did for Mary. When the time is right, the unresolved mysteries in our heart find their resolution. This is what Rilke means when he invites us to 'live our questions until one day we live our way into the answer'.[5]

The work of the heart is therefore one of connection, integration, and flow.

Like the physical heart, it opens to allow flow – of experience and people into the depths of our being – or it closes to shut it out. If it does this to external flows, it does the same to internal ones, those stemming from our own soul or the Divine indwelling. We can choose to speak or act 'from the heart' or to bury what we deeply feel and speak or act from some other place. We can have a hardness towards our own true selves, e.g. 'Don't show you care, it's a sign of weakness.' This is true also of our connection with the Divine. We have the same capacity to soften and receive the Divine Presence, whether flowing from within or without, or to harden and to choose instead to 'lean on our own understanding'.

In its pure state, the heart is a wide open, clean, clear, peaceful, almost empty vessel. In this the somatic experience can be like a vast open chamber in the centre of the chest, full of light, airy, peaceful, beautiful nothing. It can feel like a 'channel of peace', as St Francis puts it, or a 'straight way', to follow the language of the Old Testament. In this it can be a direct conduit for Divine Love, Will and Truth to manifest itself in life on earth. 'As above, so below' is the way Eugene Peterson paraphrases the line in the Lord's Prayer (Matthew 6:10, MSG). We often talk about things that God has 'placed on our heart'. As Teresa of Avila reminds us, the only way that the Divine Will can be consciously manifest on earth is through humankind's availability to receive it and channel it: 'Christ has no body now on earth but yours, / no hands but yours, / no feet but yours, / Yours are the eyes through which to look out Christ's compassion to the world, / Yours are the feet with which he is to go about doing good; / Yours are the hands with which he is to bless men now.'[6]

The simplest and most powerful statement of the work of the heart is the sixth beatitude, 'Blessed are the pure in heart, for they will see God' (Matthew 5:8). This points to the umbilical link between the heart and the eyes. When the heart is pure, so is the mind and so is our seeing. When the heart is clouded, so is our mind and our sight. At the most basic human level, it is the look in the eyes that tells us whether we have connection with another. Paul talks about this in terms of a veil (see 2 Corinthians 3:18). We can usually see it plainly in another when they are 'veiling' their eyes or 'glazing over' to defend themselves or not engage.

Finally, if the spiritual life is about the purification of the heart, then this is not a work we need to do alone. There is help available. Our primary 'work' is to open ourselves to a larger spiritual Presence that wants, I suspect very, very

PRESENCING AND SPIRITUAL DIRECTION

much, if we let it, to be at work within us, healing and transforming. Edwin Hatch's nineteenth-century hymn captures this idea perfectly:

> *Breathe on me, Breath of God,*
> *Fill me with life anew,*
> *That I may love what Thou dost love,*
> *And do what Thou wouldst do.*
>
> *Breathe on me, Breath of God,*
> *Until my heart is pure,*
> *Until with Thee I will one will,*
> *To do and to endure.*
>
> *Breathe on me, Breath of God,*
> *Till I am wholly Thine,*
> *Until this earthly part of me*
> *Glows with Thy fire divine.*

This perfectly distilled hymn describes the process we will be exploring at greater length here.

If this all sounds rather weird and 'unscientific' then, yes, it probably is. We are working with the knowing of inner experience here, rather than the knowing of science. We can see the evidence of it in our common language, where we talk about being 'hard-hearted' and 'cold-hearted' or 'soft-hearted' and 'kind- or warm-hearted'. We talk about 'speaking from the heart', of 'heartache', of being 'open-hearted' or 'guarded'. When you are pushing others away, you can actually feel your heart go hard within your chest. Conversely, when you welcome others in, you can feel your heart soften and 'melt'. We talk also about people being 'closed down', 'shut off', 'disconnected', 'absent' or, conversely, 'present' and 'open'. So presencing is very much a work of the heart.

> The Bible is a rich repository of heart wisdom. I list a series of verses below as examples of this. Before reading them, you may

want to pause, ground, and still, and then, as you read, prayerfully notice any that leap out or speak to you directly. If any do, you might spend a bit of time with them. Maybe consciously hold the scripture in your heart and notice any stirring within.

'Love the Lord your God with all your heart and with all your soul and with all your mind and with all your strength.'
Mark 12:30

'Blessed are the pure in heart, for they will see God.'
Matthew 5:8

'But Mary treasured up all these things and pondered them in her heart.' Luke 2:19

'Incline your ear and hear the words of the wise, And apply your heart to my knowledge'. Proverbs 22:17 (NKJV)

'Trust in the LORD with all your heart and lean not on your own understanding; in all your ways submit to him, and he will make your paths straight.' Proverbs 3:5–6

'Above all else, guard your heart, for everything you do flows from it.' Proverbs 4:23

'As water reflects the face, so one's life reflects the heart.'
Proverbs 27:19

'Hope deferred makes the heart sick, but a longing fulfilled is a tree of life.' Proverbs 13:12

'Who may ascend the mountain of the LORD? Who may stand in his holy place? The one who has clean hands and a pure heart.' Psalm 24:3–4

'Take delight in the LORD, and he will give you the desires of your heart.' Psalm 37:4

'Create in me a pure heart, O God, and renew a steadfast spirit within me.' Psalm 51:10

'I have hidden your word in my heart that I might not sin against you.' Psalm 119:11

'You will seek me and find me when you seek me with all your heart.' Jeremiah 29:13

'I will give them an undivided heart and put a new spirit in them; I will remove from them their heart of stone and give them a heart of flesh.' Ezekiel 11:19

'I will give you a new heart and put a new spirit in you; I will remove from you your heart of stone and give you a heart of flesh.' Ezekiel 36:26

'They asked each other, "Were not our hearts burning within us while he talked with us on the road and opened the Scriptures to us?"' Luke 24:32

'A good man brings good things out of the good stored up in his heart, and an evil man brings evil things out of the evil stored up in his heart. For the mouth speaks what the heart is full of.' Luke 6:45

'The heart is deceitful above all things and beyond cure. Who can understand it? "I the LORD search the heart and examine the mind."' Jeremiah 17:9–10

INNER TRANSFORMATION AND RENEWING – THE WORK OF THE HEART

> *'I pray that out of his glorious riches he may strengthen you with power through his Spirit in your inner being, so that Christ may dwell in your hearts through faith.' Ephesians 3:16-17*
>
> You might take a moment to let these seep in and notice any effect within you – perhaps ending with a prayer for your own receiving.

The emphasis on 'guarding your heart' in the passages above bears witness to the importance of vigilance concerning the flows of the heart. If the body is the source of the quantity of our energy, the heart is the source of its quality – and this affects our thoughts, our actions, and what we 'transmit' in our mood and relationships. Fear in the heart leads to fearful thoughts. Hope in the heart leads to hopeful thoughts. The psalmist conveys this in Psalm 139:23–24: 'Search me, God, and know my heart; test me and know my anxious thoughts. See if there is any offensive way in me, and lead me in the way everlasting.'

The dilemma is that, like the body, much of what flows in the heart happens subconsciously. The energy of instinct and of emotion is simply faster and often more powerful than the energy of conscious thought. We can do or say things before we have even realised why. We will all recognise that powerful heart surge when we say something out of anger or frustration that we later regret.

So, in our work of spiritual formation, presencing consciously in the heart becomes a crucial practice. It is literally the purification of the core channel of our being. Unprocessed experience can actually block or 'pollute' this channel and if we are not attentive, the root of our behaviour can flow from these, not our true source. In modern language, we 'act it out'.

The process of presencing and enquiry in the heart

The capacity to presence depends on whether the heart is open and available or shut down and defended. The heart hardens in states of fear, insecurity, anger, or, more simply, the felt absence of love. To open, the heart must feel safe, which is why we begin presencing with relaxation and the release of tension in the body. As the body feels safe, so the heart can come online and open. Then we can use the somatic noticing we were cultivating in our previous chapter to sense into the experience of the heart.

With the body relaxed and receptive, we can notice the true experience of our heart – what we are *actually sensing and feeling*, not what we *think* we are. Once we access the actuality of our experience, we can 'enquire' into it, presencing in it and attending to what flows and unfolds. As we 'incline the ear of our heart', we notice not only our emotions and desires but also the flows of our spiritual life – of the soul, the indwelling Divine, the promptings of conscience, and virtues such as compassion, hope, and, of course, love.

> A safe place to begin presencing in the heart is gratitude – bringing to awareness what we are thankful for, of which there may be more than we think. (That is why prayer often begins with thanksgiving, which opens the heart. In the charismatic tradition, many worship gatherings begin and end here too, liberating the heart to be in its deeper flow.)
>
> As we presence in gratitude we sense into the somatic experience of it, noticing where we feel the emotion and what it is like. It may for example be experienced as a warm softness spreading across the chest. Following our principle of feeding this with our attention, we can spend time in this direct experience of gratitude, which can have a strengthening and steadying effect.
>
> Following this, we allow ourselves to notice anything else that spontaneously makes itself known, letting things arise, rather than forcing anything. This may be experienced somatically, as sensation (e.g. a tightness in the chest), or emotionally, as a feeling that wants attention (e.g. sadness or fear).

Let us note that our hearts can contain many 'contradictory' things – joy and sadness, kindness and anger, happiness and grief. The binary mind struggles with this because it cannot deal in contradictions – how can I experience joy and sadness at the same time? But the heart can and does.

INNER TRANSFORMATION AND RENEWING – THE WORK OF THE HEART

A core principle of heart work is to welcome everything that arises, even if it feels dark or uncomfortable. This is beautifully captured in Rumi's poem, *The Guest House*, or in Thomas Keating's *Welcoming Prayer*, or in Joanna Macy's teaching on *Don't be Afraid of the Dark* in her work on *The Great Turning*.

The principle is based on the premise that all emotion is there because it belongs, with deep roots in our soul-essence and life experience. This may also include pre-conscious heart-memories of the Divine presence. To deny our feelings is to deny much more beside. We will explore this in more depth later as we address Macy's invitation not to be 'afraid of the dark'.

As we move from sensing to enquiry, I want to suggest there are two important aspects of the life of the heart to which we can learn to pay attention. Borrowing from the words of St Paul, we can view these as

1. *'Patternings'*. By this I mean unprocessed experiences – often felt as wounds, hurts, or blocks – that we are storing and are in need of processing/healing/purifying
2. *'Transformings'*. By this I mean inner 'stirrings' that are energetically moving within us – including our essential self, our deeper soul and the 'call' of the Divine saying, 'Come...'

Being 'gathered' into the recollected state is, too, the prerequisite to working with these, so that the heart feels safe. Then our somatic awareness can engage with these things in a way that is not possible for our habitual, functional state – feelings can be allowed to 'emerge' rather than be 'managed'. In this place of safety, the wary 'gatekeeper' within us can rest, remaining able to tighten the lid back down on anything that feels a little too uncontrollable. We might use the simple analogy of a bottle of 'fizzy pop'. We all know, (probably from experience!) that, if it has been shaken up, we undo the cap a little, let it fizz and release, then screw it back down quick! We repeat this gradually and patiently until we can open the heart fully.

1. 'Patternings': our unprocessed experience

I proposed earlier that our lived experience is the 'food' for our growth. However, we cannot process all our experience as it happens, especially as children, and especially experience that has wounded or upset us in some way. This generates unpleasant emotion which we would rather not feel, so we bury it. In extreme cases, this results in stored trauma.

However, what we bury stays alive within us and we stay wary, not wanting to be triggered by any subsequent experiences that may approximate to it – whether real experiences or projections (e.g. someone 'looking down on me'). This can often create the perverse consequence that we behave in a way that calls forth the very thing we are seeking to avoid. I have a friend who, as a result of childhood experience, is very wary about opening up until she has come to trust people. She embodies a certain caginess that in turn causes people not to open up to her. When she does signal a glimmer of vulnerability, often as a 'test', she does so in a way that people mostly miss, because it is so understated. When they miss her signal, it confirms her view that they 'don't understand' or 'are not to be trusted'. They have failed the test. She then rapidly closes down again, confirming her patterning.

It is not only inflicted experiences from the world that pattern and block us, but also the ones we generate. In our immature years, we do or say inconsiderate things that have unanticipated consequences and cause harm to others. We then find ourselves having to bury feelings of shame, guilt or inadequacy – or silencing the voice of our own conscience and compassion. Whatever the cause, we 'harden' because we do not want to feel these or let them through. We may rationalise this as 'the way the world is'. We tend also to bury aspects of ourselves that do not conform with our self-concept. This can be particularly true in a church or similar context where we are trying to live up to some kind of 'ideal'. This is our 'shadow' side and, as we lock it away, we lock away a lot of our own life force with it.

One side effect of this can be to limit the domain of our experience to things we feel good or safe about and avoid people or situations that make us uncomfortable. We therefore become less and less available to growth and transformation – and ultimately less available as a channel of love and peace. The difficulty of being (or being real) with people who are suffering, even people we know, is one example of this. We can feel we do not know how to cope with it, or what to say or do, so we avoid. We all, at some level, have this kind of boundary to the tolerance of experience. It can restrict our lives, diminish our sense of adventure, and leave us living in narrow tramlines.

This emotional containment takes energy and affects our wellbeing and ultimately our health. It also blocks the flow of energy within us and makes us permanently alert to anything that may invoke a re-living of the original experience. This is what we mean by 'triggering', leading us into fight/flight/freeze responses. It is body-wiring, instinctive and reactive, which short-circuits our normal awareness, sometimes leading to a loss of self-control and destructive emotional leakage. More often it takes us into apparently 'reasonable' egoic patterns of behaviour that are anything but reasonable because they are based on buried emotions such as fear or anger.

Part of my own patterning which I had to work through was a tendency to be over-strict with my children, but in a rather chaotic way. I rationalised this as necessary discipline, but the randomness and the testiness of it revealed its emotional fault lines. I discovered there was a deep, well-buried part of me that was triggered when my children got boisterous and started 'mucking around' – which was something I rarely got to do as a child. I had lost my own father when I was very young, and was an only child. I had to 'grow up' too quickly, preoccupied with being a 'good boy' and not upsetting my mother, or other significant adults. I eventually realised that part of me resented my children for being free to mess around, whereas I had not been – and was acting out this resentment in my 'strictness'.

Paul refers to it as a 'body of death' (Romans 7:24, ESV). It shuts down the indwelling Spirit and our own essential life force – we get busy intervening in our own experience and start, reactively, recreating the world in the image of our own buried fears and neediness. The psychoanalyst Carl Jung was explicit on this: 'Until we make the unconscious conscious, it runs our life, and we call it fate.'[7]

Presencing in 'difficult' emotions

So how do we release and open the 'fizzy bottle' of our heart?

PRESENCING AND SPIRITUAL DIRECTION

> Having settled our state by grounding in the body and presencing awareness in gratitude in the heart, we can become attentive to other emotions that present themselves. Whatever naturally arises, we just welcome it. As we do so, we notice its somatic quality within us and enquire into it in exactly the same way as I described above. Although maybe appearing first as an emotion, unprocessed experience is also stored in the body. It can often be sensed directly – for example as a 'lump' or a 'hardness' or 'sharpness' or some other kind of discomfort in the chest, or a queasiness, tightness, clenching or 'locking up' in the gut. Sometimes it is just plain numbness which can make it harder to access – although, if we persist, sensing into the absence of sensation in the body can be just as illuminating.
>
> As we notice what arises and 'feed' it with our attention, it can come to life and flow within us. We may face a choice – can we bear to feel it or not? – especially if it is a darker or more painful emotion, or even a powerful positive one. It is helpful to remember at this point that, although it may feel like it is 'real', it is not. It is just a feeling – we are not experiencing the event that triggered it, we are experiencing the cluster of sensation, emotion, and cognition that was our reaction to it.

Our initial response may well be, 'this is not safe, get me out of here'. Or we may experience a complete overwhelming of the ego, which can feel like a death. Both are likely to hijack us and make it feel unbearable. Grounding in the body, and in prayer, we can notice that these are just feelings – into which we can enquire and release what they contain. This is where an accompanier can be so helpful, to help us 'stay with' what we are experiencing long enough for it to yield its fruit.

Fear, for example, may be experienced as a cold, grey cloud in the chest. If we trust enough to welcome it and presence our awareness in it, without taking fright in the mind, it is not uncommon for it to dissolve and a quiet clarity arise – 'Oh, this is what I am frightened of... OK... And, yes, it's right to be attentive to this and this scary outcome is possible, but there are other outcomes... and what I am undertaking is worthy of the risk.' Fear is usually our friend, as long as we are not triggered by it. It is trying to help us stay safe. Once we embrace it, it often gives way to something else – not uncommonly excitement and strength – 'This is an adventure...' So, we learn to be curious and attentive, not reactive.

Let me bring this to life in the example of someone I was directing who was struggling with her 'sense of herself'. She described herself as being in an 'amazingly terrible place'. She was engaging in a new work that she knew she loved, resonant with her soul and her natural gifting. Yet she was paralysed with fear, indecision and self-judgment. As we presenced in this, she described the fear as a cold, hard rock in the centre-front of her chest. It made her feel sick to contemplate it. With courage she felt into the texture of the rock, which she experienced as bitterly cold, and then she started to feel something churning inside it. 'I recognise this,' she said. 'I really, really don't want to look at this...' But as she stayed a little longer, she decided she could. Feeling into the churning sensation, she experienced it like the surface of the sea, stirred up by the wind. Then she found herself dropping down below into a deep, vast, 'strong' stillness. It was neither warm nor cold, but immensely supporting, calming, and strengthening. She could feel it deep in her belly and simultaneously all around her in the atmosphere. She recognised it as the unconditional love and acceptance of the Divine that she had always 'known' but never directly experienced.

As she presenced, she realised the person who had been feeling the churning was a young child – her eight-year-old self. The sensation was her childhood panic at not being able to 'get anything right' for her very demanding father, who had been 'harsh, critical, and judgmental' of everything she did. She had learned to contain and survive this and built a successful career deploying the cold, rational, judgmental persona that resulted. But it was not 'her'. It was when she decided to make a move into a more creative work, closer to her true self, that she found herself in this 'amazing terrible place', beset by a crippling fear that she would 'get it wrong again'. All the more so, because she really cared about what she was doing.

In the session, she was able to have a compassionate conversation with her eight-year-old self, in the presence of the Divine 'Father', which was to prove profoundly releasing. She accessed a self-acceptance that she had never found before, experienced as a filling liquid warmth where the cold hard rock had been. This became an important body memory for her. She found within it a playful, confident, sociable, spontaneous creativity that had been choked by this childhood experience. Most importantly, she experienced a complete liberation from the fierce and constant self-judgment that had been with her since that childhood time. 'I can't believe the difference,' she remarked many weeks later. 'I keep waiting to be brought up short by my judgy voice, but it's not there any more.' In her work, she was able to trust this creativity and freedom. It stayed 'amazing' but stopped being 'terrible'. One of the biggest changes she noticed was a new warmth and spontaneity in her relationships.

> **'Don't be afraid of the dark'**
> It seems to be a reliable truth that below every negative emotion lies a positive energy. Beneath grief is often love; beneath anger, fairness and justice; beneath desolation, hope; beneath fear, courage and creativity; beneath loneliness, deep connection. But to access these deeper transformational energies, we must have the courage to presence in the difficult feelings and welcome them.

Even if we decide not to probe too far into an unprocessed experience, having acknowledged it we can then notice its triggering in the day-to-day. If it is, say, a tightening in the chest, this becomes something we can prime our attention with. When we notice that tightening again, it is a sign to us that something needs bringing to consciousness. Or we may just recognise it, smile and let it pass, without reacting. All this steadily increases our capacity to self-observe – and therefore our freedom of choice.

There are many forms of 'darkness' that we may seek to avoid, but which usually, when we are prompted to enquire into them, release much resourcefulness within. Anger or pain may show up as a 'stone' somewhere in the chest, shame or self-loathing as a sick feeling in the gut, anxiety as a churning in the belly. The wisdom of the heart has us welcome them all and let them be – they are all doing their work and will yield their fruits in time. The more we can acknowledge them, the less likely we are to be triggered.

As we learn to presence, in prayer and trust, in our unprocessed experience, we unlock its transforming power. We get stronger, wiser, calmer, more compassionate, better able to draw boundaries, more patient and forgiving of others, to name but a few of the fruits of this work. A 'new self', in Christ, starts to form and strengthen within us. Most importantly, we no longer need to 'hide' or shut down, we can be with what is genuinely present without the need to manage or control our experience. We can 'live to the full'.

2. 'Transformings': our 'internal stirrings'

'Internal stirrings' relate to the labouring within us of 'the life that wants to live in me', to return to Parker J. Palmer's phrase. It may be the stirring of my soul – the life I know deep down I was made to live. Or it may be the Divine Presence within 'calling us into life'.

This 'life within us' can be experienced in different ways:

- Wish and yearning and longing
- A sense that there must be more/something is missing
- The positive desire beneath sometimes negative emotion such as sadness, regret, anger
- A desire to serve, express creativity, excitement, achieve, help
- 'Spiritual' emotions, directly experienced – peace, hope, love, faith, joy...
- Images or 'pictures' in the inner life
- Tangible, somatic experience of 'flows' within – streams, fountains, light, energy...
- The direct awareness of the Divine Presence, perhaps as 'being held' or 'light within'
- A direct 'call' from God or Christ – 'Follow Me'
- A sense of 'oneness' and 'boundlessness' – connection and union with the Divine

It is in this presencing in the 'desires of our heart' that somatic enquiry can be particularly powerful. If we find ourselves yearning for the love of God (see Psalm 42), then rather than get caught into the fruitless longing, (which leaves the mind full of melancholy thoughts), we can get curious. You may try it now, even lightly. Pause, still, breathe, come into the gathered self and then see if you can sense down into a longing for 'God' or 'Divine Love' within you using your somatic awareness. If you can, now or at some later stage, try to feel into where and how you are noticing it. At first it may just feel like a faint flicker, maybe somewhere down in the deep gut. Or it might start with an ache in your heart. Try presencing in this – what is like? Warm, cold, hard, soft, static or flowing? See if you can sense into the source of it, where it seems to be arising from.

If you can find this, say, maybe a cool or a warm liquid bubbling somewhere, then drop your awareness into this and see what happens. As you feed it with your attention, it may well expand, you may feel its flow within you and notice the true quality of it. You may keep feeling deeper and deeper into the source of it... where does it flow from... maybe down deep, way beyond the floor of your gut... but try to stay with it, feel the substance of it, the energy of it. You may then decide to experiment with what it is like to consciously receive this energy, this flow of whatever it is – say a cool refreshing stream. To drink it in. As you do so, you can notice what happens in your body, heart, and mind as you welcome it fully. It may transform your perspective or, in Paul's words, 'renew the mind'. Life can begin to look very different when viewed from here.

> In my experience of this work, there is a powerful truth about the 'holy desires' of the heart. This is that the longing for the thing often is the thing... The longing for the love of God is the love of God already present in us - in fact, God's longing for us! All we have to do is presence in it, welcome it, and receive it. I imagine way, way back, possibly due to the trauma of being born onto this planet in this body, we forgot we carry this love. For years it has been trying to get through to us. All we need do, as in Psalm 42, is remember, open and receive.

So, from this perspective, the longings, the yearnings of the deep heart are pure gold, as the author of *The Cloud Of Unknowing*, quoting St Augustine, highlights: 'The whole life of a good Christian is nothing but Holy Desire.'[8] He also reminds us of St Gregory's wisdom that our lamentable human failings,

INNER TRANSFORMATION AND RENEWING – THE WORK OF THE HEART

often experienced as shame, is at source 'full of holy desire'. This is probably why St Ignatius begins his exercises by asking for the 'grace of shame' – another example of 'not being afraid of the dark'.

We can mistake holy desire for worldly desire and try to quench it through action-reward in the world. When this inevitably falls short, it leads to sorrow and shame. But the living presence giving rise to these desires is the very thing we are seeking. We do not need anything else, just to trust this. Once we learn this, we begin to access the true spiritual resources that will do the work of 'purifying our heart' – not in our own striving, but rather in our surrender to what is already present and moving within us.

We will all be on our own journey of discovery around our deepest yearnings. I have noticed it to be true also for the desire for peace, so often the living presence of Divine Peace already within, for stillness, which has a tangible, clear velvety quality to it, which, when we embrace it, flows in and around us.

I have noticed too, in relation to spiritual flows in the heart, that the 'Don't be afraid of the dark' principle above keeps resurfacing. One, for example, is the felt absence of God, or the sense of having lost contact. Another is the almost blind terror of our own insignificance and nothingness – that our life is meaningless. These take courage and presence to face into – and may be best done in the holding of a soul friend or spiritual director. One common experience of presencing in these feelings is of a 'void' or darkness within. People have described it as looking into a 'drain-hole' or 'pit'. It can be surprising, when they find the faith and courage to drop down into the void and just be there, that the experience can be strangely comforting, strengthening, and revelatory – 'a warm, cozy darkness', 'held', 'alone but not alone', 'still here', 'I am OK'.

It is worth remembering that 'in the beginning was the void'. It is strangely strengthening and empowering that I can actually experience that too – and still be 'I', the one experiencing it. There is a verse in Isaiah which catches this (45:3, NKJV): 'I will give you the treasures of darkness, And hidden riches of secret places, That you may know that I, the LORD, Who call you by your name, am the God of Israel.' It is also powerfully depicted in the poetry of John of the Cross and his 'dark night of the senses' and 'dark night of the soul'.

Whether an 'inner darkness' or a stirring of 'deep calling to deep', these experiences, when attended to in the liberating, healing presence of the Divine, are transformational – restoring us to wholeness and opening up previously blocked channels within us for the flow of love and creation energy. This of course is the work of a lifetime, and we do not set off on some vain quest for perfection, striving to 'purify our own heart'. What we do is notice and, when the time comes for something to be attended to, when it naturally surfaces within us, we listen, we presence, we enquire, we let be and let flow. I must again emphasise very robustly at the end of this chapter that this work is utterly dependent on the action of grace – in both a healing and transforming capacity.

I have spoken about 'transformations' a number of times in this chapter, and I will close with some examples about what this may actually look like – recognising it is always highly specific and personal and that we should beware generalisations that may cause us to 'expect something to happen' when we presence.

We can put these into three broad categories:

1. Healing
    a. Re-processing painful experience, releasing its grip, restoring wholeness of body and soul, unlocking the energy flow within
    b. Becoming available to the healing presence of our own life force/essence
    c. Mind/perception – seeing the world differently, as it is, not how we fear it is
    d. Being able to be with others in more undefended ways and let love flow
    e. Becoming available to the Divine help – not only healing us but transforming suffering into something that is available to us (like in Aikido), from which to serve others. Wounded healers
2. Calling
    a. Becoming available to the flow of our own true nature, the life that wants to live in us
    b. Finding the still, small voice within or God's good and pleasing will – as Paul describes it in Romans 12
    c. Unitive encounter, experiencing ourselves 'one' with the God who 'knows us by name and is pleased with us' (Exodus 33)

INNER TRANSFORMATION AND RENEWING – THE WORK OF THE HEART

      d. True perspective on what is ours to hold, and what is God's – what Eugene Peterson translates as 'unforced rhythms of grace' (Matthew 11:20, MSG)
      e. Specific invitations to 'Follow Me', perhaps into a new 'season' or 'journey'
3. The 'Re-newing' of our Mind
      a. Inhabiting a different 'I', a more expanded consciousness, more aware, more available to God, more truly 'who I am'
      b. Returning to the questions that took us into enquiry (e.g. 'What is God's plan for my life?') and framing these differently (e.g. 'How do I stay present and available to God's leading?')
      c. Understanding better our own capacity/strength/energy/resilience – a transformed self-concept from which we can act more fully and freely
      d. 'New eyes', seeing things very differently
      e. Re-patterning of the mind (e.g. a release of compassion helps us appreciate people's defendedness – making us more patient and forgiving)
      f. Our higher mind becomes available, sensing into so much more of the true life of the kingdom
      g. A new understanding of how God is present with us – for example 'dwelling in our hearts' – and learning to listen in a different way

As we move back from heart to mind, we may have to take great care not to let the functional mind take over and reduce the impact of any inner healing or revelation from our transformational experience. At this point, when I am working as a spiritual director, I always encourage people to pray for the 'illumination of understanding', so that they are *receiving* a new patterning, not trying to interpret what they have experienced from the old, pre-transformational cognitive patterns. Otherwise, we are right back where we started! But we are human and, always, we can 'begin again'.

CHAPTER SEVEN

Presencing and spiritual formation

*Do not allow this world to mold you in its own image.
Instead, be transformed from the inside out by renewing your mind.
As a result, you will be able to discern what God wills
and whatever God finds good, pleasing, and complete.*

ROMANS 12:2 (VOICE TRANSLATION)

*Sometimes
I look out at everything
growing so wild
and faithfully beneath the sky
and wonder why we are
the one terrible
part of creation
privileged to refuse
our flowering.*

DAVID WHYTE, 'THE SUN'[1]

PRESENCING AND SPIRITUAL DIRECTION

IN THIS CHAPTER, we will take a longitudinal perspective, looking at the role of presencing in our life journey – the 'work' of our 'be-coming' or 'flowering' into our full being, human and spiritual. It is a longer chapter and falls into two parts. The first, more conceptual, provides a 'map' of this journey of be-coming. The second looks at how we actively collaborate in this. There is a natural pause point between these parts.

Our soul-journey through life is often expressed as a process of 'formation' – each individual soul containing its own 'spark' of the Divine, like the seed of a tree pushing out to live in a world that may or may not be receptive to its impulses and, indeed, a world inhabited by others and by 'principalities and powers' that seek to 'con-form' and 'mould' us to their ends. It is this dance between our patterning from without and our re-newing from within that I am putting at the heart of this book. I see this as the work Paul alludes to above of 'being transformed from the inside out'. Through it we mature into fully alive human beings capable of love and ultimately a fully alive humanity capable of embodying the 'good and pleasing will' of God.

Ram Dass' classic old tale of 'Zumbach the Tailor' brings this drama of our 'patterning' to life for us in a more light-hearted way:

> *There once lived a tailor name Zumbach who had a reputation for making the finest of clothing. He used only the best fabrics, and he was especially known for his impeccable suits. A young man went to Zumbach the tailor to be fitted proudly for his first ever adult suit. After Zumbach had finished the suit, the man stood in front of the mirror to check the fit.*
>
> *At first glance he noticed that the suit jacket's right arm sleeve was rather short, and too much of his wrist was showing. 'This sleeve looks a little short. Would you please lengthen it?' he asked. 'The sleeve is not too short,' replied the tailor. 'Your arm is too long... Just pull your arm back a few inches and you will see that the sleeve fits perfectly.' The man withdrew his arm a bit, and the sleeve was matched with his wrist. But this movement rumpled the upper portion of the jacket.*
>
> *'Now the nape of the collar is several inches above my neck,' he said. 'No, there's nothing wrong with the collar,' Zumbach replied. 'Your neck is too low. Lift the back of your neck and the jacket will fit well.' The customer raised his neck a few inches, and sure enough the collar rounded it where it was supposed*

to. But now there was another problem: the bottom of the jacket rested high above his seat.

'But now my whole rear end is sticking out!' the man complained. 'No problem,' Zumbach returned. 'Just lift up your rear end so it fits under the jacket.' Again, the customer complied, which left his body in a rather contorted posture.

'But standing like this the trousers are too short.' Said the man. Zumbach answered, 'There is nothing wrong with the suit! If you'll just bend your knees a bit, you'll see the trousers are just right.' The customer tries it and, lo and behold, the suit fits like a glove – and it's gorgeous.

So, he paid the tailor for the suit and walked out of the shop in a most awkward position, struggling to keep all parts of the suit in their right places.

Later that day, he was standing in a shop, his shoulders lopsided and his head straining forward, when another fellow took hold of his lapel and said, "What a beautiful suit! I'll bet Zumbach the tailor made that suit for you.'

'Why yes,' the man said, 'but how did you know?'

'Only a tailor as brilliant as Zumbach could tailor a suit this good for a body as crippled and contorted as yours.'[2]

Let us have a look, then, at what we might call the 'journey of the soul', as it is fitted out with its worldly clothes and seeks to play its part in the world. There are many 'stage development' theories, both spiritual and psychological, but they all basically chart a journey of maturation from a beginning-of-life, childlike innocence back to a reclaimed innocence on the other side of experience. As I write this, I am reminded of Jim Cotter's lovely words in his treatment of Psalm 121 in his book of *Psalms for Pilgrim People*: 'Companion on my journey, protector at my side, I venture on the way in simple, childlike trust.'[3]

From 'con-forming' to 'trans-forming': the journey of the soul through 'life stages'

God speaks to each of us as he makes us,
then walks with us silently out of the night.
These are the words we dimly hear:

> *You, sent out beyond your recall,*
> *go to the limits of your longing.*
> *Embody me.*
>
> *Flare up like a flame*
> *and make big shadows I can move in.*
>
> *Let everything happen to you: beauty and terror.*
> *Just keep going. No feeling is final.*
> *Don't let yourself lose me.*
>
> *Nearby is the country they call life.*
> *You will know it by its seriousness.*
>
> *Give me your hand.*
>
> RAINER MARIA RILKE 'GO TO THE LIMITS OF YOUR LONGING'[4]

'I am making all things new', we hear God say in Revelation 21. 'It is done. I am the Alpha and the Omega, the Beginning and the End. To the thirsty I will give water without cost from the spring of the water of life' (verses 5–6). These scriptures, along with Genesis 2–3, can provide a rich metaphor for our journey of becoming. We begin in Eden with the 'tree of life', and we end in Revelation planted in the flow of the river of life, 'free gift'. In between, we 'thirst'. It is a journey from one kind of innocence (pre-experience) through to another (post-experience), which can also be characterised as a journey from unconscious love to conscious love. The soul at the end of our human life that has lived, willed, experienced, and transformed has a different quality to it to the one that began it – and if our soul is the only thing that travels on from this life through the curtain of death, then what happens to it on this journey is of huge significance.

If we take as our starting point the 'pure soul' in each of us at birth, this primal state of innocence has us, like Adam and Eve, wholly in the Presence of the Lord. A symbol in the book of Genesis for it is 'the tree of life' – in each of us it is the 'imaginal' self, the potential being we would become if we were to live in the way most perfectly suited to our flourishing, as in Eden, 'walking in the garden in the cool of the day' in perfect harmony with the will of God.

However, we are given a second gift – our own free will (for how else could we be truly made 'in the image of God'?). With this comes the self-consciousness necessary for us to make our own choices. In the foundational Genesis narrative, we see this represented in the 'second tree' of 'the knowledge of good and evil'. Once we have 'eaten the fruit' of this tree (been born?) we are, by definition, cut off from perfect union with the will of God. This garden of 'two trees' is thus a metaphor for the human soul. Now sent out from Eden, our only way back, of course, is to seek the Divine will again as best we can in and through our own will – 'thy will be done'.

Following our 'fall' into self-consciousness, we find ourselves cut off from the awareness of our unity in Divine Love and Being. Experiencing ourselves as separate, we have to make our own sense of who we are and what our life is for. The only mode we have for doing this is, like an echo-sounder, to sound off our own identity on the world and to see what 'pattern' returns to us. The self-conscious mind, forgetting our origin, constructs our identity from our experience. We create ourselves in our own image, as seen through the eyes of the world – our Zumbach suit.

Moving away from the biblical narrative, I am going to draw on modern developmental psychology to explore how, in our process of spiritual and human 'formation', this drama of 'the two trees' can unfold in the course of a lifetime. I represent this as a journey into and through different 'selves' at different stages. This is a summary of much more developed and sophisticated writers than I (see Bibliography at the end of this book) and necessarily simplistic.

> For our purposes here, I will characterise these stages as *the newborn self, the playful child, the wounded child, the defended self, the egoic self, the disillusioned self, the essential self,* and *the surrendered self.*

Although described as stages, these really should be viewed as 'layers' that are present in all of us as maturing adults, any of which at any time may surface and run the show, depending on what is being triggered.

The newborn self

Following birth, for a while, our original awareness of loving union may be briefly sustained but becomes gradually externalised and re-presented in the experience of our mother (sometimes father), who now becomes the 'primary love object'. Soon, one way or another, this begins to fail as we find her (or him) unable to respond to all our needs. We experience ourselves as more and more 'separate' and find ourselves 'yearning' for what we have lost. So, we have to 'learn' – at first, how to get what we need for life (and the instinctual angst of these needs not being met), and then how to show up in the world to get what we think we want – to please those we need to please, to belong, to achieve, to succeed. The original memory of our unitive state lies buried, at a visceral, pre-cognitive level, and increasingly unavailable to the developing personality.

The playful child

Alongside Divine Love, the other powerful original soul impulse is our 'life-force' – the innate, impulse to express our essential identity, our 'spark', to create, to grow in our agency. In the child, this manifests itself as play, experimentation, participation, curiosity and the moving outwards to express our nature in the world.

The wounded child

Soon, in one way or another (often in our 'terrible twos'!), we discover that the world does not respond the way we want it to. We experience rejection and frustration in various forms and sometimes even abuse by others – who will be 'dumping', consciously or unconsciously, their own patterning onto us. We get hurt, rejected, angry, frustrated. It is not a wholly uncommon experience to find a deep inner memory of ourselves at this age crying, 'What am I doing here? I don't belong!' In a child, these powerful feelings are impossible to process or even contain. So, a lot gets deeply lodged within, including what psychologists refer to as our 'primal wound', an experience so terrifying that we will do anything to avoid experiencing it again. Much of the adult ego is built upon the foundation of our wounded child.

The defended self

As we develop, we learn other ways to get the responses we need, and the things we want, and to protect ourselves from what we do not like or want. This process is often referred to as 'ego-formation'. The ego is built on layers of internal structures, or 'patterns', comprising emotional, volitional, somatic, and cognitive elements that we have learned will 'serve' us. The deepest-rooted layers are often those protecting us from harm, or our foundational fear of non-being and death. This we come to interpret in different ways – not fitting in, not being popular, not being seen, as well as not being fed, loved, or cared for. Driven by deep survival energy, the defended self starts to run the show, with its capacity to hijack our responses below conscious awareness.

The egoic self

Carl Jung, Richard Rohr, and others highlight the need to construct a 'healthy ego' to be able to handle the demands of what Jung calls the 'first half' of life. The stable ego arises out of the defended self, and if we are lucky also incorporates elements of the creative child that have flowed in our early patterning. This is the capable self that shows up in the world as a functioning, 'successful' adult – to achieve the things we seek, to build a home and family, to contribute, develop, and learn. For some, a core part of this ego-identity is their religious life, supporting our self-concept as a 'good' and capable citizen.

The ego is a regulated self, founded on a set of self-concepts, or an 'ideal self', enabling us to feel good about ourselves. The internal regulator is what Jung and others call the super-ego, which can arise vehemently in the voice of our inner critic or self-righteous judge. (A rule of thumb is to look at how we judge others, which is often a projection of our own perceived shortcomings.) In some this becomes a debilitating inner monologue that erodes the joy of life and has us (and others) constantly failing in our own eyes.

The 'I' (or indeed I's plural) that is thus 'con-formed' knows itself in its core to be made in its own image and fundamentally hollow. Its root is fear of 'death' (i.e. deprivation, annihilation, exclusion, insignificance). Paul may be referring to this in his 'body of death'. Sooner or later, we come to recognise the emptiness within, which has us constantly wary and dissatisfied – even the most 'successful' among us. The risk is that we just try to fill it with something else.

The disillusioned self

Over time, or as the result of life experiences that expose the emptiness of our self-concept or the limits of our egoic capability, we start to experience a growing inner dissatisfaction. This may be internally generated, a sense that 'there is something more', or externally generated by failures and reversals in life (which sometimes can be generated by our own unconscious drivers). This may take the form of a 'midlife crisis', of which we may experience several in varying degrees of intensity, which can result in profound self-questioning and the search for 'something more' in life. This can be true too for our religious life, which we can come to experience as 'dry' and 'formulaic' if we are not able to find the means to renew it.

The essential self

If we are able to find the means to do so, the self-questioning of the disillusioned self can take us into the 'trans-forming' re-membering of 'the tree of life' within us – our 'free gift' of talent, energy, and creative potential, which, for as long as we have breath, remains alive within us. I call this the 'essential self', as it contains the essence of our unique nature, our unique 'name' known to the One who 'spoke us into being'.

Jung and others reference the integration of the maturing ego and the essential self as the core work of the 'second half of life'. This is 'heart work' and can often require presencing in our 'shadow side' where our essence can lie buried if it does not fit the 'ideal self'.

Gradually we reorientate our lives to our 'true nature' or our 'identity in Christ' – an identity that is fundamentally mysterious to us, because it is has to be embodied and lived, as Kierkegaard reminds us, rather than defined, achieved, or understood. This invites us into a different way of 'knowing' which we gradually learn to trust. We can view this as a process of autopoiesis, or of 'apprehending' rather than 'comprehending' what lies within. We have explored this different way of knowing already in our chapter on the heart.

As we learn to access the flow of our deeper identity, we come to find ways of embodying this in the world – finding our truer vocation or expressing more of our creativity. We start inhabiting our friendships and our place in the family/community in ways more fully and naturally ourselves. We relax, letting go of our more compulsive drivers and engaging with things that bring us, and others, life. As the essential self comes online, we can notice a change in the quality of the energy that moves us out into the world – Rohr's 'drawn, not driven'.

There is also a flow and a harmony to our will. David Whyte's poem, at the start of this chapter, points us to this 'flowering' in our essential selves. Some are more blessed than others in the space they find in the world for this flowering to take place. But whether our flowering is seen or unseen, tender or hardy, the simple truth is that there is no fruit without flower. Too many people strive to 'be fruitful' before they have flowered, and what they produce can be far from their true nature – just another version of Zumbach's suit.

The surrendered self

The journey of the second half of life tends to involve growing spiritual awareness, decreasing self-centredness, and increasing self-responsibility. Flower becomes fruit and dies to release its seed. As egoic drivers lose their grip, we begin to sense more fully into the Divine Presence also at work within us. Gradually we realise that the habitual 'I' that has been running 'my' life really does not matter. In Christian terms, we 'die to self' – the *kenosis* that Paul describes in Philippians 2. This self-emptying has us open up to be available to the greater Will. In this stage of life, our primary concern becomes staying available or attuned, like a fine instrument, to this work of Love within us – famously expressed by St Francis in his prayer, 'Make me a channel of your peace'.

Mark Nepo's poem *One String* expresses these dynamics of the essential and surrendered selves in a beautiful and telling way that does not need religious language:

> *I am so busy at times*
> *trying to make it all*
> *worthwhile, that I am*
> *stunned at how easily the*
> *whole of life speaks to me,*
> *when music I've never heard*
> *or a truth I never understood*
> *plucks the one string I carry*
> *deep within.*

PRESENCING AND SPIRITUAL DIRECTION

> *I only want that string plucked*
> *and yet, it stays in a place*
> *only suffering or surrender*
> *can open.*
>
> *Still, violins in minor keys*
> *make me swallow my fear*
> *and herons flying into*
> *the end of a long day*
> *make me wish I'd led*
> *a more peaceful life.*[5]

One of the best descriptions of this journey in a non-theological frame is Bill Plotkin's *Nature and the Human Soul*,[6] where he traces the journey of the soul from the pre-experience innocence of the 'innocent in the nest' to the post-experience innocence of the 'sage in the cave', a process involving four major transitions: 'Naming', 'Initiating', 'Surrender', and 'Death'.

In the Christian mystical tradition, Bernard de Clairvaux frames this as a journey of love, from:

- 'Love of self for self's sake' to...
- 'Love of God for self's sake', to...
- 'Love of God for God's sake' to, finally...
- 'Love of self for God's sake'[7]

This is necessarily a brief and rather perfunctory delineation of what is much more richly expressed elsewhere and may warrant further enquiry if your curiosity is aroused. My purpose here is not to define this journey of a lifetime but to help us become more conscious and attentive to how we play our part in this unfolding – both for ourselves and in how we support others.

The world is full of people (all of us!), who can wax lyrical about evolved states of being, yet remain stuck in reactive ones – talking about 'love', for example, but spending much of our time pursuing our own self-interest. It is not as if I can decide in my mind to move from egoic self to surrendered self and just do it! These movements arise within me, often in a mysterious way according to the nature of my experiences and the unconscious stirring of my deeper being. So, the question is the familiar one of *how*? How do I work on myself to make myself available to these moments of transformation and growth, through grace, as they arise in their proper season? To quote Shakespeare, 'The readiness is all'[8].

I have expressed this journey of growth in a very linear way, for clarity and ease of understanding. The reality is much more circuitous than that. All these 'selves' are always to some extent 'layered' within us. At any moment in time, any one may be 'triggered' into picking up the reins and running the show. Ken Wilber's distinction between states and stages of consciousness is helpful here. We may at any time be able to access a higher 'state' in our journey, for example a state of 'flow' when our essential self comes online, say in dancing or teaching, but this state is not sustained and our egoic patterning soon kicks back in. Over time, however, as our awareness expands and our capacity to choose our state grows, we may come to a stage in which our essential self is mainly present, perhaps having consciously made sacrifices, to inhabit a way of life more congruent to it. What happens gradually over time, like a scattergram, is that we spend more time living in the later, more 'transformed' stages of this journey and less time in the more reactive or 'conformed'. Our progress along the journey of be-coming is, as the name implies, therefore less a work of doing and more a work of being, literally of 'coming into being'. It is our work of presencing that underpins and enables this.

> Before we look at how we 'come into being', this may be a natural time to pause. There are a lot of concepts contained in this chapter so far and it may be worth resting for a while to notice any that may be speaking to you more directly, particularly about where you find yourself in your own soul-journey.
>
> Where are you sensing your essential self calling you forward into new life and adventure?
>
> Where are you sensing a need to surrender, let go, and let be?
>
> No need to do anything, just notice – but do notice the energy as well as the thoughts.

'Renewing and discerning': how we participate in our own formation

The quote from St Paul at the start of this chapter points to two aspects in this work of being that underpins our formation. The first is our *re-newing*, which can also be framed as 'healing' or 'remembering' – restoring ourselves back to our 'true nature' in the image of God. The central parable for this, again, is that of the prodigal. Having spent our inheritance on the wrong things, we return 'home' to be welcomed and restored to our heritage.

The second aspect is our *'discerning'* – having returned 'home', this is how we sense and follow the 'good and pleasing' Will of God, in whatever way this is now making itself known to us – 'Thy will be done' (Father); 'Follow Me' (Son); 'The wind blows where it wills' (Spirit).

A simple metaphor for these two aspects is the loving care and restoration of a precious musical instrument so it may fulfil the purpose for which it is made. In 2 Timothy 2:21, this is expressed as a 'cleansing' to become 'instruments for special purposes, made holy, useful to the Master and prepared to do any good work.' The Sufi poet Hafiz expresses it too: 'I am a hole in a flute that Christ's breath moves through. Listen to this music.'[9]

Both these aspects, renewing and discerning, instrument and music, are necessarily the work of a lifetime, and quite probably beyond. I will consider each of them a bit more fully below before going on to explore how our work of presencing serves to support them.

Re-newing and re-membering

Viewed in the way we described above, the Fall is basically a forgetting. We forget who we truly are – 'fearfully and wonderfully made', as the psalmist exclaims (Psalm 139:4). But we still carry our Eden, our innocence, within us, in Christ. We just have to remember.

'Repent and believe' is the word of John the Baptist (Mark 1:15). 'In returning and rest you shall be saved,' says the prophet Isaiah (30:15, NKJV). Wake up, repent, return is the invitation of Christ in the parable of the prodigal, and, later in Matthew, simply to remember and reinhabit our innocence. 'Let the little children come to me, and do not hinder them, for the kingdom of heaven belongs to such as these' (Matthew 19:14).

So much of the 'work' of modern psychology and Christian discipleship can lead us into a striving to 'fix' ourselves, to make ourselves 'good', 'kind', 'strong', 'happy'. It is the absurdity of the problem trying to fix the problem, ego trying to transform ego into something it construes it should be. The wealth of biblical teaching we have touched upon above suggests the contrary: that all we need to do is re-member – to return to our true shape.

In the monastic tradition, this is *conversatio morum* – a daily, even hourly, process, almost like breath. St Paul seems to be referring to this when he urges the Thessalonians to 'pray without ceasing' (see 1 Thessalonians 5:17). This act of self-remembering is crucial to the movement out of the 'egoic' self and into the essential and the surrendered self.

This is where presencing comes in – it enables us to tune into our essential self and make contact with the Divine Presence within us, as we explored in Chapter Five. Bill Plotkin, again in *Nature and the Human Soul*, argues that only in these latter two stages are we actually a 'living soul'. Only here are we exercising a conscious 'will to be' rather than a reactive 'will to survive' in relation to ourselves, or a 'will to serve' rather than a 'will to please' in relation to others.[10]

This brings us to the second aspect of spiritual formation. As we learn to return and rest more and more in our true nature, and in Christ, so then Will, the directed Love of God, can be 'discerned' and can start to flow within us.

Discerning and following Will

If one aspect of the work is re-newing the instrument, which we might view as the first commandment, then we can view the other – what the instrument expresses, the 'music' of Hafiz's flute – through the lens of the second commandment.

'Listen carefully my child… incline the ear of your heart' is the opening of the foundational rule of Benedictine monasticism. Again, this is a daily or hourly process. I quote the opening lines of the prologue to the Rule of St Benedict below at some length because these probably speak more clearly and simply than I might do about how we learn to attend to the Will of God:

> *Let us arise, then, at last,*
> *for the Scripture stirs us up, saying,*
> *'Now is the hour for us to rise from sleep' (Romans 13:11).*
> *Let us open our eyes to the deifying light,*

> *let us hear with attentive ears*
> *the warning which the divine voice cries daily to us,*
> *'Today if you hear His voice,*
> *harden not your hearts' (Psalm 94[95]:8).*
> *And again,*
> *'Whoever has ears to hear,*
> *hear what the Spirit says to the churches' (Matthew 11–15; Apoc. 2:7)...*
> *What can be sweeter to us, dear ones,*
> *than this voice of the Lord inviting us?*
> *Behold, in His loving kindness*
> *the Lord shows us the way of life.*[11]

Let us notice that the Divine voice comes as invitation, not command – the invitation to let Will be done in the freedom and surrender of our personal will. It is the antidote to the Fall in that we exercise our will to choose to surrender and be with God. 'Not my will, but thy will', as Christ models it for us.

So, we move from a re-turning (contemplation, listening, in-breath), to a stepping out (action, speech, out-breath). The challenge of course is that this stepping out immediately invokes the same patterning we referenced above – the ego kicks in and we start to rely on our own strength, our own 'knowing', our own will, conformed to the pattern of this world.

To do anything else is instantly and viscerally to invoke fear, doubt, anxiety – it is so hard to trust the not-knowing when we step out in faith. This is where the second part of the Isaiah verse we quoted earlier speaks so directly to us: 'In quietness and *trust* is your strength' (Isaiah 30:15, my italics). So does the living example of Mary: 'Let it be to me according to your word' (Luke 1:38, NKJV). We learn slowly, painfully (and sometimes comically!) to follow the words of Proverbs 3:5–6: 'Trust in the LORD with all your heart and lean not on your own understanding; in all your ways submit to him, and he will make your paths straight.' This, then, is another key work of presencing – to trust enough to follow, often blindly...

How do we do this? How do we learn to let 'the water of life' flow within us? How do we let it be embodied in and through us in our thoughts, intentions, words, and actions, when the ego is also necessarily involved in all our activity? It is in this dynamic tussle between our 'stuck', 'patterned', 'striving' but highly functional egoic structures and the generative energy of our essential re-membered selves, in Christ, that something new comes into being, more substantial, stable, and permanent within us.

This is the miraculous 'work' of what I am calling here *'soul formation'*. By this I mean the process by which we start to find a new centre of gravity within, a new place from which to live – a new 'I' that is formed not from the patterning of the ego but from the action of the essential and the Divine within us, refined and proven in the crucible of our experience. It is primarily a work of faith. The fruit of it is what Thomas Merton calls the 'true self'.[12] St Paul talks about it as putting on 'the new self, created after the likeness of God' (Ephesians 4:24, ESV).

Again, I have put the word 'work' above in inverted commas because it is partly a matter of our own work in becoming receptive, but it is also the product of something greater 'at work' within us and around us. But this is something we need consciously to sense and receive. We have choice. We can neglect our growth, or we can attend to it, but we cannot force it, shape it, or predict and control its outcomes.

It is this 'work' of becoming truly receptive that is surprisingly often the hardest. 'Working' to 'surrender' and 'receive' seems paradoxical – a weird combination of active and passive. Coleridge in his *Biographia Literaria* uses the image of a water-boatman to express this state of being – a 'moving forward in a combination of active and passive motion'.[13] It can be difficult to do alone, because the primary mechanism we use, the ego, is often part, if not the entirety, of the 'problem'. It must be surrendered, and we have to find a different basis from which to work. So, we must be presenced and seek help. That is the 'work', and it is this 'truer self' gradually forming as a new centre of gravity within us that is the flowering and fruiting of this. It is another paradox of surrender that this is often experienced as a great freedom.

The fruits of presencing: 'soul-formation' and the 'kingdom life'

How does this 'soul-formation' work in practice? Maybe a simple example: I love art, and I want to teach my six-year-old son how to paint. I know how. I set up a desk with pencil, paper and some paints. I am thinking about how to show him to draw a face, how to paint the sky, and some simple tricks to show perspective and make things lifelike. Then something stops me. I remember what painting and fathering is all about. I put a sheet of polythene down on the ground and some tubes of coloured paint and two pieces of flip chart paper. 'Let's play,' I say.

I know that one day, once my son has learned the fun of expressing himself in colour, he will ask me to show him some techniques. But that is not this day. It's not about the art, it's about the impulse to create, to live, to love, to play. Today, we make a glorious mess. We paint 'trees' and 'flowers' and 'birds' and 'cars' – and each other. We experiment together, mixing colours to see what new colours emerge. We are of course covered in paint by the end. By the close of the day, something new has formed in both of us, something is retained. I am a different father, a different person – more playful, freer, gentler – a different artist and even a different teacher. In the tension between my egoic desire to teach what I know about art to my son on the one hand and my remembering the love of father and the life of a child on the other, something precious has come into being for us both, a true experience of connection and flow – a living memory that will never be taken away. It has 'formed us', making us more wholly who we are.

There are big moments of soul-formation in life – how we handle a setback, a loss, a rejection, or the brave decision to follow our own path or speak truth to power. There are also small ones – a moment of forgiveness, a pause for prayer, a second glance that has us truly 'see' someone. They tend to arise most powerfully when we are fully committed and buried in something 'important' and then we notice or remember that something else, more subtle and precious, is needed. In the book that I co-authored, this was the stand-out feature of people who were seen and known to be 'leading with love'.[14] These were people who remembered to be kind in the small things as well as focused and effective in their mission, often in pressured environments, against the dominant culture.

If the key to this is presencing, it is not a presencing that denies the ego; it includes it and transcends it. I have noticed so often it is the ego-striving that takes us to the place of surrender and the being fully in what 'drives' us that awakens us to the truth of what 'draws' us.

Julian of Norwich points to this: 'Sin is behovely... but all shall be well and all manner of thing shall be well'.[15] And Christ was starkly clear that He came for the 'sin-full', not the 'righteous'. To explain a little further, neither I, nor, I am sure, St Julian, are advocating a path of conscious sin! What is meant by 'sin' here is the action we inevitably fall into when we strive too hard and long in our own will, pursuing our own ends. However 'noble' these may be, it is almost inevitable that we lose our presence and connection with the Greater Will. In the metaphor of the vine in John 15, this is what must and will be burned off. But it is in this constant waywardness and falling short that, like the prodigal, we learn to re-turn, re-new and find the 'Way' in which 'all shall be well'.

In this process, something permanent becomes formed within us that starts to create a more mature centre of gravity at the core of our being – 'fully human and fully divine' and capable of being simultaneously in both. Thomas à Kempis expresses this as 'The Imitation of Christ'.[16] St Paul would perhaps talk about us growing into the 'fullness' or the 'likeness'. As we remember, too, that our soul is the only part of us that survives beyond death, this is truly the 'work of a lifetime' and perhaps, if one considers the impact of soul-formation on our collective humanity, it is the sole purpose and meaning of our life on earth.

This, then, is our work of 'living sacrifice'. We strive to be who we think we need to be and then we let go into who we simply are – heart, soul, mind, strength – embodied in vulnerable connection with God and with others. It requires strength, faith, and presence to stay this vulnerable and this trusting for long, but I suspect you will have met people who have – do any come to mind as you read this? I suspect you may recognise them by their quiet, clear, attentive strength.

As we live more from our soul, we change. In the early stages, this is a calmer, more centred 'state', less 'caught' by reactivity. As it forms and 'condenses' within, it becomes a stable 'stage' in our maturity as our behaviour flows from this new centre. We become kinder, more patient, more available to others and to Love. We see more clearly. We also find a natural authority flowing from the ground of our being.

As we learn to live in our own 'truth', our soul more embodied in 'heart, mind, and strength', we begin to experience more of the wider 'truth' of the spiritual dimension, which is present everywhere if we but notice it. This is one way we might interpret Christ's references to 'the kingdom of heaven'. As we live less from 'self' and so become more available, we are more likely to have direct experience of the kingdom at work around us and within us. We shall explore this more in our chapters on prayer and relationships.

Experiences that seem remote or infrequent in the egoic phase of the journey become more present in the surrendered phase – for example, unitive experiences or the presence of Love as a tangible force at work in the world. Other biblical truths start to become available to us in our daily experience, to 'feed' and 'direct' the soul more clearly – for example, the 'voice of the Lord' speaking in nature. We become more attuned to the synchronicities of the Will of God at work. I have alluded already in Chapter Four to how we may experience the Love of God. Other common aspects of what is often termed 'mystical' experience include:

- Being enfolded in the tangible peace of God
- The experience of 'awe': the immensity of God and the vastness of creation
- The 'welling up' of joy inside – a spring of living water welling up to eternal life
- The experience of 'beauty' and 'transcendence' and the interconnected flow of life in all things
- The direct experience of Christ, with us, behind, beside, before, within – gazing at us, relating and connecting directly with us, sometimes silently, sometimes with words
- The experience of 'union' and the dissolution or 'marriage' of the soul into the Divine
- Hearing 'God speak' to and in the soul
- Receiving a direct 'word' or prophesy or guidance or invitation to 'Follow'
- An 'emptiness' and a 'nothingness' in which 'I am' – *Todo y Nada*

Such experiences can be 'transformational' in that they change us forever, both our way of being and our self-concept. They remain a part of us forever, a 'living memory', part of our embodied soul, as in the *Memoria Dei* exercise in Chapter Four.

The more we can be open and available to this kind of direct contact with the Divine, the more Will can be at work in us and through us. But there are two major risks with these experiences, which of course still hook our human patterning. The first is that we 'react' to them in our old egoic nature. I remember my own conversion experience and my immediate response: 'Why have I been chosen, what should I do?' The obvious answer was to become a priest, so I entered that process. Eventually, I ended up in a monastery and met one of the monks who gently enquired what had brought me there. 'Testing a calling to the priesthood,' I replied. There was a pause and a compassionate smile. 'Yes,' he said, 'God has great ways of using our pride for His ends.'

The second risk is that the 'feel' of these experiences can have us thirsting for their repetition – a kind of spiritual gluttony, as though the experience of God *is* God. For many years after my first experience of Divine Love, which I now know was 'just' a healing from shame, I would sit in prayer devotedly trying to conjure up similar experiences. And yes, God ultimately did use my pride for His ends. I found the contemplative path, but it took another ten years before I began to recognise that all I had to do was follow. It was only then, for example, that I was able to accept the 'free gift' of being welcomed into the Benedictine Oblature rather than having in some way to 'earn my place' amongst the Abbey Community.

As in all experience, as previously described, we learn just to welcome it, receive it and collaborate with its work within. If there is a yearning to repeat the experience, we practise the wisdom of somatic enquiry to sense into the true energy of the yearning, rather than attach it to any object, even if that object is a repeat experience. The yearning, or the undistorted part of it, is usually the very thing, alive within us, that we are seeking elsewhere. We have just forgotten, or not yet consciously received it.

In this work, something of our old nature will have to 'die', voluntarily. We let go and trust what is unfolding within us in its own time according to its Will and our readiness to receive and collaborate with it. This is the fusion of our own efforts and the greater 'Work' that I alluded to earlier. All we have to do is stay awake and allow what we receive to do its work of 'renewing of our mind'.

'Why do you seek the living among the dead? He is not here, but has risen,' the angel says to Mary after the resurrection. This is so often the experience of the functional mind after a powerful experience. It does not have the cognitive structure to make sense of it. I find so often in my experience of spiritual direction that a person's true being has already changed profoundly in response to the transforming force within, but the 'old mind' has not realised it yet and is still trying to run the show the way it always has. This can be very confusing for people, and I will say more on this in my chapter on spiritual direction at the end.

It is probably why Paul had to spend three years in his own wilderness as he adjusted to his new reality after his road to Damascus experience. Possibly he had the luxury, in becoming a tent maker, of being able to step off the treadmill and catch up with himself. Indeed, I wonder whether the reason Paul 'persecuted Christ' so fiercely in the years before his conversion was because deep in his soul he already knew who Christ was, but his egoic identity could not admit it, nor afford to? Hence the question that 'undid' him: 'Saul, Saul, why do you persecute me?' That, I sense, is another truth of this work – that the more we resist the still, small voice within, the more energy we have to expend to fight, avoid, deny, or contain it – with consequences both for ourselves and those we love until, one forthcoming day, it's heard...

> Let us pause for a moment to breathe and to 'Listen... incline the ears of our hearts'.
>
> What is the ear of your heart saying to you now as you just rest and quieten for a moment to hear your own 'still, small, voice?'
>
> Just presence for a few moments in breath and body and listen, not 'for' anything, just opening the ears of your heart to what is here, present, 'just' waiting...

So, in summary: my proposition in this chapter has been that this 'work' of presencing, in which we consciously attend to, receive, and 'digest' the 'daily bread' of our inner and outer experience, is what 'feeds and strengthens the soul' as the necessary centre of our journey of formation. It is not just in prayer or in powerful spiritual experiences, it is potentially in every moment, in the 'daily bread' of our lived experience – if we can 'just' bear to be present to it and be transformed by it, 'fully human, fully divine'.

As seems to be happening quite frequently as I write this book, I notice Barbara Brown Taylor is writing directly to this point in the Center for Action and Contemplation blog:

> *According to the Talmud, every blade of grass has its own angel bending over it, whispering, 'Grow, grow.' How does one learn to see and hear such angels?*
>
> *If there is a switch to flip, I have never found it. As with Jacob, most of my visions of the divine have happened while I was busy doing something else. I did nothing to make them happen... I play no apparent part in their genesis. My only part is to decide how I will respond, since there is plenty I can do to make them go away, namely: 1) I can figure that I have had too much caffeine again; 2) I can remind myself that visions are not true in the same way that taxes and the evening news are true; or 3) I can return my attention to everything I need to get done today. These are only a few of the things I can do to talk myself out of living in the House of God.*
>
> *Or I can set a little altar, in the world or in my heart. I can stop what I am doing long enough to see where I am, who I am there with, and how awesome the place is. I can flag one more gate to heaven—one more patch of ordinary earth with ladder marks on it—where the divine traffic is heavy when I notice it and even when I do not. I can see it for once, instead of walking right past it, maybe even setting a stone or saying a blessing before I move on to wherever I am due next.*[17]

I have suggested here that each step of growth moving us forward in our soul journey involves us embracing the two core activities highlighted by St Paul of 'renewing' and 'discerning' in a presencing pause of 'living sacrifice'. This increases as we move to the latter stages of our maturity where the essential and the surrendered selves start to come more online. This therefore is where a spiritual director, or 'soul friend', can be so helpful – it is hard to do this 'work' alone.

What also happens, though, is that as our own inner 'centre of gravity' changes, so do our relationships – often seismically. This becomes the substance of our next chapter.

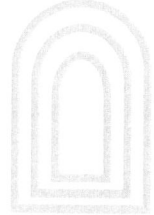

CHAPTER EIGHT

Presencing and our relationships

Then we will no longer be infants, tossed back and forth by the waves, and blown here and there by every wind of teaching and by the cunning and craftiness of people in their deceitful scheming. Instead, speaking the truth in love, we will grow to become in every respect the mature body of him who is the head, that is, Christ. From him the whole body, joined and held together by every supporting ligament, grows and builds itself up in love, as each part does its work.

EPHESIANS 4:14-16

I SUGGESTED IN THE LAST CHAPTER that as our work of 'renewing' and 'soul formation' continues apace, the world of our relationships must inevitably undergo its own transformations.

The stages of development I described in that chapter can be just as profoundly applied to our relationships, each of us present in the wider 'body of Christ' that we all inhabit. In earlier stages of development, we are more likely to experience our separation. The functional mind will tend to reduce others to 'objects' of our own consciousness and will. Martin Buber famously termed this 'I-it' relationships, rather than 'I-thou'. However, in the later stages of our life journey, the boundaries between us start to dissolve as we learn to let love flow and 'die to self'.

Christ Himself is very explicit, as we have alluded to earlier, about the essence of true relationships 'in the body': 'When two or three gather in my name, there am I with them' (Matthew 18:20). When we are 'gathered' and available in our inner life, and also in connection with others, equally available in their inner lives, we become a 'channel'. Something powerful and precious can flow through us into this world – a 'peace which passes all understanding' and the 'good, pleasing and perfect' Will of God. So often in the Bible, it is in and through relationship that great things flow into the world. Christ sent the disciples out in pairs. Paul never travelled alone. Even with Christ, something very substantial, but different, came into being through His different relationships – with Peter, John, Mary Magdalene, Thomas.

However, the converse can also be true, as many of us will have witnessed in church, organisational, or family relationships – when fear and misunderstanding take root, these can rapidly magnify into discord and conflict at worst or a wariness and 'closed' space at best, where only superficial engagement is possible. In fact, we could go so far as to say that one of the biggest issues for church life is that, under the imperative to be 'good Christians', true connection can be subsumed by a mask of polite-talk and superficial relationships. I am always grateful and humbled on our Crossroads Retreats to have people from outside the Christian faith who can often be much more 'real' in their expression of their life-challenges and questions and open up the space for others to follow. In the same way, people with a living faith (when they express this as an integral part of their lives and without an agenda to 'convert') arouse the curiosity of those without.

This embodiment in relationship can be experienced as an energetic presence, as the living substance of our relational life – which has indeed a life of its own in the inevitable reciprocity of being. Some today, particularly those who are 'constellations' practitioners, describe this substantive presence as the 'field', with its own presence and intelligence. At a more day-to-day level, we often talk about the 'climate' or the 'atmosphere' or the 'mood' of a gathering or group or even a single relationship. It is infectious – but always, of course, the question is what it is 'infected with'.

We do not live alone, we live in connection with every other soul that, to some extent, we 'let in' to our lives. This is the wisdom of *'ubuntu'*, which I have referenced earlier. People affect us and we affect them. The teenage daughter of a dear friend, talking about school life, said this very thing to me, talking rather sadly about one of her friends who had lost her way: 'We become who we surround ourselves with.' We sense and connect in an energy that flows, and it becomes infectious – others become drawn to us too. We invite each other forwards on our journeys and we hold each other back. It can be a very specific dilemma of the Christian walk when someone enters a relationship with Christ and faces the inevitable change in life patterns that follows when friends and family do not.

It is no surprise that in the ego-dominant phase of our lives, we find ourselves surrounded by ego-dominant people – nor, when the 'essential self' starts to come online, that we find ourselves drawn to others who are operating more from essence than ego. The more 'surrendered' soul is naturally able to be more generous and deeply inclusive, but will also need to be rigorous in maintaining her space and not be 'crowded out' by the many who are drawn to her.

As we journey towards our fuller selves, whether through subtle or dramatic changes, those people still firmly wedded to our former 'patterns', which may include some of our closest or most important relationships, are likely to be fiercely resistant to the change that is starting to come alive in us. They may experience it as 'losing us', or rather 'us losing touch with ourselves and them' as we change. This can be the cause of significant challenge, confusion, and pain. I have already alluded to Paul's conversion, and one can only imagine what played out in the pattern of his relationships and his place in the social fabric of his time.

Yet, if that is true, it is also true that Paul was sent his Ananias, and several others later, to accompany him on his journeys. As our soul-life starts to come more and more online, our soul-companions start to appear too. In later stages of the journey, as we inhabit more of our surrendered self, we start also to discern and open to those we are being called to come alongside to serve and support, however surprising, as Ananias found when he was 'nudged' to befriend the one who had been leading the persecution against him. This becomes much more fine-tuned as we mature and recognise it is God doing the work, not us. So, it becomes less about the breadth of vision, or a 'calling' to 'serve suffering humanity', and more about the depth of contact with specific people who are brought to us on the 'way'. Witness the people Christ helped amidst the many He inevitably had to walk past.

I am not going to attempt in this chapter to cover all the relational issues that play out in ego-to-ego connection. This has been written about ad infinitum elsewhere. Nor will I delve into how we 'serve' in relationship, which is a subject so vast and explored elsewhere by wiser writers than I. My focus for this chapter will be more personal and experiential – on what can happen when we learn to become more presenced, and available to Presence, in relationship.

One thing that can happen relationally, as we grow in our inner awareness, is that we start to sense the relational field as a living presence around us – 'the body of Christ' – a greater 'being' of which we are a part, not a separate actor. There is a paradox which it is not uncommon to experience – when we are more fully presenced, we are simultaneously a separate being and an indivisible part of a wider whole. People who describe some kind of unitive experience often describe a feeling of being 'part of the ocean'. Rather like Heisenberg's wave/particle duality, we seem to be able to choose to experience and 'know' ourselves as either individual 'drop' or vast 'ocean'. We are all of the same whole, but just like the surface tension that causes a part of the ocean to become a drop of water, for whatever mysterious purpose, so we can assume the distinct identity of an individual soul.

Ramakrishna Paramhansa's delightful parable about a salt doll (paraphrased here) illustrates this beautifully:

> *A salt doll journeyed for thousands of miles over land in search of its true home and identity. Finally, it came to the sea. It was fascinated by this strange moving mass, quite unlike anything it had ever seen before. 'Who are you?' said the salt doll to the sea. The sea smilingly replied, 'Come in and see.' So, the doll waded in. The farther it walked into the sea the more it dissolved, until there was only very little of it left. Before that last bit dissolved, the doll exclaimed in wonder, 'Now I know who I am!'*[1]

The capacity for boundlessness in relationship can be very important in spiritual direction and indeed in the running of retreats. It allows aspects of each other's experience to become available in the field of connection, and therefore discernible to each other. It also enables us to become 'channel' for

Will and Love and Peace. One of the most important things we can do for one another in the spiritual life is to act as 'mirrors' to each other.

It is notoriously difficult to see our own true nature, because for us it is as natural as breathing, and therefore the self-concept that we form as part of the narrative of our functional self often excludes some of the richest and most essential parts of our nature. This is how we start to inhabit what Thomas Merton refers to as the 'false self'[2] – we make our choices and live our lives from our ego, patterned by the world rather than the truth of who we are. That is why one of the most powerful and deeply transformational gifts we can give to each other is to 'be seen', truly seen, by the other. The soul knows when it has been seen and it bursts into life within. For some indeed this can be too scary and the eyes glaze and avoid for fear of being invited into who they truly are. For most it is powerful, emotional, and an overwhelming relief.

This, I imagine, was the essence of Christ's ministry. He saw people, and in His gaze, He called them into being. This is epitomised by the account of His dinner with Simon, the Pharisee, in Luke's Gospel. 'A woman... who had lived a sinful life' came into the room while they were at dinner and Simon was appalled that Jesus welcomed her. Christ's challenge to Simon was direct and simple, 'Simon, do you *see* this woman?' Christ saw her for who she was, not for her 'patterning'. 'I came into your house. You did not give me any water for my feet, but she wet my feet with her tears and wiped them with her hair.' The draw of so many to Christ will have been this experience of a gaze that 'just' simply saw them and awoke them into life. It will have been the same gaze too that evoked such defensiveness and resistance in the Scribes and Pharisees (see Luke 7:36–50).

It is a simple and wholesome challenge for all of us. Can we see beyond the limits of our own preconceptions and conditioning? This requires us to be presenced and sufficiently 'surrendered' ourselves, so that we can learn to see and connect with each other through the eyes of Christ – and to be available as 'channel' of the greater Presence to and for each other. It is always a wholesome principle to be asking in prayer when we are with someone, 'Please help me see this person as they truly are.' The answer to this request can rarely, if ever, come to the cognitive understanding. It will be at best a felt, energetic awareness of their deeper soul presence beneath the layers of their own egoic patterning, which we so often mistake for their being.

To be able to connect at this level, therefore, it is imperative we do what we can to have our full being online, as described in Chapter Four. This involves keeping grounded in sensation and breath so that the mind can remain clear, and the heart come online, which is the faculty most central to 'seeing people as they are'.

Sometimes a spiritual directee will talk about experiencing a sense of the presence of Christ and, when they 'turn' and receive his gaze upon them, it is always profoundly and deeply transformative. 'You have searched me, LORD, and you know me,' says the psalmist (Psalm 139:1), and that searching gaze is one of pure Love (and truth, for there is no distinction in that gaze) – if we can bear to receive it.

To be seen is to be released into being, if we can bear it and not rush to hide. Richard Rohr expressed this powerfully:

> *The true and essential work of all religion is to help us recognize and recover the divine image in everything. Our job is to mirror things correctly, deeply, and fully until all beings know who they are. A mirror by its nature reflects impartially, equally, effortlessly, spontaneously, and endlessly. It does not produce the image, nor does it filter the image according to its perceptions or preferences. Authentic mirroring can only call forth what is already there.*
>
> *Consider the very 'Mind of Christ' as a mirror. The Christ-mirror fully knows and loves us from all eternity and reflects that image back to us. I cannot logically prove this to you, but I do know that people who live inside of this resonance are both happy and healthy. Those who do not resonate and reciprocate with the inherent dignity of things around them only grow in loneliness and alienation and invariably tend toward violence in some form, if only toward themselves.*
>
> *Whatever you call it, the 'image of God' is absolute and unchanging. There is nothing humans can do to increase or decrease it. And it is not ours to decide who has it or does not have it, which has been most of our problem up to now. It is pure and total gift, given equally to all.*[3]

This can enrich our understanding of Christ's words in John 8:31 (NKJV): 'If you abide in My word, you are My disciples indeed. And you will know the truth, and the truth shall make you free.'

If we are each of us the spoken word of God, then to abide in this word wholly, in the wider Body of Christ, is to be set free to be who we truly are, as

PRESENCING AND OUR RELATIONSHIPS

Christ reinforces later in John 15:4,11 (NKJV): 'Abide in Me, and I in you... that My joy may remain in you, and *that* your joy may be full.'

Thomas Merton, in *New Seeds of Contemplation*, also describes this process of 'being seen' in a complex but powerful passage:

> *Within myself is a metaphorical apex of existence at which I am held in being by my Creator. God utters me like a word containing a partial thought of Himself. A word will never be able to comprehend the voice that utters it. But if I am true to the concept that God utters in me, if I am true to the thought of Him I was meant to embody, I shall be full of His actuality and find Him everywhere in myself, and find myself nowhere. I shall be lost in Him: that is, I shall find myself. I shall be 'saved.'*[4]

As I have said before, this is a work we cannot do alone, for the 'I' that is seeking to see and know myself is blinded by its own patterning. It has to be surprised! It is perhaps one of the most fundamental truths of human life that it is only through the loving gaze of another (human or Divine) that we come to truly know (and love) ourselves. It frees us from the relentless striving to perfect ourselves in our own eyes, or to be 'doing' the work of Christ and to release us into 'being' ourselves, in Christ.

This is the essential work of spiritual friendship – the Cistercian monk Aelred of Rievaulx describes this powerfully and movingly in his treatise *On Spiritual Friendship*:

> *Moreover, it is no mean consolation in this life to have someone with whom you can be united by an intimate attachment and the embrace of very holy love, to have someone in whom your spirit may rest, to whom you can pour out your soul, to whose gracious conversation you may flee for refuge amid sadness, as to consoling songs; or to the most generous bosom of whose friendship you may approach in safety amid the many troubles of this world; to whose most loving breast you may without hesitation confide all your inmost thoughts, as to yourself; by whose spiritual kisses as by medicinal ointments you may sweat out of yourself the weariness of agitating cares. Someone who will weep with you in anxiety, rejoice with you in prosperity, seek with you in doubts, someone you can let into the secret chamber of your mind by the bonds of love, so that even when absent in body he is present in spirit... you alone*

> may repose with him alone in the embrace of charity, the kiss of unity, with the sweetness of the Holy Spirit flowing between you. Still more, you may be so united to him and approach him so closely and so mingle your spirit with his, that the two become one. Let anyone who finds it pleasant to enjoy his friend see to it that he enjoys him in the Lord, not in the world or in the pleasures of the flesh, but in joyfulness of spirit... all flattery and fawning are checked... patting each other on the back and conniving with each other... taking care not to offend one another, they incur each other's ruin because they do not enjoy themselves in the liberty of justice or in the Lord. (3.39.109: 300).[5]

Coming back to my earlier comments about the substantive energetic 'field' that arises in the true connection of 'gathered' souls, nowhere is this more apparent than in those 'in love'. The atmosphere around them is tangible and it has a palpable impact on those present. I recall recently two people walking through London, exuding such an atmosphere, and a complete stranger came up to them and just said, 'You look so amazing together, you two. Just a beautiful energy,' and walked straight on, with the couple's rather bemused thanks following him as he did. As referenced in my earlier chapter on the heart, this is largely because 'in love', the heart is able to open, and its transformational resonant energy can flow – well beyond the body, and some would say beyond time too.

Mark Nepo captures this in his poem, 'For Joel at 94':

> They say that miners in South America
> strap small lamps around their chest, that
> this works better than the light coming
> from the center of your head.
>
> They say the head can be fooled,
> but the heart can't turn without
> the body. This makes me think of you
> digging your way through your long life,
> lighting everything with your heart.
>
> It's a good way to live. And when we
> sit at the end of the day, our hearts

> *illumine the day and we see each other*
> *in its radiance. I can tell, it reminds you*
> *of many circles you've been a part of.*
> *It's a good way to measure time.*[6]

In a spiritual direction or retreat setting, and indeed perhaps in any life setting where great care has been taken to create a boundary in which this quality of 'recollected being' is not intruded upon, this capacity to 'mirror' the truth of who we are begins to create and hold a 'thin space' in which 'the kingdom of heaven' may truly be present in this world. An essential part of this, in my experience, is that everybody enters into a conscious and intentional presencing practice along the lines described in Chapter Four, so that the mind can be freed and the heart comes online.

Particularly important is the capacity to be able to 'sense' what is happening energetically and the ability to 'speak from the heart'. Given what we were saying about the heart in the Chapter Six, this allows for the much freer movement of transformational qualities such as joy and love and peace and hope and faith to be felt – and quite literally infuse the atmosphere in the room. This is not about making anything happen, it is about an opening awareness to what is already here. As we explored, these qualities are 'infectious' because as human beings we have been formed to resonate with these infused virtues. As we become more and more 'awake' in the fullness of this presence, so our minds become available to the wisdom we are meant to receive – which may be for ourselves or indeed a 'living word' for another. This then enables all four spheres of knowing to be available in the shared space – in relation to each other and to the Divine and, indeed, to nature. This in turn enables a much deeper and more 'present' layer of wisdom to be accessible and to flow.

As I write this, Psalm 133 comes to me:

> *How good and pleasant it is*
>   *when God's people live together in unity!*
> *It is like precious oil poured on the head,*
>   *running down on the beard,*
> *running down on Aaron's beard,*
>   *down on the collar of his robe.*

PRESENCING AND SPIRITUAL DIRECTION

> *It is as if the dew of Hermon*
>   *were falling on Mount Zion.*
> *For there the LORD bestows his blessing,*
>   *even life forevermore.*

The wisdom that can thus flow is characterised in the Wisdom of Solomon 722–24 (NRSVACE):

> *...a spirit that is intelligent, holy,*
> *unique, manifold, subtle,*
> *mobile, clear, unpolluted,*
> *distinct, invulnerable, loving the good, keen,*
> *irresistible, beneficent, humane,*
> *steadfast, sure, free from anxiety,*
> *all-powerful, overseeing all,*
> *and penetrating through all spirits*
> *that are intelligent and pure and most subtle.*
> *For wisdom is more mobile than any motion;*
> *because of her pureness she pervades and penetrates all things.*

It is not uncommon, in my experience, for people to comment in the retreat space that 'this must be a taste of what heaven is like', where there is no need for boundaries, where people may 'shine', where they feel safe enough to be able to explore, release their patterns, and heal their wounds in the manner described in Chapter Six, and, most importantly, where they may be available to the movement of true Will in their lives. The living experience of this kind of presenced encounter seems to me to be very close to what Paul describes in 2 Corinthians 3:18: 'We all, who with unveiled faces contemplate the Lord's glory, are being transformed into his image with ever-increasing glory.'

    I remember vividly, on the last morning of a recent retreat, people being invited in the freshness of the morning to take an 'awareness walk' around the garden. On their return, they each shared something of the experience, and each had, in their own way, encountered different facets of the Divine as they walked. One person described in minute detail an experience of being completely absorbed in the micro-world of tiny insects and spiders at work in the damp, long grass. Another came back ablaze with the colours she had seen. Another felt called to explore the rubbish dump at the back of the garden. One had been lost in awe at the sight of a red kite overhead, another had been paddling barefoot in the flow of a stream. Each returned, hearts wide open, connecting their experiences to deep movements in their retreat journeys. As they shared, facets of the presence and 'glory' of the Divine shone out of them – peace, life, love, joy, awe, compassion, humility, reverence, strength – and mingled and infused the space in an almost tangible manner, till the air was thick with Presence. No one was inhibited, each spoke from the heart, beautifully reflecting back what was being transmitted as people shared. At the end we paused for a moment just to notice what the atmosphere in the room was like. There was a liquid silence. 'This is the kingdom,' someone said – and no one dissented.

These 'soul to soul' experiences and encounters, however fleeting in time, have a powerful effect on the processes of formation described in the previous chapter. Something is sown in the soul, again often intangibly, that feeds a different 'centre of gravity', a different reference point from which to view and inhabit our experience. We become more and more of our 'true selves', to pick up on Merton's wisdom again. This true self is less likely to be 'tossed back and forth by the waves and blown here and there' by life's turbulent ephemera, and is more able to sense the deeper tide. It is also a self that is more secure in itself and therefore less likely to be seeking to have its ego-needs met in and through 'deceits and devices' in relationships. It is therefore more able to give and receive graciously to and from others in the intended and necessary reciprocity of life, as expressed in the second commandment.

In fact, I would go further and say that these soul-to-soul experiences must necessarily be fleeting and bounded in this life. They are intended to feed and strengthen the soul in Love. We are not meant to cling onto them, as Christ so movingly bids Mary not to cling to Him outside the empty tomb. Nor can we exist with this kind of boundarylessness much of the time in a functional world that so easily intrudes and distorts. So much harm can be done when one person's egoic patterns, however unintentionally, intrude into the wide-open heart of another – the most obvious effects being of violation, betrayal, or deep hurt. The beauty of a well-constructed retreat or one-to-one space is that boundaries are clearly demarcated and there is no expectation that we will continue to have this kind of open access to each other's lives (however tempting it may be to cling on there).

In the normal flow of life, this process is much harder to negotiate, and a crucial part of our work of presencing is to be attentive to how and where our own boundaries are being intruded upon in some way and to gently, lovingly, put in a boundary marker at that point. I remember myself receiving spiritual direction many years ago, being in deep, very emotional inner work around a buried response to a bereavement, which just opened up out of the blue towards the end of a session. My director very gently asked, with five minutes to go, 'How do we want to bring our time together to an end, Chris?' Left to my own devices, I would have carried on much longer, but as soon as she asked, I was able to draw to a wholesome close that left me able to continue in the work in my own space – and I was fine with that.

I remember this because prior to that I had got into the habit of allowing my sessions to overrun if there was a lot of emotion around – and rarely did it help, indeed it was often counter-productive. I had thought people may be upset by having to close. I realised the opposite was true. The space is the space, and it is enough. The Benedictine rhythm of the hours reflects this truth. Everything has its bounded time and space.

So much unnecessary suffering is caused by misaligned expectations around 'what is mine and what is yours'. It is in these conditions, of course, that our work of grounding and presencing becomes most important and most difficult. Nowhere do we get more 'caught' in our reactivity than in the sphere of relationships. We receive others' projections and act them out, we feel other's emotions, mistake them for our own and react accordingly. We lose perspective and find ourselves saying things in the heat of the moment that we would never dream of when we are grounded. And of course, we come into every relational encounter with our preconceptions primed and ready to be triggered in a self-fulfilling cycle of inference and action. Being able to ground, breathe, and return to a 'clean' place of grounded presence in the heat of human contact and activity is one of the greatest life skills that we can muster. This is something we will look at further in Chapter Eleven when we look at 'sustaining presence'.

The other crucial facet of human relationships is that, whilst probably in Christ our true relationships exist beyond time, we live the patterning of our relational experience in time – and therefore in the temporal reality of birth, life, and death. Very few relationships may be for a lifetime, some are for a season, many may be for just a fleeting moment of connection. Returning to where I began this chapter, the capacity to handle (delicate) beginnings, (full-on) middles, and (releasing) endings in relationships, with all the emotional flows inherent in these, is one of the most formative aspects of human experience: being able, for example, to discern who is being sent to you on your path, being able to bid farewell with love and gratitude when the path is done. Much heart softening and hardening can take place within these life passages, with all the consequent potential for soul-formation or soul-stunting that can occur. It is everywhere in the Gospels: 'Leave everything and follow me,' Christ says to the disciples. Their whole journey is bounded between Christ's 'come and you will see' and 'where I am going you cannot come'. 'Do not cling onto me,' he says to Mary.

Our capacity for presenced awareness and deep, sensitive discernment at these times can be fundamental to our capacity to find and stay on our own 'good way'. It is too easy to stay too long, and too easy to leave ahead of time, and it is here that we most often need the help and perspective of a greater Love than our own – one to help us sense the season and find the right response.

In respect of this, we can end this chapter with some words from the Cistercian Bernard de Clairvaux, on the flux of life and the constancy of Love: 'I love because I love. I love that I may love. Love is a great reality and if it returns to its beginning and goes back to its origin, seeking its source again, it will always draw afresh from it and thereby flow freely.'[7]

CHAPTER NINE

Presencing and prayer – life as prayer

> *May the Divine help remain with us always...*
> *And with our absent brothers and sisters.*
>
> BENEDICTINE PRAYER

THIS SHORT PRAYER, used daily across the Benedictine and many other orders, highlights the fundamental premise of the spiritual life – that there is a 'greater help' available to us than anything we can summon ourselves.

In a way, our work is simple: to make ourselves available to this Help. But this is a work that we must learn, or re-learn, because we forget it in our separation and egocentricity. Therefore, I treat prayer here as an opening up of our full being, along the lines of the first commandment, to the Presence of God. This implies that at some level of our being we can know or sense this Presence, or at least the way in which it chooses to make itself felt to us. As such, it assumes that God can be experienced and that this experience can, like all our experience, change us or re-new us – if we want to receive it.

The first half of this chapter will explore the nature and practice of prayer, and the second half will then focus on our core theme, which is how we inhabit our *experience* of prayer and are 'fed' by this.

The nature of prayer

Prayer, from the perspective above, brings us into a true and loving relationship with the Divine. Our own life experience of love and friendship teaches us what a loving relationship is all about:

- Being fully open with each other, nothing hidden nor needing to be hidden
- 'Being there' for each other, in good times and bad
- Doing things wholly together, the exciting and the mundane
- Inhabiting our own truth whilst fully allowing the other to inhabit theirs
- Giving each other space and trust and freedom to make our own choices, celebrating when these go well and being there as a source of support and comfort when they do not

'Being there for each other' is probably the key phrase in all of this. Of course, the Divine is always here with us and in the whole of the created order – 'The whole earth is full of his glory,' as it says in Isaiah 6:3. Or, as the poet Gerard Manley Hopkins puts it: 'The world is charged with the grandeur of God. / It will flame out, like shining from shook foil.'[1] Paul is equally adamant that 'neither death nor life, neither angels nor demons, neither the present nor the future, nor any powers, neither height nor depth, nor anything else in all creation, will be able to separate us from the love of God that is in Christ Jesus our Lord' (Romans 8:38–39). Christ himself was unequivocal: 'I am with you always, to the end of the age' (Matthew 28:20).

Not only is the Divine present around us, but since we are 'creatures', the Divine is also present within us. If the Divine is always here, present with us, the only question, therefore, becomes whether we are present to the Divine. This is where presencing and prayer come in. 'Therefore, I will remember you,' the psalmist says, and returns to the essential truth of his 'indwelt' being: 'Deep calls to deep in the roar of your waterfalls; all your waves and breakers have swept over me. By day the LORD directs his love, at night his song is with me – a prayer to the God of my life' (Psalm 42:6,7–8). In a similar vein, St Paul talks about the Spirit at work praying within us: 'In the same way, the Spirit helps us in our weakness. We do not know what we ought to pray for, but the Spirit himself intercedes for us through wordless groans. And he who searches our hearts knows the mind of the Spirit, because the Spirit intercedes for God's people in accordance with the will of God' (Romans 8:26–27).

So, in many ways, our work of prayer can be as simple as consciously allowing the prayer that is already happening to have its way within us.

We tend to view prayer as time set aside, often in quiet, to direct our attention towards God. But it does not have to be that way. Brother Lawrence invites us to 'practice the presence of God' by consciously including the Divine in all the aspects of daily living – doing stuff together as well as being together. Frank Laubach, following Lawrence's lead, set himself the task of remembering God once a minute, and used the simple mechanism of talking to God as though God were present all the time: 'This year I have started out trying to live all my waking moments in conscious listening to the inner voice, asking without ceasing, "What, Father, do you desire said? What, Father, do you desire done this minute?"'[2]

The critical factor in the life of prayer is not the time we give to it, but our presence in it – i.e. the quality and focus of our attention. Firstly, do we even remember that God is present? Secondly, how do we direct our attention to God? If we are using our mind, we risk just focusing on our own idea of God. Thirdly, how able and ready are we to listen and receive God's invitations and responses to us? Are we truly open, or are we filtering what we can receive by what we are expecting? Behind this is the more fundamental question, as we explored in Chapter Seven, of which 'I' is the one doing the relating. Is it my functional or egoic self or my 'whole', surrendered self?

This is where our work of presencing becomes so important in our life of prayer. Indeed, some would say, it is the essence and entirety of prayer.

There is a wealth of teaching on prayer practices, especially in the contemplative and Ignatian traditions. It is not my intention to examine them here, but they all aim to take us into a space where we find ourselves 'with God'. One is the practice suggested by the anonymous author of *The Cloud Of Unknowing*, subsequently developed by Thomas Keating as 'centering prayer', which captures the essence of most of what we are discussing here:

> *But now you will ask me, 'How am I to think of God himself, and what is he?' and I cannot answer you except to say, 'I do not know.' For with this question you have brought me into the same darkness, the same kind of unknowing where I want you to be! For though we through the grace of God can know fully about all other matters, and think about him – yes, even the very works of God himself – yet of God himself can no man think.*
>
> *Therefore I will leave on one side everything I can think and choose for my love that thing which I cannot think! Why? Because God may well be loved, but not thought. By love God can be caught and held, but by thinking never.*
>
> *Therefore, though it may be good sometimes to think particularly about God's kindness and worth, and though it may be enlightening too, and part of contemplation, yet in the work now before us it must be put down and covered with a cloud of forgetting. And you are to step over it resolutely and eagerly, with a devout and kindling love, and try to penetrate that darkness above you.*
>
> *Strike that thick cloud of unknowing with the sharp dart of longing love, and on no account whatever think of giving up... A naked intention directed to God, and himself, alone, is wholly sufficient...*
>
> *If you want this intention summed up in a word to retain it more easily, take a short word, preferably of one syllable, to do so. The shorter the word the better, being more like the working of the Spirit. A word like 'GOD' or 'LOVE'. Choose which you like or perhaps some other... and fix this word fast to your heart, so that it is always there come what may...*
>
> *So, lift up your love to that cloud. Or, more accurately, let God draw your love up to that cloud.*[3]

Of course, our familiar question emerges – *how?* How do we do this, or be this, in the minutiae of our own experience? We have already explored the practice of presencing in previous chapters and I won't repeat it, but I will invite you to remember our core practice in Chapter Four: to make our bodies 'living sacrifice' and open up, as much as we humanly can, in all our faculties – heart, soul, body, and mind – to the ever-present greater Presence.

In order to do this, we detach our attention from all the ways it may be distracted. The four principles for this are the cultivation of *stillness* (body), *solitude* (heart), *silence* (mind), and *surrender* (will). The effect is to free our attention to a place where we can simply witness what is actually present within and around us – i.e. the lived experience in the 'now' of our state of prayer.

The traditional way to do this is to take ourselves to a quiet place and remove exterior intrusions, as Christ often did. This helps, but it is not strictly necessary and may not be possible for much of the time. We can learn to do this anywhere. The core of it is the inner work of consciously releasing and presencing a balanced awareness in each of these centres.

Practice

I would suggest always topping and tailing any prayer time with an expressed intention to surrender to the greater 'authority' of the Divine – e.g. 'May all my thoughts, words, actions, and intentions be directed purely to serving and glorifying Your holy name.' We then begin, as ever, with a conscious presencing of awareness in breath and body. Then, as described in Chapter Four, we 'gather' ourselves into the recollected state. As we practise this, at first in a conscious, fairly lengthy process, we develop the capacity to presence prayerfully in these different centres with more ease, speed and familiarity. We can just breathe and touch awareness into each and allow a stilling, even just for a minute or so. As we do so, our awareness expands and our capacity to 'receive' is substantially increased. We are available – and being available is all God asks of us. If it helps to settle we may use a meditative word, (e.g. '*Maranatha*') or a phrase (e.g. 'Be still and know that I am').

The first thing we will notice as we still is often the busyness of our mind, then the needs of our body (maybe for sleep!), then the things that are most present to us emotionally, the feelings we are often desperately trying to 'manage', or maybe desires and frustrations that have a grip on us. We can easily get 'caught' back into any of these things and identify with them. As soon as we catch ourselves doing this, we just bring awareness back to breath and body and feet and let them be. The centering prayer tradition suggests using a word, such as 'love' or 'peace', as an aid for this.

Gradually, if we follow the practice above, the 'cacophony of my fragmented self' (as I remember Pete Greig once describing it in his morning blog)[4], starts to quieten and settle. I am then able to deploy my faculties to the true purpose of my prayer – 'just' being with the One who is always here.

PRESENCING AND SPIRITUAL DIRECTION

Inhabiting the experience of prayer

Finding this 'gathered' state of pure receptivity is the beginning. The next movement is into *active* receptivity, which the phrase from the Benedictine rule, 'Incline the ear of your heart', captures beautifully. As we settle into this 'active-receptive' state for prayer, we can allow our awareness to be drawn into an enquiry of the actual experience of prayer.

If we follow the wisdom of St Paul, this prayer is going on continually within us, but the functional mind is too coarse to pick it up and words are too clumsy to interpret or express it. 'We do not know what we ought to pray for, but the Spirit himself intercedes for us through wordless groans'(Romans 8:26). Those who pray in tongues will be familiar with the experience of this. Jesus Himself is equally clear on the point: 'I will ask the Father, and he will give you another advocate to help you and be with you forever – the Spirit of truth. The world cannot accept him, because it neither sees him nor knows him. But you know him, for he lives with you and *will be in you*. I will not leave you as orphans; I will come to you' (John 14:16–18, my italics). Not only is the Holy Spirit within us, but Paul confirms what some reading this book will already know: that we also have 'Christ dwelling in our hearts'.

The literal mind cannot grasp this presence within – we need a more subtle intelligence and perception. So, we presence our awareness in our more subtle centres and listen. In a prayerful state, we can allow our awareness to be drawn to what arises. The simplest and probably most reliable place to start, as I have said, is with sensation. For instance, as I pause and presence now in the middle of my writing, I am conscious of a fullness in my chest, around the base of the sternum – a gentle upward pressure, a bit like a filling with a warm liquid. As I drop my awareness to sense into this, I experience the rising of a soft light up through the chest and into the head. I feel it at work in my mind, subtly and soothingly changing the patterns of my thought. A feeling of peace spreads in the head and down though the neck. I am immediately aware that I am not alone. A word pops up: 'Comforter'.

My evaluative mind clicks in at this point. Is this real, or is this just an association, a fantasy, because I quoted the John scripture a few lines back? But the presence remains, warm, strong, in front of my chest. 'I am here, always.' I feel the warmth flowing down my arms as I write. I am now slightly disembodied, as though I am watching myself as I type. 'You can trust yourself in Me' – these words, given to me in prayer on an Ignatian retreat many years ago, pop up from nowhere: 'Show them what you have'.

As my writing blends with my prayer, I pause. What is this experience? I check my grounding and feel the strong, warm, rooted connectedness to the solid earth beneath. The energy flowing through my feet is palpable. My breath is calm, cool, deep, rested. There is a warm, soft, pinky-orange soothing light in and around my head. I feel a smile upon me, and within me. The light is clearer and brighter towards the top of my head, and it cascades like a cool, soft, gentle, subtle liquid down over my shoulders and all the way down to my feet, like a flowing mantle.

'I am who I am' – words form in the increasing clarity of my mind, like a still, yet gently flowing, pool. 'This is enough. You do not need to seek to know me. I am who I am, and I am here.' 'This is enough.' 'You are enough.' The Presence remains, clear, warm, luminous. I can feel there is a work going on in a deeper layer of my mind. I sense the invitation, 'May I...?' I consent. I do not need to know the nature of the work. I trust the hands of the potter. But I am being invited to rest and still and allow. So, I stop writing.

Returning to this page after a walk, I know there has been a work going on within me. I feel lighter, calmer, freer, clearer about what matters and what doesn't. Some very important relationships in my life have become clearer, including my relationship with myself. The feeling is of an increase in equanimity. But there is still a work in progress, actually a greater surrender, being invited. There is 'undigested' material here that I may need to bring to my own spiritual director.

This was an unexpected turn in the writing, and I shall leave it here by way of a living example. Of course, the 'truth' of such experience is entirely subjective and of relevance and significance only for the one experiencing it, although there may be aspects of the process that I hope are of a wider relevance.

I will now move onto some consistent principles that I have noticed to be particularly valuable in helping process the *experience* of prayer – both my own and my directees'. This will take us into the more practical, less personal or theological, content for this chapter and is therefore a natural 'break point' if you want to pause in your reading and do whatever serves you to recentre so you can come back to this refreshed and uncluttered by what has gone before.

1. **Beginning with and returning to the somatic experience.** This has proved a reliable guide to me over many years. There is an 'objectivity' to the embodied experience in that I can actually sense it physically in my body and it is therefore largely (though not entirely) free from imaginative distortion. I also tend to find, when I am settled in my 'gathered' state, that presencing awareness in whatever arises first is a reasonable place to begin. It will flow to where it needs to once I open to it. This can be in many and varied places.

   A person I was working with recently began by sensing a 'heavy feeling around the head'. As she presenced her awareness in it, it softened and yielded and the head opened to a soft, pale white, almost creamy flow of Divine presence that flowed down into her chest in a sweeping movement, blending there with a stream of rising, harsh, red substance, which she recognised as anxiety. As she witnessed this, the heart became a kind of container for a process of transformation. 'It looked like raspberry-ripple ice-cream,' she said laughingly. Something new was being formed in this blending process, a different quality of strength and capacity to be. 'This is not just for me, it is for others,' she noticed. 'I am being invited to serve from this place… it's raw, and beautiful… and so real… so 'just as it is'… there is wisdom and understanding here…'

2. **Presencing in the experience.** By 'presencing', I mean dropping our attention to sense and feel directly into whatever is sensed. We can feel right into the middle of something, even impenetrable rock or empty pit, or we can sense its surface and how it sits with what is around it. The effect of doing this is to liberate whatever it is containing. Quite often this will be experienced as an expansion or transformation of the substance and almost some kind of 'flow' – liquid, energy, light, warmth etc. As this occurs, we may also receive emotional or thought impressions. Feelings, words or insights may arise.

   These need to be treated delicately, as the mind will seize on them and, if we are not careful, our neutral witness will be hijacked, and the ego will start making sense of the experience according to its own priorities and preconceptions. As a rule, the principle of 'arising' is a good one. If thoughts or feelings surprise us then they are more likely to be trustworthy than thoughts or feelings that play to some existing pattern of judgment or preference. The 'Comforter' word above is an example. As I am writing, I now realise that a big element of that experience was receiving – allowing myself to be comforted/settled in my deep being – in a way I would never have thought of, nor been able to manufacture myself, i.e. not a self-soothing or placating, but a wholesome state of self-acceptance that I can allow myself to trust and live in more, 'just as I am'.

One significant phenomenon in the experience of prayer can be the oft-lamented experience of 'getting nothing back'. We push our attention to the Divine, as we think we know it, and articulate some kind of initiation of contact. Then... nothing, not a word. One reason for this may be our expectation of what a response should be. At the most basic, we may expect a conversation, like a telephone call – or maybe a feeling, such as calm or reassurance. If we do not get what we are expecting, we assume nothing is being communicated. This may be a result of praying to our 'idea of God', and one practical response can be to let go of this and start praying to 'nothing', to the unknowable God, and see what then our experience becomes.

If the basic reality of our prayer is that, in response to our reaching out, nothing is being experienced, we can still attend to that – because that actually is our experience! It can be mysteriously fruitful to sense into the experience of 'nothing'. What does 'nothing' actually feel like inside? It may be, as we pause and notice what we are actually experiencing, that we begin to realise there is a lot more going on than we thought. For example, we may feel a subtle yearning, desire, or frustration inside which contains the real feeling or impulse that had us reach out in prayer – the prayer that was already at work within. As we allow ourselves to experience this and what lies within it, we may notice, as with any 'holy desire', that the Divine is much more present than we thought – that what we were looking to receive is already here.

Alternatively, it may be that our experience genuinely is of nothing – a kind of emptiness or void within. If so, that is our real experience – we are feeling 'nothing'. What is 'nothing' really like? As we locate it, we enquire into it by dropping awareness into the void within, the hole maybe where 'God used to be', or the dark cave where our voice-cry echoes, unanswered. What is it like in here? What happens when we drop into it? What does it feel like: warm, cold, dark, airy, fluid, solid, spacious, hemmed-in etc? As we spend time inhabiting the experience of nothingness, it can be surprising what we find. But we must be careful to sense or feel our way in there, not think our way in. What seems to the mind like nothing can often be very substantive indeed. 'In the beginning... the earth was formless and empty.' (Genesis 1:1).

3. **Staying open and attentive** to the Presence of the Divine at work within us and around us ('Where are You, Lord?'), however we experience it. If and when we become aware of the Divine Presence, we consciously collaborate with it. We will know it when we feel it. (Though in the early phases of the work, our mind will register a certain incredulity or distrust.) Gradually, as 'the gatekeeper opens the gate', we learn to hear and trust the 'voice of the good shepherd'. It can take many forms – in some cases, literally a felt experience of Christ or some other aspect of the Divine actually present with us in our experience, sharing it within us. Or it may be a hand upon the shoulder, a touch on the heart, a sense of enfolding, perhaps accompanied by peace, a flowing light, or an awareness of love, sometimes felt almost as a physical force, like a melting, or dissolving, or a tidal flow.

Again, the simple principle of presencing and surrender applies: just to let be and let go. In my experience, as we do this, we become able to notice wherever and however the Divine Presence is at work (though we may not always be able to make sense of it). It will always be accompanied by a very gentle sense of invitation and asking permission – 'Let Me', or 'May I', or 'Do you want this?', or 'Do you want me to...?' This for me is what Christ is really saying when He says, 'Follow Me.' It is not so much the Christ without, as the Christ within, 'guiding our feet on the way of peace'. Conversely, anything that is clamouring or seeking to 'push' our will is, in my experience, most certainly not of the Divine.

4. **Being aware of the functional mind** 'grabbing' at the experience and taking off with it. In the early stages of this work, it is almost impossible not to do this. The mind is excitable and wary – excitable when something reinforces its sense of agency, identity, and control, and wary when something threatens it. We will very likely be carried off by it. One sign I have observed in myself and others when the functional mind starts taking over is that it is often accompanied by a lot of head movement. This can be a helpful trigger to catch ourselves at it and to return to our stillness by grounding in the body and presencing in breath and/or returning to the awareness of the Divine Presence, who will be patiently awaiting our return.

Another more insidious form of this grabbing can occur when we receive an image in prayer. For example, someone I was working with recently received a picture of herself being led by the hand by Christ along a wild clifftop path.

Fairly quickly she started following this in her imagination and picturing the scene around her and what was ahead and behind. It was only when I asked her to place her attention in her hand and to feel the connection with Christ and what was flowing in the clasp that she began to truly receive what was being transmitted in the prayer. This was His invitation to close her eyes and let Him lead. As she did this, she began to feel inside what it was actually like to trust the leading of Christ, to feel the sensitivity and subtlety of His guiding 'touch' within and to begin to see with His eyes, not her own – a different kind of seeing, not dissimilar to that I quoted earlier in Chapter Four, a seeing with the eye of the heart.

The effect for this person was an awakening of this very capacity – to see at the heart level, a kind of radiant spiritual seeing, rather than the head. It helped her begin to learn to experience the events and interactions of her life very differently – to see the 'deeper purposes' at work and to be much more subtle in her interventions. She said:

> 'I could see so clearly what others could not. For a while it was deeply frustrating. Then, as I learned to remember to feel His hand in mine, I began to realise I did not need to try to act on everything I was seeing. Many times, I had to let things play out as they would, for better or for worse – except on those occasions when the right words just arose within me, almost without effort, so clear, and therefore calm, however challenging they might be to utter. Those words I knew to speak, and let them be what they were – to have the effect for which they were intended, which sometimes was rejection, a rejection which others noticed, including the ones doing the rejecting. Before long, it was amazing. People whom I had struggled with in the past started including me, inviting me to things – sometimes just for my presence in the room; coming to me to sound things out on me, really listening when I spoke. Often I did not need to say anything. I ended up getting so much more done with so much less angst.'

5. Being patient. As in the example above, we do not expect transformational illuminations, even though these will sometimes come. Much of this work is opening our being at pre-conscious levels to the One who just wants to be with us as our friend and guide in this life. It is also about inner formation – creating a new centre of gravity, a more stable base of perception and awareness. It is not uncommon for the fruits of prayer to pop up months, even years, later. If something arises, or a word comes, that we do not understand but sense is of God in some way, we just receive and remember and let it lie. It will surface when it is needed. For the lady above, it was simply the felt remembrance of that hand clasp.

6. Staying grounded. If we can, at all times we keep a fraction of awareness in a 'neutral' place in the body – maybe feeling the sensation of our feet connecting to the ground, or else the tips of our fingers connecting in the light clasp of our hand. Even if we are blessed with powerful unitive experience in prayer, in which the individual soul seems literally to dissolve back into the vast ocean of the Divine, we try to stay grounded and aware of the body. It is easy to get carried away in the heart response to this and soar into rapture. Then, when we return, we will forget. If we can stay attentive to our personal embodiment as well as our unitive enlightenment, we may notice the extraordinary grace that we can actually choose to be both 'ocean' and 'drop', personal and Divine, simultaneously, effortlessly flowing from the one to the other. Similarly, we can experience the pure joy of life, or deep grief and compassion for the suffering of humanity. Our task is to fully experience these things and, as much as humanly possible, fully receive them in the 'living sacrifice' of our bodies – not to be transported by them. Whatever the truth of our experience in prayer, the simultaneous truth is that we are still here, sat breathing the air of this planet in this now, and digesting this morning's breakfast! That way we can receive and metabolise the 'daily bread' of our prayer too.

7. Being active, conscious, and fulsome in our receiving. This is the heart of what prayer is all about. Communion. There is a tendency of the mercurial (avoiding) mind to move on and miss the experience. So, so often in my work as a director, when I ask people what they are experiencing, say in the heart, they will say, 'Oh nothing really, just a sense of peace and lightness.' This golden rule of 'just' – something immense always follows... 'Just' peace, 'just' the one thing that is the deepest yearning of the vast majority of the whole human race! As I ask people to pause and receive that peace and let it flow to where it wants to flow, transformation happens, the heart warms, insight stirs, strength and determination flow, the body lightens, the mind clears, awe arises. 'Stay,' Christ is forever asking us. 'Abide in Me.' But we can be so quick to move on, or skit away.

8. Revisiting the flow – as the prayer time draws to a close, inviting the Divine Help as we do so, taking awareness back over the entirety of the experience, from the first place of somatic presencing and the flow that ensued, it is possible new wisdom will arise as we do. We invite Help in remembering – prayer for a Divine 'seal' on all that is intended for our growth. We remember, not as a piece of written or verbal 'memorising' but as embodied experience – we feel it, sense it, and allow it to be stored as body or heart memory. These become 'living memories' that endure and work within us, reconnecting us to all we accessed through grace in our prayer time. As we learn to remember these places of encounter, of being touched in our innermost being, they start to become more and more available in our lives so that, for example, we can presence awareness down in the belly, or towards the back of the head, and access a different state, with a quality of awareness and presence way beyond the habitual ego.

Again, it is St Paul who draws our attention to this conscious work in his prayer for the Ephesians:

> *I pray that out of his glorious riches he may strengthen you with power through his Spirit in your inner being, so that Christ may dwell in your hearts through faith. And I pray that you, being rooted and established in love, may have power, together with all the Lord's holy people, to grasp how wide and long and high and deep is the love of Christ, and to know this love that surpasses knowledge – that you may be filled to the measure of all the fullness of God.*
>
> EPHESIANS 3:16

Like everything in this work, we learn to co-operate wilfully and consciously in this, otherwise we will exit our time of prayer and just 'forget', or at best have a two-dimensional stored memory that we try in vain to conjure back into life by our own efforts.

So, these are the three key 'active passivities' in prayer: *open surrender, collaborative receiving, embodied re-membering*.

9. Making conscious connection back to the functional mind and the habitual understanding. It is only at the end of prayer that we do this – and not by trying to make sense of it, nor memorising it. That is the surest way to kill the fruits of prayer, because this would be done using the cognitive patterning that we perhaps need liberation from. Our habitual mind would interpret, compress, and store the experience into an intellectual confirmation (e.g. 'God loves me'), but miss the subtlety of what is really flowing into the mind from the love within (e.g. 'Look! See and know yourself as I see you... notice what it is like to let this inform your experience of yourself'). The most effective thing as we close our prayer therefore is to ask prayerfully that our understanding may be 'illuminated' in this kind of way. Then we wait in trust and allow the brain to receive whatever comes.

I sense this is what Paul means when he talks about the 'renewing' of our mind. It is sometimes possible to actually experience this as a flow of light or warmth – either flowing up from the body into the underside of the brain, as the fruit of the work that has been happening deep within, or flowing in through the top of the head as a direct infusion. At other times, you may experience nothing, but if you have made the prayer, you can trust that the necessary renewing will be happening, often in your sleeping and dreaming, and may only become clear a while later when you find yourself being able to think and see in new ways.

So often the fruit of this kind of transformational prayer experience is a shift in seeing – as Proust famously puts it, 'The real voyage of discovery consists not in seeking new landscapes but in having new eyes.' Christ is explicit in this: 'Your eye is the lamp of your body. When your eyes are healthy, your whole body also is full of light. But when they are unhealthy, your body also is full of darkness' (Luke 11:34).

So much of the work of the cleansing of perception happens deep within us as we let go of old wounds and habits that fundamentally impact how we see the world. It took me five decades to learn to look at life not out of wariness and distrust but out of expectancy and hope – to actually believe deep within that the Divine wants only our good and is at work everywhere around us. Only then could I begin to see it. The capacity to trust is not a cognitive thing, it is visceral – heart, body, mind, soul.

10. Experimenting with moving in and out of state. Finally, as we exit the prayerful state, I always encourage people to take a few minutes to feel what it is like returning to their more habitual state of existence. So, we open our eyes really slowly, allow ourselves to take in everything, with wide-open peripheral vision, letting the light find us, seeing it as it is, rather than focusing and placing our perceptual classifications upon it. Similarly with the body: when we move, we do so really slowly, consciously. Then we may settle back into our stillness again and drop briefly back into the state of prayer to re-member it. Doing this two, three, or four times as we exit prayer can again build the 'muscle memory' that will allow us to remember and return to our prayer-filled state.

As we return to our daily life, we can experiment with making this same shifting between states in the day-to-day – not forcing anything, just simply re-membering. In this way, gradually we learn to let our lives *be prayer* – to pause and exit our striving to do things in our own will, to breathe and release accumulated 'stuff' that we may have unconsciously been imprinted with and to allow ourselves to receive the 'Divine Help' that is there all the time waiting to work in us and through us.

11. Letting this become as natural and humble as breath. One thing I am always conscious of in this subtle work of transformation from egoic states to essential and surrendered states is the temptation to invent a new dualism – 'essential is good and must be encouraged, egoic is bad and must be eliminated'. The reality is so much more subtle. Our egoic or 'patterned' self is the one that helps us show up and function in the world. Returning to the analogy I used in Chapter Five, it is an 'instrument', however imperfect, through which the greater Will will seek to flow.

I find Paul's language very helpful here. It is not that we are 'patterned' – we cannot not be. It is only when we 'conform' to the patterning that we lose our way. Similarly, it is not about reprogramming the mind, but 'renewing' it – restoring the original purity of the flow of perception, so that we see and embody our patterning with clear eyes. 'Be thou my vision, O Lord of my heart.' This is no quest for perfection, or 'Christlikeness'. It is a humble, and grateful, acceptance of our human-ness, even our 'sin-full-ness', and an opening to the renewing 'breath of God' within. We let that breath transform us, not our own efforts. Our only work is to open, receive, remember.

I have tried to spend most of my time in this chapter focusing not so much on *how* to pray (i.e. how to enter a state of genuine receptivity) but on how to *be with the experience of prayer* and how to fully receive and 'digest' it – following the same principle described earlier about the digesting of experience as 'food' for the growth of our inner being. Prayer, of course, is one of the most powerful modalities of experience we can enter as we seek consciously to open ourselves into direct relationship with the Divine (rather than the indirect, mediated though life events, written material, or other people). The experience of prayer is, however, much more subtle and less immediate on the senses, and it takes a more patient refined attentiveness than that which we deploy in 'normal life', where experiences and impressions thrust themselves upon us. It is a particularly fine dance to sustain a 'neutral witnessing presence' in prayer that is able to observe and receive without egoic distorting. That is why maintaining a state of groundedness, bringing awareness constantly back into the body and breath in the 'now' is so important (or the centering prayer 'neutral word'). This keeps the functional mind occupied on something and prevents unhelpful or even dangerous distraction. Sometimes, the best prayer you can make is one where absolutely nothing notable happens – it is a sign of your honest, undistorted capacity for self-observation.

As we progress with this work, something is deposited within us that nurtures a new centre of gravity. From this place, not only do we become more sensitive to the work of the Divine within us ('Oh, that today you would listen to His voice...'), we also develop a subtlety of perception that allows us to be much more balanced and discerning about how we respond to our daily experience. Gradually, we learn to occupy our being as a more sensitive instrument, attuned to the subtle resonance of the 'spiritual' at work in the created order. We often tend to think of the spiritual as something 'other', a different plane, to this world. But this chapter is predicated on a knowing that we can and do inhabit the spiritual, or in Christ's words, 'the kingdom', in this earthly life. As above, so below... Therefore, its effects are palpable and knowable – we just need to remember our finer capacity to sense and respond. Sadly, this capacity has been eroded by the patterning of our childhood 'education', still so firmly rooted in empirical positivism.

Finally, though, we always remember that we have humbly to return. We come out of prayer and back into life – however transforming the desert, or transfiguring the mountaintop, and however much we may long to 'remain'. Thomas Merton in his autobiographical writing, *A Search For Solitude*, embodies this almost agonisingly for us in his desperate yearning to disappear into the life of a hermit and the simultaneous relentless pull back into community and the world:

> *Everything hurts me. I want to turn away from everything, lose everything, throw away the world, shake off time, lose all the things that are trying to grow on me like barnacles. Of course I can't do it. There is only One who can do it for me, and He is making me suffer in order to open the way for the love that is the means by which He intends to do that work. My God, how much is there to be done!... I cannot be a solitary until my heart has been laid open to the four winds and has been trampled on by the whole world.*[5]

In many ways, this is the very heart of this work of 'spiritual direction': how we return and remain simultaneously, living in a permanent state of prayer, whilst acting in the world – somehow managing to fit in and be accepted/acceptable and still being a channel for the Will, grace, and challenging, healing, loving, joyful presence of God. This is our daily experience of the eschatological perspective articulated by Tom Wright and others as 'living between the now and the not yet'.

I remember recently being with a directee who saw herself literally held in the arms of God, wrapped and comforted, whilst simultaneously sat in the middle of a very tense and unpleasant conflict situation. Her body experienced the complete dissonance of this, wanting to tense and be alert in every nerve ending whilst simultaneously wanting to soften, melt, and let go. As she sat in this, something started to happen within her. She was able to 'see herself' in both states – her capacity to witness expanded. As it did, something new and quite tangible began to arise – a new quality of presence. 'I am actually wholly in both,' she said, 'feeling both simultaneously – my body can do this. I can do this. Gosh, it is *so* clear...' The sensation that arose was a new, clear, almost liquid calm, where she was no longer captured by her body's reactivity. She felt free, and whole. This is a good example of something new being sown into the 'fertile ground' of her being – and it seems to have taken root. She texted me to comment on how very different her daily experience has become since that encounter.

PRESENCING AND SPIRITUAL DIRECTION

This then brings us to the topic of our next chapter. How *do* I live in this, how do I exercise my own will at the many 'crossroads moments' in life when I have to make choices – 'my will or Thy Will'? This takes us into the practice of 'discernment'.

Again, please do pause to ground and pray before you read on.

CHAPTER TEN

Presencing and discernment

*There is a divinity that shapes our ends,
rough-hew them how we will.*

HAMLET V.II

*For God has bound everyone over to disobedience so that he may have mercy on them all. Oh, the depth of the riches of the wisdom and knowledge of God! How unsearchable his judgments, and his paths beyond tracing out! 'Who has known the mind of the Lord? Or who has been his counsellor?' 'Who has ever given to God, that God should repay them?' For from him and through him and for him are all things.
To him be the glory forever! Amen.*

Therefore, I urge you, brothers and sisters, in view of God's mercy, to offer your bodies as a living sacrifice, holy and pleasing to God – this is your true and proper worship. Do not conform to the pattern of this world, but be transformed by the renewing of your mind. Then you will be able to test and approve what God's will is – his good, pleasing and perfect will.

ROMANS 11:32–12:2

I HAVE QUOTED ABOVE the full flow of Paul's exhortation to the Romans. This often gets lost because of the chapter division in the Bible, which is placed before his dive into an awe-struck hymn of praise. I imagine Paul, mid-way in his writing, being suddenly caught by awe and gratitude because, in and through the craziness of his own adventures, he has glimpsed and remembered his own direct experience of the miraculous agency of the Divine Will at work in the world. This book is, in so many ways, just a laborious expounding of what Paul expresses so cleanly and perfectly here, i.e. that:

- There is a bigger Will at work in the world – good, pleasing, perfect
- The gift of our own free will causes us, like the prodigal, necessarily to wander 'disobediently' off the path
- In noticing that we have wandered, we return. That, as I quoted from Julian of Norwich, 'Sin is necessary' to keep reminding us of this
- The greater the wander, the more joyous the return, and the more fulsome the surrender...
- As we keep wandering, we learn more and more quickly to return...
- Until gradually we learn an attitude of continuous surrender – 'living sacrifice' – that has us capable of discerning and collaborating with this Will
- And how joyful this can be, to participate in the 'good pleasure' of the Living God!

This is the 'active passivity' I spoke about in the previous chapter. In this way, each day can be an act of pure offering, as Ignatius expresses in his beautiful 'Suscipe' prayer: 'Take Lord, and receive, all my liberty, my memory, my understanding, and my entire will, all that I have and call my own. Thou hast given all to me. To Thee, O Lord, I return it. All is Thine, dispose of it wholly according to Thy will. Give me only the Grace to love Thee. That is sufficient for me.' In this lies our true liberty. It is another paradox that what in religious language can sound so 'heavy' to the ears of the world – 'sacrifice and surrender' – is in fact the source of such freedom, lightness, and joy. This is our theme for this chapter.

The true and constant nexus of our whole journey of soul-formation and becoming lies, it seems to me, in the exercise of our will. At its most obvious,

PRESENCING AND DISCERNMENT

this is visible in the decisions and choices we make. But it is also true in how we choose to respond to what life puts our way – hope or despair, trust or doubt, hard heart or soft heart, clenched fist or open hand. Our soul journey in life as I described it, from innocence through experience back to innocence, gradually teaches us to exercise our will *less in deciding and more in discerning*. Rather than coming up with ideas and intentions from our own understanding and impulses, we learn to use our will to clarify what is present, so that we can see and understand what is already in place and already moving: the greater Will that is in flow, 'Thy will be done.' Frank Laubach describes this movingly in his writing on practising presence in *Letters To A Modern Mystic*:

> *As I analyse myself, I find several things happening to me as a result of these two months of strenuous effort to keep God in mind every minute. This concentration upon God is strenuous, but everything else has ceased to be so... I think more clearly, I forget less frequently. Things which I did with a strain before, I now do easily and with no effort whatever. I worry about nothing and lose no sleep. I walk on air a good part of the time. Even the mirror reveals a new light in my eyes and face. I no longer feel in a hurry about anything. Everything goes right. Each minute I meet calmly as though it were not important. Nothing can go wrong excepting one thing. That is that God may slip from my mind if I do not keep on my guard. If He is there, the universe is with me. My task is simple and clear.*[1]

This is the essence of it. If life, lived to the full, is doing God's 'good, pleasing and perfect will', which, when Paul glimpses it, ('the mind of the Lord') takes him into rapture, then our true work lies in the steps he outlines in the Scriptures. This is derived, no doubt, from his own first-hand experience as one of the first Christians trying to live this way in the world. I am trusting, therefore, that the practical steps he speaks of can be used to shape and channel the entire shape and flow of the enquiry that we have been following in this book:

- To make our bodies 'living sacrifices' – fully alive, fully available to the indwelling and surrounding Presence of the Unitive Divine. (Body) (Chapter Four)

- No longer conforming to the patterning of this world (Functional mind) (Chapter Five)
- Being transformed – *trans-formed* as opposed to *con-formed*. Deep change within our being. Chrysalis to butterfly. (Heart and soul) (Chapter Six)
- By re-newing of our mind – literally making new again – a whole new way of seeing, perceiving and thinking. (Higher mind) (Chapter Seven)
- Then we can sense into what we are truly here to do, His Will.... (Strength) (this chapter and the next)

So, again, our perennial question in this book is, 'How?' Firstly, how do we discern what is of the greater Will? Secondly, how do we find the strength to embody it and the clarity to sustain it?

We have already covered the first question in earlier chapters. If we are able to remain presenced in the recollected state as 'living sacrifice', with heart, mind, soul, and body knowing available to us, freed from our reactivity to ego-patterning, then we can use this awareness to sense into and trust what we find arising. The flow of true Will within is, in my experience, nearly always received as clarity in the mind, peace in the heart, solidity in the gut and, most significantly, a sense of alignment or congruence in the soul. Some people have described it to me as a kind of 'pregnancy'. Others describe it as a sense of conviction or inner knowing or sometimes a palpable force and impetus into movement arising from within the belly or the solar plexus. It may not have a verbalised or concrete intention attached to it, it may just be a knowing that 'I am on the right path' or the 'good way', as referenced earlier from Jeremiah 6:16.

Writing this, as I am, on Easter Saturday, I wonder whether Mary Magdalene had a sense deep within her as she returned to the tomb on the morning of the third day. Not knowing why or what, but knowing somewhere within her that she had to return and, like her namesake, 'birth' Christ once more in the eyes of humanity – by being the first human to re-cognise Him. The invitation she received to move from transformational recognition to purposeful action was direct: 'Do not hold on to me – Go... tell' (John 20:17). Mary was the first apostle whose task it was to awaken the others. Part of her, somewhere deep in her soul, perhaps already knew what was awaiting her as she set out on that dawn. She had a choice and yet she had no choice: the pure Love within her could do no other, and this pure Love gave her the eyes to see and the ears to hear what was obscured to others – the risen Christ. 'There is a divinity that shapes our ends, rough-hew them how we will.'[2]

So, we could go so far as to say that nowhere is our work of presencing more important than in discernment. Do we listen to the 'still small voice' within? Do we allow it to be wholly received and digested and to move us into sustainable action? It is only when we are present that we can be available to a Will that we cannot comprehend but can apprehend as we attune to its deeper, resonant flow around us and within us. Probably the most famous example of this is Elijah in the cave, sitting, waiting, in his interior solitude, silence, and stillness, sifting the signs of his experience, the earthquake, wind, and fire, until he heard the quiet, gentle sound and he knew – he knew in a way far beyond cognition – that it was a deep soul-knowing (see 1 Kings 19:12).

It seems to me that it is only when we are fully present to what is actually happening within us that we can be 'testing and approving' in the way Paul describes. Thomas Merton expresses this wisdom with a beautiful clarity in *The Ascent to Truth*:

> *The voice of God brings peace. It does not arouse excitement but allays it, for excitement belongs to uncertainty. If He moves us to action, we go forward with peaceful strength. More often than not His inspirations teach us to sit still... the inspirations of the Spirit of God are not grandiose, they are simple. They move us to seek God in works that are difficult without being spectacular. They lead us in paths that are happy because they are obscure. His inspirations make us clean. They deliver us from coarseness and from limitation... One last thing: the light of the Holy Ghost does not leave us pleased with ourselves but pleased with God only. If it permits us not to be displeased with ourselves, it is because it has brought us into a deeper union with Him.*[3]

This attentiveness to the inner state in discernment is completely different to trying in the cognitive mind to work out, or more usually second guess, what is being Willed for us. So many times in spiritual direction, I find myself holding for people in the turmoil of trying to figure out 'what is God's plan for my life?', or, even worse, in their surveying the wreckage of the 'plan' that was disappointed – or, even more insidiously, the hollowness of it being 'achieved'. I know, I have spent many years in this turmoil myself!

The answer in prayer to this 'what's the plan, Lord?' is nearly always the same: 'Come... and you will see.' The call is into relationship, not activity: 'Follow me...'

So then, our next 'how' question: 'How do I know I am following?' That is everything we have been exploring in this book. Imbued with trust, we become living sacrifice, incline the ear of our heart, and wait until we hear. It is important to note at this point that 'waiting' does not mean inactivity. Waiting means we carry on living, doing what we need to do, being in what we are, with who we are with, as wholeheartedly as we can – whether that wholeheartedness involves pain and frustration, or playfulness and joy. But we also do it as presenced as we can – then, as we presence, what is waiting to become clear becomes clear.

The end of the Anglican Sunday Communion liturgy is so fitting in relation to this: 'Almighty God, we offer you our souls and bodies to be a living sacrifice, through Jesus Christ our Lord. Send us out into the world in the power of your Spirit, to live and work to your praise and glory. Amen.' I love it that the first requirement is 'just', simply, to *live*. Too often we make our discipleship to be about 'work'. Instead, as we go about living, we are invited to presence... and listen for the 'voice that brings peace'.

We can practice in small things and, as we do so, start to become able to discern the nature and origin of the subtle movement of Will within. Just as Frank Laubach practised in his daily banter with Christ, so we can practice discernment any time we want: 'Lord, does this job will to be done?' 'Does this food will to be eaten?' 'Does this word will to be spoken?' To pose these questions is to pause, breathe, pray, and bring them into a deeper, more presenced, place within us and to rest there for a while to let knowing emerge. This is a powerful, simple practice. It develops the 'muscle' of a discerning will, putting the ownership of it into the right relationship.

Often, there will be no strong indication, and so we rely on our own will and judgment. Sometimes something else will arise – a deeper yes or no. In this way, we learn to listen. This is not a recipe for paralysis, by the way! It is just a practice that can be included in your morning prayer and your evening examen. I will say more on this in the next chapter.

> In this work of presencing in discernment, we follow the same precepts as laid out in the previous chapters, coming into the gathered state and with all our centres of knowing open and available – heart, soul, mind, body – beginning, as laid out in Chapter Four, with the body and awakening our somatic knowing. With your inner sensing activated, if, for example, you are facing into a specific choice or question, you can then sense the degree of alignment between the different centres, sense where there may be disturbance, blockage, or flow and prayerfully presence your enquiry in these. It is often the 'gut' which contains buried knowing, and presencing there can sometimes have an illuminating effect in the heart or mind. The feeling of relief and release that flows when the centres come into alignment is palpable.

One important, further element of discernment can be to speak it out loud. Giving voice, full voice, to something and noticing what the experience is like of doing so is one of the most valuable things we can do. This allows us to feel the resonance of our intention and 'test' it before we act it out. This again is where the help of a spiritual friend or spiritual director is invaluable – they can reflect back to us the energy that we are embodying.

We tend to think of 'discernment' as being needed when we have a particular decision or choice to make, but this really is too crude, and probably often too late! Discernment is an ongoing work of learning to sense into the energy that is moving us into being and, as we explored in the last chapter, allowing ourselves to 'receive', align, and embody impulses that flow from our own essential self or from the Divine. Psalm 37:4 expresses this 'immersive discerning' very clearly and simply: 'Take delight in the LORD, and he will give you the desires of your heart.' St Ignatius' teaching on the 'discernment' of spirits and the interior movement towards 'consolation' or 'desolation' (which probably has its roots in his immersive experience of reading biblical and other texts during his long lay-up in hospital) is another helpful example of this.

Unfortunately, the identification with different inner energies is so visceral that it often only becomes noticeable by its fruits. One classic aspect of this is what we find ourselves 'taking responsibility for'. If you are not conscious of it, you can find yourself very quickly caught in deceptive patterns, assumptions, and expectations, which soon become 'burdens'. I am reminded of a directee who is a priest with a particular gift for holding funerals. Time and again people come to her and express their gratitude, whether they are religious or not, for the quality of presence that flows when she is holding the service. Therefore, she is very much in demand and always has a diary full of funerals. She came into spiritual direction overwhelmed and exhausted by the burden she was carrying. When we presenced and remembered her previous experience of this ministry, she described a familiar pattern – a feeling of overwhelm and helplessness: 'How can I hold for a grief, or a tragedy, as huge as this?' Then, in the service, an awareness of 'something flowing through me... I know it is all going to be all right... the church fills with a Loving Presence.... the space is 'thin'... the words just come...' I remember asking her, 'Whose work is it...?' There was a pause of recognition. I asked, 'Then why are you holding all the responsibility?' She laughed and literally saw Christ's outstretched hands. 'Let me have it,' she heard Him say, and then, with a smile, 'or, at least, can we not hold it together?'

For those in Christian ministry, this is one of the most frequent and debilitating issues with which people present. Christ's famous invitation in Matthew 11:29 to 'take my yoke' is speaking directly into this.

Julian of Norwich says something similar, which also highlights the limits and joys of trying to 'discern ourselves': 'It is easier for us to get to know God than to know our own soul... God is nearer to us than our soul, for He is the ground in which it stands... so if we want to know our own soul, and enjoy its fellowship, it is necessary to seek it in our Lord God.'[4]

This is pointing us back to a foundational truth in this work of discernment, that our first move is always into relationship with the Divine, ensuring that all we are carrying is wholly shared. We find ourselves back with Ignatius' 'Suscipe' again, teaching us how to release everything to its proper Owner: 'Take, Lord and receive...' – our burdens as well as our blessings. The simplest way to do this, whatever we are doing, is to remember for whom we are doing it. If it genuinely is the Divine, we may soon, if we pause to listen, hear within us a 'let me...' ('carry this...', 'take this...', 'show you...' etc).

The most reliable fruit of discernment then is not our particular decisions, but rather our clarity of intention – being clear about the energy that is moving us, where to, and why. Intention drives attention and attention feeds what gets actualised in the reality of this world. Perhaps, for all of us, our primary intention might simply be to 'remain in the Vine' as Christ puts it in John 15. That is our core work of prayerful presencing described in the previous chapter. But, of course, out of this, more specific intentions will arise for each of us, in its season, and each may flower (or wither), bear fruit, and be pruned.

An example of an intention to illustrate this, which currently for me serves as a guide for my daily life, is my desire and impulse to seek to find and hold 'space for encounter' – for and with others. This has become clear to me through a process of many years' formation, but is something, as I look back, that I see has been an essential quality of my being which, in various ways, I have been manifesting since my childhood – for example, in my love of long walks in the wild with close friends, with space for deep conversation. Or sailing. Or dance. Or running retreats. I remember when I was at college, writing a children's story about what I called a 'pryat' mysteriously opening in a nearby woodland – a sacred, thin place where all sorts of beautiful things can happen, but one which needed careful attention and protection from the blundering ways of adults! When I first started going to the monastery, one of the clearest words I heard in prayer was, 'Protect this space' – a voice just resonating in the very centre of my head like a bell.

When I keep 'space for encounter' present in my daily awareness, I am always amazed at the 'little' encounters that quite 'randomly' open up. Only yesterday, I was sat at a public dinner with a complete stranger who shared that she was struggling with a sense of 'not doing enough' in a new role. As she shared, and released, in a gentle, flowing conversation over our food, a peace began to flow and she realised that the impulse, the sense of call, that was beneath her sense of 'failing' was enough. We both noticed the clarity and the beauty of the energy at work in her – and that that was enough. 'Trust this' was the thought that took hold and, immediately, freed from the shadow of all she had come to believe she was not doing, she began to see the things that were opening up. All I needed to do, quite naturally and in a relaxed way, was listen and 'see' her.

> It may be worth pausing here to notice. What clear intentions are you 'living from'? How have you seen these at work in your life, even unconsciously?
>
> Are there intentions that need bringing into a clearer focus? Perhaps try speaking them out aloud once you have done this? What does it feel like within you when you do?

If our intention is clear and flowing from our being, not from our striving ('drawn not driven'), our words and deeds will follow quite naturally. Being thus present in our own intentions allows us to trust ourselves and to seek to understand and be present to the intentions of others. It also leaves us open and available to the movement of Grace. This frees us from the tyranny of trying to perfect the right course of action, which can lead us into endless speculation about how others might respond and how we might in turn respond to their response. If I am clear in my intention, but my actions fall short or go astray, I can learn and realign. I can speak my truth, invite others to speak theirs, and work creatively with what emerges. This may be a synergy if the Will is at work in a congruent way within us. Or it may be a clash of opposites, through which a transforming Will can dynamically flow. A healthily primed intention, with presenced attention from a rooted personal centre of gravity, becomes a 'charged', powerful, and creative force for growth, emergence, and change. I remember the fierce difference of opinion I had, in the early days of my business, with the person who was eventually to become my best client and the source of some truly creative and generative work together.

It is worth saying a bit more here about the nature of our own human will, which is of course the energy that moves us into action. What we call 'will' can flow from many different sources. The will that flows from the 'egoic self' is different to that which flows from the 'disillusioned self', is different to that which flows from the 'essential self' or 'the surrendered self'. Also, at any moment in time, we may be in the grip of energy from different sources, from:

- Our ego-patterning and the superego as 'shoulds'
- The influences or manipulations of others as 'serve', 'perform', 'deserve', 'deliver', 'make good' etc
- Instincts and desires as 'need'
- The amygdala as 'fight' or 'flee' or 'freeze'
- The unconscious as 'compulsion to...'
- Conscience as 'right action'
- Essence as 'be...'
- Compassion as 'help' or 'care'
- Love as...
- The Divine as...

The truth of our condition is that most of the time we genuinely do not know what is moving us to action (or inaction). We may think we do, but our motives are so massively and subtly mixed. It is so often only in retrospect, sometimes well after an event, that we understand more of what was moving us to action. Kierkegaard again comes to mind: 'Life can only be understood backwards; but it must be lived forwards.'

Only when we are fully conscious can we fully know. But to be fully conscious is to know the mind of God, which is impossible to us, as Paul witnesses in the opening quote of this chapter. The good news is that we do not need to know fully (though of course we seek humbly to know what we can). What we can do is sense when we are in the greater flow and trust, 'walking by faith, not by sight' (2 Corinthians 5:7). The measure of that trust is, usually, the 'peaceful strength' that Merton talks about. This has us able to act with limited knowing and, recognising our blindness, to trust in the 'living way' (Hebrews 10:19–20) that we are following.

A final matter to raise in relation to the process of discernment is our reactivity to what arises as we pause and presence. This is often referred to as 'resistance' and usually stems from a part of us that does not, for whatever reason, want to go where we are being invited to follow. In other words, 'My will, not thy will'. In our spirit of noticing, resistance is gold dust – it reveals to us energies and aspects of our personality that we have not yet brought to conscious awareness. So, like everything, we learn to welcome resistance and to feel into it. As with much inner work, it is likely to show up as a somatic effect – for example, a tightness in the chest or the throat or a sicky feeling in the tummy. In the heart, it can be felt as a hardening and, in the mind, it can be felt as a buffering, a numbing refusal to think or face into something. Or sometimes the mind just goes blank, often the sign of a silencing of conscience.

Resistance can take many forms, but one of the most insidious, especially in the early stage of our journey, is a resistance to 'noticing' itself. In this form, life may pose us a significant question in our experience, and we simply ignore it. We distract ourselves or change the topic and quickly bury the stirring feeling inside of us. The more we do it, the more shallow and easily distractable our attention becomes. In this instance, our primary intention has actually become the avoidance of discomfort, and we become more and more addicted to external forms of self-soothing.

> As you are reading this, you may want to pause and briefly notice some of your patterns of resistance. What are your favourite ways of distracting yourself?
>
> No judgment, just a friendly noticing and perhaps even a smile as you greet an old friend.

Resistances tend to crystalise around something a part of us wants to keep 'hidden' (as in Genesis 1) – from ourselves, from God, from others. I am always conscious that a very clear one for me is the avoidance of poverty, not in myself necessarily, but in witnessing the physical poverty of others. I do not like the soul discomfort it induces. So, ironically, the noticing and welcoming of our patterns of avoidance provides a powerful source of enquiry and inner discernment, and a great opportunity to practise doing the very opposite of what my inner resistor would have me do – for example, for me to engage with people living rough and to realise the simple truth that a 'space for encounter' for many is 'just' to be seen, spoken to, and not walked past.

As I write this, my conversion experience, some 28 years ago, comes to mind. It was triggered by a conversation I was having in a group about how, when, and why we give to people begging on the street. One lady said: 'How do you measure the currency of love? How do you give it? How do you pay it back?' These words triggered, right there in the café that we were in, a vision of a 'cloud' of pulsing light above me and an overwhelming realisation that this was the unconditional love of God. A voice came into my head: 'Do you want this?' (Always, that respect for our sovereign will.) I said yes, and my life was reset... I have never until now made the connection between my conversion and what I found myself writing above on poverty. Some further presencing and discerning, I suspect, is being invited!

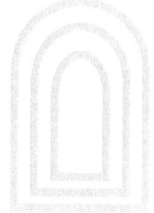

CHAPTER ELEVEN

Sustaining presence in daily life

'Were not our hearts burning within us while
he talked with us on the road...?'

LUKE 24:32

'Blessed are those whose strength is in you,
who have set their hearts on a pilgrimage.
Passing through the valley of Weeping, they make it a place of springs.'

PSALM 84:5-6 (WEB)

THIS CHAPTER is where the rubber meets the road. We have covered much about the practice of attentive presencing in prayer and in spiritual direction encounters, but is it possible to stay presenced when we are immersed in the daily 'patterns of this world'? This is fundamentally what we are called to be, and it perhaps represents the highest state of spiritual intention to be wholly human in the world and wholly available to the Divine Will. Life as prayer, prayer as life, no separation. Of course, this is what Christ so perfectly modelled for us. For us, simply, we do what we can – trusting in Christ's words to St Paul: 'I am with you; that is all you need. My power shows up best in weak people' (2 Corinthians 12:9, TLB).

So, how do we make ourselves 'living sacrifice' as we go about our daily lives and work in the necessary exercise of our own will, agency, and strength as we do so? The foundation of this is to 'Be alert! You do not know when that time will come' (Mark 13:33). This is primarily, as we have been emphasising in previous chapters, a conscious work of *attention*. To do this, we must train the attention, otherwise we will be 'caught' and triggered by our own reactivity and by distractions and deceptions. This is what 'sustaining presence' is all about. The best way to train the attention is with a regular daily practice. I will therefore outline below a series of ways in which we can practice presencing attention in different aspects of our lives.

> You may want to notice, as you read these practices, any that speak to you, making these your 'long list'. You can then pick just one or two to be 'short-listed' for your conscious practice over a defined period. This is something for which you can make yourself accountable to your spiritual director, if you have one.

Rule of life

A basic starting point, and structure, for sustaining our practice is what in the Benedictine tradition is expressed as a 'rule of life' – a daily rhythm of spiritual practice, study, and prayer, with a regular pause, whatever we are doing, to enter formal prayer. This, of course, is enshrined in many Islamic nations by the public call to prayer. The pause for prayer is one of the most powerful ways of 'shifting state' and restoring us to the ground of our being from where, in the words of St Benedict, 'Always, we begin again.'

Most of us, at some stage, will have attempted some kind of rule, with varying degrees of 'success'. The inverted commas are the most important thing in that last sentence, for the beauty and elegance of this rule of life is that it is *'practice,* not perfect' – no quest for perfection and no judgment when we stick to our rule or break it. There is only simple self-observation and curiosity. 'Oh, I haven't prayed for over a week, whereas last week I prayed every day – what is going on? What might I do to help sustain or reinvent my rhythm of prayer for the circumstances or state I now find myself in? Or do I just give myself a break?'

We all have certain stable rhythms, even if it is just eating, drinking, waking, and sleeping. In my experience, whatever your own spiritual 'rule of life', if you have one, there are a couple of foundational precepts worth noting. The simplest is to build any rule around the natural rhythm of your day. It just makes it so much easier to follow. This is why so many religious orders have prayer on waking, before bed, and before meals.

Another precept is the importance of the morning. So much deep work goes on overnight, when our ego is decoupled and the dream life does its thing re-ordering the brain, sifting the experiences of the day and the liminal contents of the unconscious. That means there is always much wisdom available to us after a good night's sleep. Unfortunately, the first thing that happens on awakening (sometimes after a momentary and slightly panicky 'where am I and who am I?'), is that the ego reimposes itself. At its crudest, this may take the form of running through in our minds all that the day has in store and remembering all the things we are worrying about or, sometimes, excited by. Therefore, the natural state is to start the day at this level of consciousness. You may have noticed how, if you wake up in a particular state, or 'get out on the wrong side of bed', that pattern will play itself out during the day – this is the self-fulfilling quality of our pattering. It can be essential, therefore, to take charge of your state before you engage in the day. Some people suggest doing this in bed before your feet touch the ground, whilst I tend to suggest doing your morning practical routines then setting aside some time, even if only ten minutes, to re-empty or re-orientate your state by a presencing or prayer practice that we know works for us personally. This may be a silent, stilling meditation, a walk in nature, or a time in prayer. But we try to make it something that will bring us into the gathered state with heart, soul, mind, and body all opened, relaxed, and online.

The corollary, or an additional practice, is something in the evening or before bed, which can also help with sleeping. Two elements are particularly useful here. One is some kind of quick review of the day in which we simply, intentionally, notice a couple of significant moments during the day in relation to a core intention. If this was around peaceful presence for example, you may just notice when your peace was most present, and what it was like when it was, and when it was most absent and what seemed to trigger that. This practice of self-reflection will substantially strengthen our capacity for self-observation and thus our ability to 'catch ourselves in the moment' when our peace is being disturbed, enabling us to respond more choicefully. The Ignatian examen is an example of this kind of process. The other element is some kind of 'melt into the darkness' prayer or meditation, usually involving gentle relaxing of the body and a 'letting go and letting be' in the mind and heart. You may also have a favoured nighttime prayer to help with this. This is different from the kind of 'actively receiving' state of rest we described earlier. This is more of a 'relaxing and emptying'.

Attention

I want to propose something slightly different in this book for our daily practice, which hopefully will be entirely complementary to whatever spiritual practice and rhythm that you have chosen. That is simply to pay attention to our attention. To 'keep awake' by keeping an element of freedom in our *noticing* – so that we are more and more conscious of how we are being.

The way we liberate our attention is through the process I outlined in Chapter Four, of sustaining a 'gathered' or 'recollected' state. The simplest and most fundamental movement that helps us do that is to bring awareness into breath, and I make no apology for repeating this. Just taking five conscious belly breaths, into that still centre I spoke of earlier, can change our state. Feeling into your hands and feet and softening your face as you do so, will amplify the effect. Even if you sense no need to enquire, the pause for breath will reset your state and ground you and you will be more aware of your own energy and presence.

> With your awareness thus freed you can enquire, even just once a day, but hopefully more, maybe using any or all of the following questions:

> 'Where is my attention being drawn and what does this feel like (in the body)?'
>
> 'What else am I being invited to notice?'
>
> 'How and where am I sensing the Presence of the Divine?'
>
> 'What am I being invited to remember... about who I am... and about my intentions?'
>
> What is it like, what is the effect, when I do this?

Breath is by far the simplest and most effective route for presencing that we have. To presence in breath is to restore awareness instantly to the basic origin of our being, as represented in Genesis 2:7: 'Then the LORD God formed a man from the dust of the ground and breathed into his nostrils the breath of life, and the man became a living being.' To presence in breath is to return to our origin and 'begin again', free in our undistorted will.

The enduring work therefore is for a 'free will' and this, in many ways, is the 'pearl of great price' that we learn to treasure more and more as we find and re-find it – a clarity of awareness and an attention free of distractions, attachments, associations, and reactions. A conscious and awake soul that can be available to the Divine in whatever we are doing.

Richard Rohr speaks powerfully of this soul awakening in his daily meditations:

> *I think of soul as anything's ultimate meaning which is held within. Soul is the blueprint inside of every created thing telling it what it is and what it can become. When we meet anything at that level, we will respect, protect, and love it. Many human beings simply haven't found their own blueprint or soul, so they cannot see it anywhere else. Like knows like! When we only meet reality at the external level, we do not meet our own soul and we have no ability to meet the soul of anything else either. We clergy would have done much better to encourage Christians to discover their souls instead of 'save'*

> *them. While everything has a soul, in many people it seems to be dormant, disconnected, and ungrounded. They are not aware of the inherent truth, goodness, and beauty shining through everything.*[1]

Just as breath is the transformational force that feeds the life of the body, so attention is the transformational force that feeds the life of the soul. What we give our attention to flourishes, for where our attention goes our energy flows, often unconsciously – and ultimately where our energy flows our life goes. The capacity, therefore, to pause and notice what we are giving our attention to (and not to), is the foundation of freedom. This must be cultivated.

This work is essential in both accessing and further feeding the new 'centre of gravity' that forms within us as we progress in our journey of becoming. It is only from this place that we can be awake to, and potentially act in support of, the greater Love and Will at work within us and around us. It is the essence of the first and second commandments and the Lord's Prayer – 'Thy kingdom come, thy will be done.'

Remembering

Gradually, as we do this work, re-membering (literally putting ourselves back together again) becomes a habitual spiritual practice. The most important facet of remembering is perhaps 'soul-remembering' – to remember who we truly are (in God). That requires us to bring our awareness out of the functional mind, our identification with the stuff of our lives and our limiting self-concepts, to locate it in the true source and substance of our being. This is the root of the 'tree of life' within us, or the 'image of the Divine' that we were actually born to be, as well as the formative experiences that have fed our soul. Then, in turn, we can let it flow into the day-to-day stuff of our lives.

As a brief aside, it is perhaps worth saying a few words on 'memory' at this point. Memory, like intelligence, belongs in all our centres, not just the functional mind, and we can learn to be conscious in how we use and access this too. The obvious understanding of the word is the recall of thoughts or data stored in the mind. We tend to think of memory as remembering names or facts or recipes or the time, place, key aspects and significance of certain experiences. But I view this more as 'memorising', a '2D' experience compared to the '3D' of allowing our whole being to be imprinted with a powerful living memory, as we notice in the 'Memoria Dei' activity. Just as we can store it in different ways, so we can access memory in different ways too. We can recall an experience or we can re-live it – that is to presence ourselves back in the time when it was occurring and to see, hear, feel, sense, even taste or smell (like Proust) the actual experience in its fullness.

A simple practice, therefore, is actively to remember the things that have shaped and formed us (e.g. 'Memoria Dei'). This is particularly helpful in our relationships, especially our close ones. We often forget what has formed us in our togetherness and take each other for granted. The act of reminiscing with a friend can be a powerful and beneficial practice of soul remembering, rather than, as some may perceive it, a nostalgic indulgence – as long as we do not get stuck in the past and remember to be present, in the rich experience of this living memory, in how we are being with each other in the now.

In re-living memory, we become aware that we have emotional memories too – feelings can resurface from significant events, sometimes powerfully and surprisingly, triggering what we think of as 'buried memories', connections, and associations. We also have body memory, well known in developing certain skills or habits, but also powerful sensations that we may re-experience when triggered by certain events or memories, such as cold or trembling or warmth or softness. Much of our work in presencing and enquiry in our earlier chapters is actually re-engaging with these memories to re-access them and process them properly, so that the full wisdom of the experience is available to us and the fullness of our being, that is often locked away with them, can be released and allowed to flow.

Most of our significant memories are so because of the power of emotion that is associated with them, whether positive or negative. These are the memories that shape us and become a part of our becoming. They may be 'formative' memories that have shaped and strengthened and matured us into a more conscious being, or they may be 'raw' memories, unprocessed and 'buried alive', and therefore triggering and driving our thoughts and actions unconsciously. These 'raw', unprocessed memories become the substance for the work described in Chapter Six of purifying and strengthening the heart. The 'formative' ones become part of our practice of constant re-membering – who we really are rather than who we think we are.

As we saw earlier in the book, this 'work' of surrendering and developing a new centre of gravity for our being is basically a process of learning to digest our unresolved experience so that we are not living in the fractious energy of the structures that we have built to defend against that. Then we can be living as wholly as we can from this place of source, integration, and wholeness. To 'resolve' an experience, as we have seen, is to bring it and receive it into the essential 'light' of Being shining within our soul. This will often feel excruciatingly vulnerable or downright impossible. The more this happens, however infrequently, the more our 'I' gradually becomes aligned with our true Being – and therefore available to the greater Will that is seeking to work in and through us – as Paul attests in Romans 12. We start to develop a new centre of gravity, the hallmark of which is a growing sense of inner knowing and peace.

Finally, in terms of re-membering, one foundational and practical way of collaborating with this work is to regularly drop our awareness, our sense of 'I', down from the mind and into our deeper belly presence, our 'core' or literal centre of gravity, and to allow our sense of being to flow from and in there. This, like much in this book, is a practice, and we need to take the time to do it regularly. If we do, we gradually come to notice the intelligence, the 'voice' of our 'gut', usually reminding us in its grounded way what really matters. Alongside this we might notice if, where, and how we sense the presence of God within this 'core' – 'Deep calls to deep' (see Psalm 42:7). Be patient; it may take a while before we are able to let go in the mind and tune in down there.

Wisdom

Over time, we start to develop a different, sustained 'level of presence' from which to live our lives than the habitual thinking of the functional mind. A dear friend of mine described this beautifully as we were discussing a forthcoming retreat on Bardsey Island in North Wales, one of that country's most beautiful and powerful 'thin' places (where the veil between heaven and earth is somehow thinner). 'We often talk of "thin places",' he said, 'and that is my constant hope, that I too may become a "thin place".' It is subtle at first. We may not notice it, though others may. We will find ourselves, calmer, less reactive, less easily 'triggered' by situations, and more able to hear a different voice, a voice of wisdom, from within.

The voice of wisdom, the mystery of where the human meets the Divine in flesh and time, speaks quietly and deeply inside us. It is easily ignored and, gracious as it is, will never seek to intrude or override the more pressing voice of the ego. But gradually, as we develop our centre of gravity, we learn to hear and recognise this voice and to notice how and where it tends to speak within us. It speaks from a very different place than our 'inner chatterer' or even our usual 'thinking voice'. You are more likely to hear it in a deeper place of experience, sometimes at the back or base of the brain, sometimes in the core of the heart, as David seems to reference in Psalm 51:6 (ESV): 'Behold, you delight in truth in the inward being, and you teach me wisdom in the secret heart.' The same is true of that other Divine-imbued voice within, conscience. Both wisdom and conscience, like essence, flow from the deeper soul, and it is a sign of our growing maturity in presence that these voices start to make themselves heard within us.

Once we have developed the capacity to hear and recognise the voice of wisdom speaking within, an important practice can be consciously to check in with it, particularly when we find ourselves in a situation or conversation where we recognise that we need to access a different knowing.

> This practice involves stilling and locating awareness in the place where you have found wisdom speaks in you, and sensing into the simple enquiry of 'what is wisdom saying in relation to this, if anything?'
>
> It is important not to grasp for any answer. As we discussed in the previous chapter on prayer, we just let the voice, or sensing, emerge or arise. If nothing comes, we revert to our more habitual cognition and judgment. If something does surface, then of course we remember to self-check, in prayerful discernment, 'How do I know that this is the voice of wisdom?'
>
> We can do exactly the same in listening to conscience.

Prayer

We can experiment with other simple techniques that free our attention. One, of course, is to keep focusing attention on the Divine. So, in addition to presencing in breath, we may simultaneously use a word or phrase, as in the Centering prayer tradition. This must be a neutral word or phrase, so that the mind does not get immediately caught into a stream of religious or other associations. One of the most effective is just 'I am' which, with its echo of the Divine 'I am who I am' can be powerful in a combined work of God and self-remembering.

A technique which I have found particularly effective is to use a prayer word simultaneously in the heart and the mind. This begins as a formal practice, maybe included over several weeks in our daily prayer rhythm. After that it becomes an embedded habit, such that we find we are less praying the prayer than 'the prayer is praying us'.

> To do this we need to ground and come into the gathered state so that our full being is online. Having done that, we spend a bit of time presencing our awareness somewhere in the body, for example feeling into our feet or our hands, so that this bodily sensation is present to us always in the background.
>
> Then we bring awareness into the centre of the heart and start breathing a prayer silently within the chest. The best thing is to use a foreign language, for example *'Kyrie eleison'* (a Greek phrase, meaning 'Lord, have mercy') and just to keep repeating the words for a few minutes, spoken as deep in the heart as we can, so that it becomes an embodied rhythm within us (all the time still feeling our feet on the ground).
>
> Then, allowing that to continue in the background, we can bring awareness up into the head and silently speak the English (or your own language) version of the same prayer words, in this case, 'Lord, have mercy', right in the centre of the head, again allowing

> this to become a rhythmic chant. Then we pendulate between the two until we become gradually settled in the awareness of both continuing simultaneously, all the while aware too of our feet on the ground.

This will feel cumbersome and awkward at first, but gradually, if you persist, you will find your awareness being greatly expanded, with attention capable of being in prayer simultaneously in body, heart, mind, and yet still free to attend to other things. Once this has become a habituated practice, we can start into this prayer rhythm anytime and anywhere – walking down the street, moving between meetings, eating a meal or attending church. Our attention may need to be given to something, but as it returns we will realise that the prayer is still going on inside us.

Expanding and freeing attention

Anything we do that has us presence attention simultaneously in two or more activities or aspects of our being has a powerful effect on expanding and freeing the attention. Like any physical training activity, it develops the muscle for more varied, versatile, and stronger use. Presencing in the body or the senses is particularly powerful and relatively simple. Examples of this might include:

- Actively feeling into the sensation in your hand every time you clasp a door handle
- Touching and feeling the sensation of things, plants, brickwork as you go about your day
- Conscious eating – bringing awareness into the experience of taste in your mouth, eating slowly and noticing the change in texture of the food as you eat. This can be done with a prayer of gratitude too for the sacrifice of what has given its life that you might eat. 'Taste and see that the LORD is good,' the psalmist says, 'his praise will always be on my lips' (Psalm 34:8,1)

- Conscious drinking. If you drink, say, a sip of water, stay with it as it descends through your throat, down your oesophagus and into your tummy. See how far down you can follow the sensation of the coolness within
- Expanding your seeing – notice the experience of sight, include your peripheral vision, look up, see the sky when you walk down the street
- Experimenting with periods of silence with friends or family if it is possible to do that – maybe the occasional meal in silence to allow awareness to flow into other aspects of the experience

If all these seem simple, almost trivial, my only invitation is to try them and see. Anything that helps free our attention helps us stay awake, presenced, and available. Once we are available, the 'Divine help' can do its work within us and Grace can move.

Our inner self-talk

Brother Lawrence's famous book *The Practice of the Presence of God* provides us with a living witness of this process of everyday presencing and is certainly to be recommended if my book is speaking to you in any way.[2] Brother Lawrence emphasises our core theme of 'active passivity', what he calls a 'hearty renunciation'. A few quotes from his writing provide us with some important principles for this work. It is evident from these how important a well-trained attention is for what he is commending:

1. Be clear about our motives and intentions and keep this in mind in all we do:

> *That the most excellent method he had found of going to GOD, was that of doing our common business without any view of pleasing men, [Gal. i. 10; Eph. vi. 5, 6.] and (as far as we are capable) purely for the love of GOD.*

> *We ought not to be weary of doing little things for the love of God, who regards not the greatness of the work, but the love with which it is performed.*

2. Pray for the Divine help. We could do worse than start each day with Brother Lawrence's simple prayer, or our own version of it:

O my God, since thou art with me, and I must now, in obedience to thy commands, apply my mind to these outward things, I beseech thee to grant me the grace to continue in thy presence; and to this end do thou prosper me with thy assistance, receive all my works, and possess all my affections.

3. Stay in the connection:

We should establish ourselves in a sense of GOD's Presence, by continually conversing with Him.

Think often on God, by day, by night, in your business and even in your diversions. He is always near you and with you; leave him not alone.

> One of the most simple and powerful practices that Brother Lawrence invites is making our self-talk, or 'inner chatter', prayer, simply by including God in it as much as possible. A straightforward practice in this, if a thought, or particularly a self (or other) judgment starts to gain force within us, is consciously to pray, 'Lord, all these thoughts I return to You. Please give back to me only that which comes from You.'
>
> Or we may, as Frank Laubach suggests, 'just' include God in the conversation. 'What shall we do now, Lord?' 'How am I going to prepare for this meeting, Lord?' 'I wonder what my friend would most like for her birthday, Lord?' Clearly, the risk with this is that we feed the voice of the chatterer, when silence may be the better way, but if we catch ourselves at it, it can be a helpful way of making it a 'hearty renunciation'.

Nature

Another powerful aspect of daily life into which we can presence our attention is, of course, nature. As the psalmist sings out in Psalm 19:1–4:

> *The heavens declare the glory of God;*
> *   the skies proclaim the work of his hands.*
> *Day after day they pour forth speech;*
> *   night after night they reveal knowledge.*
> *They have no speech, they use no words;*
> *   no sound is heard from them.*
> *Yet their voice goes out into all the earth,*
> *   their words to the ends of the world.*

A well-tried method for becoming available to the greater Presence at work in all creation is an 'awareness walk'. We start, again, by becoming present in our gathered state, with a particular emphasis to bringing all our senses online, and then going for a walk in nature, whether mountains, woods, fields, parks, or a simple garden. It is something I use on all my retreats and I have been doing so since day one. At Waverley Abbey, it is almost guaranteed that people will return with some kind of epiphany, revelation, or transformational insight just in the short walk through the garden across the bridge by the lake and into the ruins of the old abbey. Swans, trees, kingfishers, leaves, flowers, rain, sun, wind, snow, lightning and thunder, light in its many forms all seem to conspire to yield their fruit in season. It was almost embarrassing when we were running our corporate leadership programmes in the House, at some expense, that the most powerful learning activity proved to be a free, untutored stroll around the grounds!

The Divine in nature is speaking to us all the time – it cannot not be, because the Divine Presence is incarnate within it, God's Will 'being done on earth, as in heaven'. And nature has not experienced the 'Fall' in the same way as man. It cannot deny its own flowering, to paraphrase the David Whyte verse I quoted earlier in this book. As Gerard Manley Hopkins says, it will 'Flame out, like shining from shook foil'[3] and re-mind us who we are and who God is. As such, it becomes a powerful mirror for our own soul. All we need to do is open up our awareness and allow ourselves to 'see and be seen'.

Richard Rohr makes explicit the role that nature plays in our own soul remembering, drawing inspiration from his Franciscan heritage:

> *Through extended time in nature, Francis became intimately connected with non-human living things and came to recognize that the natural world was also imbued with soul. Almost all male initiation rites—including those of Jesus and John the Baptist (see Matthew 3:13–17)—took place in nature, surely for that reason.*
>
> *Without such soul recognition and mirroring, we are alienated and separated from nature, and quite frankly, ourselves. Without a visceral connection to the soul of nature, we will not know how to love or respect our own soul.*[4]

Relationships

The other crucial area for practising presence in daily life is, of course, in our relationships. I have said much about this already in a previous chapter, but there are some relatively simply techniques that we can deploy to remain awake and receptive to what is truly flowing to-and-from in our connections with others. Again, this can be a matter of some simple precepts we have covered already:

1. Being clear in our intent so that our attention is positively 'primed'. The simplest is a quick 'bullet prayer' for the Grace 'to see them as You see them'. St Patrick's lovely 'breastplate prayer' with its close, 'Christ in the hearts of those that love me, Christ in the mouth of friend and Stranger' is a lovely reminder to us to re-spect, and therefore look attentively for, the hidden depths in people we meet. One of my mentors went so far as to claim that 'when two people meet, it is like two universes colliding'.

2. Being presenced in the gathered state, with heart and body knowing online. This enables us to sense into the energetic flows that are going on beneath the façade of words and behaviour. The heart and gut have the capacity to discern through resonance and 'mirror neurons' what is being transmitted at the emotional, unconscious, and spiritual level. This can communicate infinitely more than what is being spoken. We have the capacity also to respond with the heart and body without saying a single word. But we

have to exercise great care when we do revert to words – they can maul the subtlety of what is being exchanged.

> A very simple exercise to access presencing in relationship can just be to sit in silence with someone for five minutes or so, facing each other – eyes open, but in an expanded field of perception with peripheral vision online, rather than focusing on each other – and just noticing energetically what you are sensing in the field of connection between you, however subtle or apparently insignificant.

3. Using our body. If someone touches you, even a simple shake of the hand, be there – have your awareness in your hand and feel what flows in the touch. Feel warmth, texture, substance, flow. Keep your awareness there, as in the example above of drinking, feel the sensation of the person's touch on your skin until it fades. Notice what is being transmitted.

4. Likewise, sensing into the energetic 'field' of presence that is the atmosphere between people. Anyone who has been in love or seen people in a relationship of love will know what this is like. The 'atmosphere' is pervasive. This is true for other atmospheres – what we sometimes call 'mood' or 'climate'. If we allow ourselves to become aware of these, and prayerfully presence into our experience of them and enquire into them, much wisdom can be released. Many a time I have sat with someone, or a group, in prayer and we have all felt something palpably flowing within and between us. Sometimes it can be helpful to comment on it because our noticing can inform someone else's. I remember being on a leadership programme with a large Christian charity and becoming aware that something was moving. In a break, one of the participants drew my attention to the 'thick', 'warm' presence that was their experience. Immediately, I was able to recognise it and attune better to what was at work. Sometimes, however, the opposite can be true, and our words can distort the experience of others.

Levels of presence

I hope by now it is clear that it would be impossible and quite ludicrous to attempt to embody a fully awake, soul-shining, wholly vulnerable presence in all our activities. Much of what we call 'ordinary life' would grind to a halt! (Maybe that's not a bad thing, but it would be a massive trauma for those who still identify with that as their primary business in life! And, of course, they would just ignore you.) We are all operating at different levels of 'awakeness' and at different times. I can only connect with you and you with me at the lowest common denominator – and there is no judgment in that. 'Those who have ears to hear', as Christ is so often recorded as saying in the Gospels, is not a statement of judgment, it is a statement of compassionate understanding and acceptance. It is why Jesus uses parables so that we can find the level of meaning intended for us when the time is right, which may be the twentieth reading of an all-too-familiar biblical verse. Everything happens in its own time, according to the greater Will.

John Wimber's testimony about his own conversion comes to mind: 'I knew something revolutionary was going on inside of me. I thought, "I hope this works, because I'm making a complete fool of myself." Then the Lord brought to mind a man I had seen in Pershing Square in Los Angeles a number of years before. He was wearing a sign that said, "I'm a fool for Christ. Whose fool are you?" I thought at the time, "That's the most stupid thing I've ever seen." But as I kneeled on the floor I realised the truth of the odd sign.'[5]

We need to find the level of presence that serves the activity we are in, but we can still stay intentional about it. The miracle of my egoic self will do just fine for many things in life. Christ reminds us of this in His guidance to 'render to Caesar that which is Caesar's and render to God that which is God's' (Matthew 22:21, NIV). That means I am intentional when, say, I go to watch my beloved Wales play rugby with a group of friends: intentional about having fun, letting go, enjoying the rugby, having a few beers, not talking religious stuff that will alienate my friends – but staying awake enough to notice 'spaces for encounter' when they open up.

When I am presenced in my driving, I can seek to adopt the practices of the advanced driving test, noticing all that is going on around me, even commenting on it in my mind, rather than becoming distracted by preparing the talk I am giving at my next teaching session!

PRESENCING AND SPIRITUAL DIRECTION

When I am in spiritual direction or running a retreat, I am presenced by a much more thorough immersion in a deep stillness that has me able to be mostly 'surrendered' and available to what is flowing spiritually as well as humanly. All these are fundamentally different levels, or configurations of presence, but all conscious – that is the core work.

> Whatever I am in, I can seek always to be presenced in the basics (recognising I will 'fail' much of the time!) – holding my main intentions, conscious of breath, as both Divine and human, aware of sensation in the body and emotion in the heart and able to notice my thoughts, not be identified with them. Then I am free.

And so we must 'return to where we started' and hopefully 'know the place for the first time', as Eliot puts it in the *Four Quartets*.[6] I will fail in this, constantly and sometimes spectacularly foolishly. That is the whole point. That is the essence of this life of 'formation' by which the soul grows in Love through its immersion in the messy imperfection of a human life – mainly by getting it wrong... and noticing!

It goes without saying, therefore, that possibly the major quality of anyone pursuing this life of presenced awareness is a robust sense of humour, mainly the ability not to take ourselves too seriously and to laugh, time and again, in recognition of how we allow our consciousness to be colonised by something other than that which is needed. I am reminded of the time I was running a team away day on a set of canal boats and delivering a very fierce 'safety-awareness' reprimand to the crew of one boat, only to step around quickly, having finished, lose my footing on the deck, and fall headlong into the water. There was a pregnant, suspense-filled silence as I clambered back aboard. Nobody said a word, nobody needed to, the eyes said it all. Then we all collapsed in laughter.

We are meant to fail in this – *practise*, not perfect. To fail is to succeed because it is all about being fully human, and each time we do, it strengthens our noticing and feeds our awareness. The only failure is to give up trying.

As I write, I notice in this, as in so much, the fractal nature of it all. The work of 'keeping awake' is itself a microcosm of the bigger work of our journey of soul formation. 'Sin is necessary.' We get it right by getting it wrong. Our growth happens in the courage to stay in the dynamic tension between a Divinely-imbued soul seeking to embody itself in a wayward world. Sometimes in my work as a spiritual director, I catch a glimpse of the true nature of the vast spiritual being sat before me, and it is awesome to behold. But for this life, we are called to live in the in-between, the 'kingdom of heaven' and the 'earth below', the 'now and the not yet', and to live as fully as we can in both, wholly human, wholly Divine. Barbara Brown Taylor's gentle wisdom comes to mind: 'Becoming fully human is the greatest homage we can bestow to the One who showed us how.'[7] To this we can add the words of T.S. Eliot: 'Humankind cannot bear very much reality.'[8]

We live on the cusp between our Divinely-infused nature and the egoic structures we have formed for this life. That means the messiness, the imperfection, the brokenness, and the ordinariness of everyday life are just as real and important as the yearning to love, to serve, to 'magnify the Lord'. The sailor in me sees it as the necessary tension between the heavy, rusty keel beneath my aged boat and the wind-filled sail above. It is the squeeze of these two forces on the hull that produces the forward motion. The (less than) firm hand on the tiller is the awake attention, steering my best-intended, frequently-tacking, course through the foamy sea.

CHAPTER TWELVE

The role and experience of the spiritual director

> '*Were not our hearts burning within us
> while he talked with us on the road?*'
>
> LUKE 24:32

IN THIS CHAPTER, I will explore the role and experience of a spiritual director in supporting the different aspects of spiritual formation outlined in this book. This is another 'how to' chapter, for which I draw primarily on my own experience, with the aim simply of sharing my own learning. Please do write to me if you want to add to this, and we will find a way to share this collective wisdom.

The first part of the chapter is on spiritual direction as a process, with thoughts on how to hold space for a presencing-based approach. This is followed by thoughts on how to support directees in relation to the specific content of the earlier chapters. As I indicated at the start, especially if you are an experienced spiritual director, you may want to read the relevant part of this chapter as a footnote to each of the previous chapters as you work your way through. Or you can read the whole book and then read this as a separate standalone chapter.

This makes it a longer chapter, so I would suggest you pace your reading of it. There are two natural breakpoints which you might want to take advantage of as you read: one before we begin the commentary on Chapter Four and another before we comment on Chapter Seven.

The spiritual direction process

Definition

I take as my starting point for the chapter a core definition of the role of the spiritual director that has already been expressed by many writers, and is well put by Barry and Connolly:

> We define Christian spiritual direction, then, as help given by one believer to another that enables the latter to pay attention to God's personal communication to him or her, to respond to this personally communicating God, to grow in intimacy with this God, and to live out the consequences of the relationship. The focus of this type of spiritual direction is on experience, not ideas, and specifically on the religious dimension of experience, i.e., that dimension of any experience that evokes the presence of the mysterious Other whom we call God.[1]

Theirs is an excellent foundational book, and one I would strongly recommend to anyone seeking to learn a 'spiritual direction' approach to their ministry. I say 'approach' here to emphasise that spiritual direction is not just restricted to formal one-to-one sessions. It can be used in any encounter, including of course 'spiritual friendships', where we make ourselves available, however fleetingly, in the capacity Barry and Connolly describes.

The spiritual direction relationship is a tripartite process. The primary relationship is between the directee and the Divine. The secondary relationships are those between the director and directee and the director and the Divine. The sole focus of the director is to help 'widen the channel' of connection between the directee and the Divine – then get out of the way so that the 'Work' of the real spiritual director, the Divine, can flow, transforming, renewing, and inspiring true Will.

More precisely expressed, following the logic of this book, our 'work' (inverted commas again because we can only do this if we are available to the flow of Grace ourselves) is to help the directee inhabit an 'I' in their relationship with the Divine that is as fully open as possible to the Divine Presence that is here, 'permeating the present', wanting and so patiently waiting to be at Work in and with them.

Our role in getting out of the way

From the perspective of this definition, any 'directing' we are doing is purely to help the directee attend to their direct experience of the Divine, however it manifests to them, and, when connection is made, to get out of the way. I have repeated this because it is just so important. We should be aiming to be an empty vessel in the work (impossible of course, except through Grace).

I remember, many years ago, going to a Benedictine House with a group, and one of the Community gave a talk on spiritual direction. 'So, what do you all do, then?' he asked us. We told him we were all coaches and counsellors. 'Oh no!' he exclaimed, 'You are the worst!' We were rather taken aback! There was a pause… followed by a beaming smile and the words, 'You think you actually know what you are doing!' His words were a beautiful gift that I have treasured to this day. The scripture for his session was Matthew 4:18 and the title: 'Lay down your nets and follow Me.'

This reminds me of a time, too, when I was holding for someone in direction who, after presencing and enquiry, had found his intimate, expanded place of connection with the One he called God. He had come 'home' and there was a powerful communion going on. I knew it and knew I was now redundant. But in my keenness to add value, I asked him another question – something like 'How's it going in there?' 'Fine,' was his slightly surprised and rather put-out answer, 'but what are you doing here?' I left him to it and learned a very helpful lesson.

A practice to honour this is to begin and end every session, where possible, with a prayer of conscious surrender and an invocation of Divine Will and authority over the encounter. This may be done aloud with the directee if they are amenable, or silently. The simple, radical, one is the Lord's Prayer, for example: 'In this time set aside to be here with You, may Your Kingdom come and Your Will be done.' Another helpful foundation is gratitude – even as simple as, 'Thank You for the gift of this time to attend to You and Your Presence at work in our lives.'

A typical structure for a 'presencing-based' spiritual direction encounter

Before we go on to look at how we hold for the 'work' described in each chapter of this book, it is worth saying a few words about the 'container' for the work. In doing so, please accept a reminder that I am drawing on my own practice and I make no claims beyond saying that it seems to work. I present this as a formal spiritual direction session, but I hope you will be able to make the leap to how this can be translated into more informal interactions:

> The process I use is one which James Finley, in his audiobook *Following The Mystics Through The Narrow Gate,* attributes to Thomas Merton. This centres around three questions:
>
> 1. 'How is it going waking up in your life and relationships?'
>
> 2. 'How is it going surrendering to the Mystery that has intimately accessed your heart and brought you to this place so that it might transform you into itself?'
>
> 3. 'How is it going allowing the answer to the second question to percolate up through the first?'[2]

These three questions seem to capture the drama of our prodigal nature. We 'wake up'. We re-member who and whose we are. We re-turn.

So, having bounded our time in prayer, we can invite the directee to share whatever is present to them in answer to Merton's first question. As they do so, we both listen attentively to what is arising, paying attention to emotional, spiritual, and somatic experience alongside the more cognitive 'download'.

At some stage, when we both feel it is right, we can pause and consciously still and presence using a guided meditation, like that in Chapter Four on becoming 'living sacrifice'. This involves presencing in breath and body and then bringing awareness into sensation, emotion, and thought. A good preface to this can be Psalm 139 with its invitation to be 'searched': 'You have searched me, LORD, and you know me.' We recognise that this is done with a gaze of Pure Love. It is also a reminder of the greater holding that is present in the Holy Spirit which 'hems us in behind and before' (see Psalm 139:5).

As we still, we pay attention to the direct emotional and somatic experience that is arising in the spirit of 'welcoming prayer'. We can then follow the process of 'enquiring' into what arises, in the 'patternings' or 'stirrings' of our heart as described in Chapter Six and allowing a 'surrendering to the Mystery' that is at work in these. We close this phase with a conscious 'receiving' of any Divine infusion or invitation. This may result in a significant shift in state and awareness.

Rooted in this awareness, in the final phase we allow what has been at work to 'percolate' back into what was shared and expressed at the opening. What does life look like from now? What has changed? What are we seeing differently? What has been opened up or resolved?

> Three prayers are very helpful in this third phase:
>
> 1. That our habitual understanding may be 'illumined' by what is present. This I take as what Paul refers to as the renewing of the mind. We do not seek cognitively to interpret what has taken place, which would reinstate prior cognitive patterning. We ask for illumination, with the potential for new, Divinely inspired, 'patterning'
>
> 2. That we may wholly receive and remember, in body, heart, mind, and soul, what has been sewn within during the encounter. This is a holistic remembering, not just 'memorising', so that what is remembered can work within us in daily life

> 3. For a Divine 'seal' upon all that has taken place – see Song of Songs 8:6: 'Place me like a seal over your heart, like a seal on your arm, for love is as strong as death.' For example, we might pray, 'May all that is of You in this, Lord, be forever sealed within, and may all that is not blow through like chaff on the breeze and be gone, so all that remains is more and more of You in us and us in You'

Finally, there is a crystalising of intention around what next – in terms of conscious 'practices' between sessions. How do you live life from this state of awareness having received what has just been given? How do you stay conscious and attentive to this? What help might you need? How might you stay in this quality of connection with the 'Mystery that has accessed your heart'? This leads into a closing conversation about any practical changes to the directee's rule of life and their personal practice of prayer, presencing, and self-reflection.

We do not need slavishly to follow this format. Sometimes, for example, particularly if there is no 'burning issue' occupying the directee's mind, we may begin with stilling and presencing – and let what arises inform the session. Sometimes we will encounter a Divine 'hijacking' and let this flow where it Will.

> As a simple summary, this process looks like:
>
> - How are you arriving and what with?
> - Stilling and presencing
> - Enquiring: What is present and how is the Divine at work within it/you?
> - (Getting out of the way!)
> - Receiving: What are you being invited to re-member, receive, and say 'yes' to?
> - Returning: How do your opening questions look from here?

THE ROLE AND EXPERIENCE OF THE SPIRITUAL DIRECTOR

> - Closing: How are you leaving? What are you going to do to stay in this?

Having explained this basic framing, I will now look at how we work with the different aspects outlined in this book, a chapter at a time. This will look both at the content of a spiritual direction encounter and at the pattern and practice between sessions. It will build cumulatively into more 'advanced' work, but this is to do with the structure of the book rather than real life, where it will be more iterative and cyclical.

How to support the process of 'gathering' and self-recollection (Chapter Four)

This is the groundwork – the conscious, constant 'becoming living sacrifice' – fully awake, fully receptive. To follow Merton's process above, we seek, as best we can, to be present and surrendered to the 'Mystery' that is at work within.

This begins with our own practice as directors, and our attentiveness to our own rule and 'gathered state'. Before any encounter, we 'gather' into presence ourselves. My hope is that, however experienced you are, this book will have provided some additional insights for this. My practice is to presence in all our faculties as the first commandment invites. Even if we find ourselves in an impromptu 'spiritual direction encounter', we can pause 'just' to breathe, ground awareness in the belly, feel our feet, and touch into heart, soul, mind, and gut, asking for the Grace to be available to the greater 'Work', so we are held and not relying on our own nets. If we have only a moment to gather, even just a word of invitation, like 'Lord, have mercy' or *'Maranatha'* spoken in the centre of heart and mind, combined with a single deep, whole body breath, can make all the difference.

From this baseline, further elements which we may cover concerning this initial work of 'gathering' include:

1. Explaining. Introducing people to the different centres of knowing – head, heart, body, soul – and inviting them to practise with these. This can be introduced by inviting people to place their hand on the three physical centres – top of forehead (mind), centre of chest (heart), and just below the navel (body/'gut') – and simply noticing 'what it's like in there'. Some people, especially the more cognitive by preference, can struggle with 'letting go of the head' and bringing awareness into the body. If so, we may just leave it at coming into breath and grounding the feet. Scripture is helpful with this: God's 'breath of life' in Genesis and Christ's washing of feet are two lovely ways to bring people into body experience – also Paul's words on the body as 'temple of the Spirit'.

2. In-session practice. If people are amenable, it is most helpful to lead them in a guided relaxation, presencing their awareness in each of the three centres as described in Chapter Four. I tend to leave 'soul' as something of a mysterious unknown with an invitation to stay curious to how 'soul knowing' pops up. Having come into the recollected state, we then enquire what their experience is of this. This nearly always yields something of substance to spend time with. In early sessions, I often find that some aspect of Divine Presence will arise – possibly a feeling (e.g. 'peace' or 'calm') or an experience (e.g. 'stillness', 'holding', 'light') or an image or word. We invite them to notice what happens when they presence attention in this. It may expand or flow and yield an experience of encounter with the One who is waiting to greet them. However, whilst these encounters do often occur, I must emphasise that we absolutely 'expect nothing'.

If more complex or disturbing material arises, we may want to leave these alone in early sessions – unless there is clear guidance and willingness to go there. We can agree to 'notice that popped up' and keep it in mind to see if it arises again in future sessions.

Having established this, holding a time of guided presencing and stilling can become standard practice in all sessions. (I usually run 90-minute sessions with 20 minutes or so for this.) Gradually, people familiarise themselves with the recollected state and how to access it in the day to day.

3. The core work of strengthening 'awareness'. In this early work, the most important thing in my experience is to develop people's capacity for a 'neutral', 'witnessing' awareness (in Christ) – i.e. simply to notice what is present in all aspects of consciousness. It is this that enables the directee to find freedom from their own reactivity and the draining presence of the superego, or 'inner critic'. The practice that supports this is stillness, recognising that stillness is never 'still' – there is always breath and the pulse of life in the body. (I often talk of it as the stillness of standing by a flowing river, or the swell of the ocean.) Two scriptures that are helpful are Psalm 131:2 (NKJV): 'Surely I have calmed and quieted my soul, Like a weaned child with his mother' and Psalm 46:10, which can be included in a meditation: 'Be still, and know that I am.'

The purpose is 'noticing the noticing' that is available when we still – the capacity to attend to any aspect of our experience and not to identify with it. So, if someone laments that 'my mind is so busy with "stuff"', our response can be: 'Congratulations! This is awareness – seeing your thoughts. This is the beginning of freedom.' We give reassurance that there is no need to 'stop' the mind – just to let it be and not identify with it.

4. Rule of life and practice between sessions. A good initial practice is to encourage presencing in the body and the senses – for example, walking in nature, conscious eating, touching, looking, hearing. Just a pause a couple of times a day to notice sensory experience is helpful. They might also include stilling and grounding in the body (feet and breath) as part of their daily prayer rhythm.

5. Self-observation and 'examen'. As soon as people experience an aspect of the Divine – whether it is peace or joy or stillness or simple gratitude, we encourage them to notice what it feels like in body, heart, and mind, and the effect of this as they inhabit and receive it. They will then be in a position to notice this as 'state of being'. It can be helpful to give it a name (e.g. 'peace') and notice what it is like to move in and out of it this state. Having 'found' this quality, a useful work is a daily self-reflection on it. This is not trying to grasp after the state or 'achieve it', it is just to cultivate awareness. For example: (i) 'When was my "peace" most present to me today, even if only slightly, and what was it like when it was?'; (ii) 'When was the opposite true; when was I most "caught", and what was it that triggered me?'

This is a powerful practice to establish in someone's rule, and is central to the conscious work of presencing – similar to the Ignatian 'Examen'. It has no other purpose than to refine our attention. If it is sustained for a few weeks, it develops the capacity to 'self-observe' – which is noticing in the moment that our peace is being stolen. We are then free to pause, breathe, and choose, or pray, to find a different response. If we find there is a long period of absence, we just stay curious with absolutely no self-judgment. No 'why am I so useless at this?' or 'what is wrong with me?' Just: 'How interesting – I was in it last month and this month it has completely gone. I wonder what might be behind that…? Was there *any* time when it was there? What is this telling me?' This can, of course, be done as a prayer: 'Lord, what are You showing me?'

Presencing and attention (Chapter Five)

Much of what supports the basic 'work' in Chapter Five has already been covered. Our role here is encouraging the 'becoming aware of what you are aware of' – whether in emotional, mental, somatic, or spiritual experience. As a director, you soon notice which aspect of someone's experience is less accessible than others, and you can give them practices to strengthen this (acknowledging it will be neither easy nor 'natural' to do so!). The simplest practice for this is a conscious pause, three or four times a day, just to ask, 'What am I aware of right now?' and to check in with their 'centres' – especially their least favoured one.

Another helpful attention practice is 'morning pages', where directee just fills a page with freeform writing of whatever crosses their consciousness first thing in the morning, with the instruction not to read it until weeks have passed, if at all. As they do, they can play with writing from heart and gut (and even soul!) as well as head and imagination.

The main work of this phase is learning to attend to the Mystery – to emanations and intimations of the Divine, in themselves and in others. Obviously, if people have come with some pressing issue which is overwhelming their attention, then this may not be possible. But this in my experience is by far the most important building block at this stage. Once people have tuned in to their capacity to 'be still and know', the next thing is the noticing 'that I am God' (as in Psalm 46).

This is a gentle work, but so significant – to be done with sensitivity and an honest reverence for inner experience. Some people who have mystical or unitive experiences, however beautiful, can find them discombobulating – even to the extent of willing to forget them. They see them as a disruption to the functional mind and everything it has learned about what is 'real'. One of the greatest gifts we give, especially to those with strong, but often 'buried', contemplative awareness, is the reassurance that they are not 'mad' – that there is indeed a rich inner life, an experience of being, alongside and coterminous to our daily experience of functional reality. The Christian Gospels are explicit about this. It is what Christ calls 'the kingdom'. We *can* experience this and, when we do, it disrupts our certainties. So, the more gently we do this, helping people gradually to notice, and trust, their 'intimations of immortality' as Wordsworth calls them, the less disruptive and more readily integrated their awakening will be to the Divine Mystery at work in their lives. We could call this strengthening the soul, though it is really strengthening belief in the functional mind that this inner life is real and trustworthy.

A very useful activity to prime this is the 'Memoria Dei' exercise described in Chapter Five, with our role being to help the directee notice what their somatic heart experience is as they do it. With this as a living memory, we can invite people between sessions to notice hints of God, the Mystery, the Beyond, and how they experience them. Again, it is important they do this as an act of pure reflection and curiosity, not a personal quest to 'discover God'.

A simple self-reflection, or 'examen', can support this. For example, 'When was I most aware of any hint of the Divine today, if at all? How? What was it like?' and 'When did I feel most distant from the Divine today? What seemed to trigger me into that?' Over time, this will sharpen their attentiveness to the Divine Presence (or felt absence).

It is quite possible, as a director, that in this work you will find yourself holding for, and in, more direct 'unitive' encounters with your directee. Your own somatic noticing and 'field awareness' become more important in this. For example, I may find myself in a Memoria Dei exercise feeling a welling up in the deep belly and/or a feeling of light flaring upward from the heart into the mind – often indicators in my experience of the presence of Joy. Or I may also feel the tangible presence and substance of Love – perhaps as a 'strong softness' on the skin, or expansion in the heart, or as a colour, say, a blue/lilac wafting silky material, or a 'melting' and 'melding' in head, heart, or body. Whatever the experience, you can use your own experiential awareness to direct the directee's attention to this (having checked internally that it is not your memory or projection). This could be as open as, 'What are you feeling?' or 'What are you sensing?' Or it could be slightly more directive. 'Are you sensing anything in the atmosphere right now?' Sometimes, when I am more confident that something is present, I will be as direct as to say, 'I am finding my awareness being drawn down into my belly, are you sensing anything down there?'

If they do discern somatic (e.g. warmth) or emotional (e.g. joy) experience, we invite them to presence in it by asking questions around: 'Where are you feeling this? What is it like? Colour? Texture? Substance? Movement and flow?' This is by far the best opportunity to help them practise the process of somatic enquiry that will become so important in the more challenging work of 'transformation in the heart' that we will explore shortly. Since this enquiry is into the experience of the Divine, it feels safe, illuminating, empowering – if a little strange!

Using our own prayerful discernment, we invite them literally to 'drop' awareness into whatever they are experiencing and to 'soak in it' or 'inhabit it'. If it is an experience of joy, I tend to invite people to travel against the flow, otherwise joy tends to flood upwards and dissipate. Dropping down into the source of joy can be a very profound experience – the source of a 'spring of living water welling up to eternal life' (see John 4:14).

The purpose of this presencing is to fully experience *and receive* what is at work within. Always, there is a choice to receive or to reject and squander. Always, where the Divine is present, there will be a gentle voice saying, 'Do you want this?' Probably, because it is so gentle and natural, people may just move on and say, 'Well, that was nice – now what?' So, we invite them to 'abide':

- 'So, this is joy... What is it like to be in the presence of joy?'
- 'How does joy want to flow within you? What happens if you let it?
- Where is the Lord/Divine/Christ in all this? What is being shared/communicated?
- Where is there invitation to receive? What is it like when you do?'

The result can be a growing awareness that the Divine is actually *this* close... a brief re-membering away. This kind of experience can start to form the new 'centre of gravity' that I spoke of in earlier chapters, so learning to attune and collaborate with it is a fundamental task of spiritual direction. As directors, we help most simply by holding people in it, if only for a few seconds more than they might do themselves. We might view this in the light of the closing verses of Revelation: 'Come... take [*receive*] the free gift of the water of Life' (Revelation 22:17, my addition). To the functional mind, this has no relevance, and it will want to move on. But with help, people come to re-cognise that they are more than they 'think'. They can be present to their essential self, 'made in the image of God' (see Genesis 1:26).

Once people have confidence in this process of enquiry into the inner life and, hopefully, the sensitivity to notice that Divine is as present 'in here' as 'out there', they will be ready to presence and enquire into some of the more emotionally and ontologically challenging 'transformings' that are also at work in the heart. This is the invitation we framed in Chapter Six: 'Don't be afraid of the dark.'

Transformation and the work of the heart (Chapter Six)

This is sensitive work, the transforming of unprocessed experience, sometimes deep hurt, and the egoic 'patterning' that has arisen to protect and enable the self to function in the world – a world (and possibly even a 'God') which, as a result, may be viewed as untrustworthy or even hostile. This work is referenced in the Bible as the 'purification' of the heart: 'Create in me a clean heart, O God, and renew a steadfast spirit within me' (Psalm 51:10). In this, again, we recognise our complete dependence on the Divine.

It is harder work because of the pain and patterning that gets triggered. We want people to feel safe and to reach out to help. The temptation to rely on 'our own nets' is therefore stronger. We should also recognise this is the territory of therapy/counselling, and we will need to be clear about our boundaries. We may recommend people access therapy if appropriate alongside their direction or pause direction if it is confusing for a client to be in multiple holdings. (In my experience, there is a healthy complementarity. Therapy can be important in opening up new layers of the ego and unconscious to the 'inner work' of spiritual direction.) However we contract, the Divine will not be so bound and will act as therapist too – transformationally liberating people from past hurts, blocks, and 'stuckness'.

Here, the 'don't be afraid of the dark' theme comes to the fore. Having accessed the recollected state, grounded in sensation in the body and gratitude in the heart, this is the work of presencing and enquiry into 'difficult' emotions, such as doubt, despair, anger, sadness, loneliness, abandonment, or emptiness. It is important only to engage in this when someone is ready and willing to 'go there'.

If a strong emotion arises (which a person may still instinctively want to repress), we can invite them to allow it and to be attentive to the experience. This is an invitation to 'release' the emotion and the past event that has triggered it – ideally using their somatic noticing as a grounded way of doing so:

> 'Where are you feeling this?' (e.g. chest); 'What does it feel like in there?' (e.g. hard rock).
>
> Having accessed this, we work as before, inviting them to feel inside it: 'What is it like, temperature, texture etc? What is around it or beneath it?'
>
> 'What starts to happen as you just allow it to be here? What is arising with it?'
>
> 'What else is present? Is there an intelligence in it? Where is the Divine/the Lord?'

If people feel safe enough, this enquiry into their 'darkness' can be powerfully transformational. I have spoken about this in the chapter and won't repeat it here, but the effect of presencing can be that the 'containing' sensation ('rock', 'hard', 'cold', 'tight', 'knotted', 'twisted') eases and the energy in flow beneath can release – this can be an essential quality or a virtue, such as hope or courage, or the direct work of the Divine.

Sometimes, strong emotion when welcomed will take us back to earlier trauma, and the surfacing of a part of ourselves that is trying to protect us, e.g. a young child frightened of a father's anger or disapproval. This can provide the opportunity for a conversation between these parts and an integration, releasing the soul-life locked away in the protective part. But we are always careful to let it be their conversation, not intruding in any way – except to invite them to notice how and where the Divine may be present.

As directors, we trust that if this has surfaced and someone wants to stay in it, the Divine will be at work. We will often sense this somatically ourselves, which further settles us and them. This implies that, whatever arises, we stay with it.

> 'Deep calls to deep' can be a guiding principle – i.e. enquiring 'what lies beneath' what they are experiencing and allowing what wants to flow within from the Divine indwelling.

This can be a long work, and old fears and habits will resurface. But once people have learned to trust that they can be with this, welcome it, and allow it to be transformed or integrated, they can form a stronger centre of gravity from which to self-observe and unhook from old patterns. This can be experienced as a huge release.

Spiritual formation and becoming (Chapter Seven)

It is in this broader 'journey of the soul' that a spiritual director, or soul friend, has such an important part to play. It is very hard to take ourselves through some of these transitions without help. It likely that people will seek you out as a director when they find themselves in such times – maybe a sense of their old religious life starting to feel 'hollow' or 'dry', or a sense of disorientation or disillusionment at old patterns and relationships. These are sometimes referred to as 'ego-alien' times, when habits and assumptions are challenged, either by the complexity of life without or a stirring of the soul within.

One thing we can immediately provide as directors is the reassurance that this is not 'abnormal', that there is 'nothing wrong with them', and that the feelings they may be experiencing, such as disillusionment, doubt, hollowness in prayer, even loss of 'faith', are all natural stages in any evolving journey. Feelings are just feelings, and we can trust and enquire into them, holding fast to the principle of welcoming all experience as food for growth, not trying to deny them or manage them away.

PRESENCING AND SPIRITUAL DIRECTION

One key theme in the 'soul-journey' is the increasing need to 'surrender' and 'trust'. As a general rule, I find the mind is usually the last faculty to 'catch up' with what is already well advanced in the deeper parts of the being. This is possibly what Paul is onto in Romans 12 when he highlights the re-newing of mind. So, our capacity to help people open the mind can be important here. This is enhanced, as I have indicated, by prayer for the 'illuminating' of the mind following depth work.

This can be done somatically by inviting people to sense into how and where the mind is 'containing' or striving to 'figure it out' and inviting them just to 'let go'. This can be felt as a pressure in or around the skull. Consciously relaxing this can enable the functional mind to let go and the 'new mind' that Paul describes to open. As in Paul's own story, we may need to help people hold in a place of vulnerable, 'blind' not-knowing until the new knowing can emerge. The sign it has will be a visible 'lightness' and a release into freedom. Some people have described this as an 'opening of the top of the head' or an expansion of consciousness.

Helping them notice what it is like to be in 'this mind' is important. Old cognitive patterns return, and people will literally have no memory of what they have accessed. It can take time before people transition into a more permanent 'new self'. As I said in Chapter Five, these different selves can live alongside for many years. We can help people notice, and choose, which one is 'running the show'. This can be a useful self-reflection between sessions: 'When was I most/least present in my true self this week, and what was it like?'

Related to this is the importance of noticing and welcoming 'resistance' as the ego fights back and refuses to 'go there' or surrender. The same principle applies, which is to welcome it and gently hold people there, in the various forms I have described in this book. Resistance is the 'base metal' in the alchemy of transformation because it helps surface patterns that may well have gone unnoticed – a feature of resistance which thrives in the dark.

Examples of resistance might be:

- Preferring to stay at a cognitive, discursive level and not to want to go into prayer and presencing

- Diverting into 'disembodied' states such as imagination ('I am getting a picture of'), or the superego ('I should...'), or scriptural 'instruction', ('the Bible says...')
- Doing and saying things to 'please' the director
- 'Forgetting' powerful and important insights that have arisen in previous sessions
- 'Sticking' in patterns that no longer serve and re-presenting these in a different guise each session

There is nothing wrong in any of these per se, but over time we come to recognise when an individual is using these to divert, and we gently bring them back: 'I sense we have been here before...'; 'What are you actually feeling right now?'

Relationships (Chapter Eight)

Most of our significant transitions will involve others. Helping people notice and pay attention to key relationships in their journey is self-evidently important. But there is so much variety in this that there is little I can highlight here, except perhaps the following:

- During times of transition to notice relationships and patterns of connection that are no longer serving and to help people be with these bravely and compassionately. Sensing into 'truth in the heart' (see Psalm 51) is particularly important here – also the discerning of emotions that are arising from imbibed expectations and perceived 'needs' of others, e.g. 'not wanting to disappoint' someone
- Helping people prayerfully notice and welcome the 'people of peace' they are being 'sent' at transitional stages in their journey, or people they are 'being drawn to', and helping them discern what is really at flow in these relationships
- Helping people notice and presence in relationships they are either 'clinging onto' or 'holding back from' in some way. This can reveal deeper childhood patterning that may be wanting to be released

Working with different experiences and types of 'love' is huge here, warranting a book in itself. Suffice it to say that when love arises, so also does the opportunity to presence in it and experience its true substance. This can be very powerful in distinguishing between the energy of human 'eros' and the force of unconditional love, *agape*. Again, this will involve heart-presencing and helping people welcome what arises. The experience of Divine Love at work within will often be the transforming power in the soul-journey, which, as I describe in Chapter Five, is a journey into greater and greater capacity for Love. We can help people 'let flow' and 'let go' into this, learning to recognising that 'we do not have Love, Love has us'.

Just as with the mind, it takes time for the 'new heart' to come more permanently online. Old patterning kicks in and 'catches the heart'. It can take years and deep surrender to develop a patient heart able to recognise that everything it is yearning for it already has – and to allow this quietly and generously to 'flow into being'. Our role as directors in this is often one of helping people re-member and re-access the 'bigger Love' within, perhaps presencing in their 'thirst,' as the psalmist describes in Psalm 42.

Presencing and prayer (Chapter Nine)

This takes us to the very core of our work as directors, which is helping people come into their connection, or communion, with the Divine and then get out of the way. The core premise of this book is that the Divine Presence is always present, seeking to be in communion with us to help us live 'life to the full'. But we forget this, and our response to our experience is to construct a false ego-narrative about who we are and what is 'real' or 'true'. In the Old Testament this would probably be referred to as an 'idol'.

The fundamental precept of this presencing-based approach therefore is that *the Divine Presence can be experienced and 'known', or rather re-membered*. Not only that but the Divine *wants* to be experienced and known. But this can only be through faculties that are 'pure'. By this I mean capable of receiving and purely embodying – rather than, however subtly, trying to grasp or possess, as part of the ego's project to 'create ourselves in our own image'. As soon as that occurs, the Divine Presence, in respect for our sovereign will, desists: 'By love he can be grasped and held, but by thought, neither grasped nor held.'[3] This is very subtle and often unconscious. But if we are sensitive in prayer, we can feel the shift in the spiritual energy as we try to grab at God's meanings and 'plans'. This is where spiritual direction is at its most helpful because it is actually very difficult to discern between 'my thoughts and your thoughts' (see Isaiah 55:8). We help people develop this sensitivity by helping them attune to their experience of Presence (being careful not to impose ours).

This means that constantly in the process of direction we help people in:

- Releasing egoic patterning in body, heart, mind, helping people 'let go' and open
- Encouraging active presencing – sensing, feeling, opening, trusting, offering, receiving, asking, listening…
- Bringing their attention to how they are noticing aspects of the Divine – in areas less prone to cognitive and emotional distortion; soul, body, deeper heart, higher mind
- Helping them learn, in body, heart, and soul more than mind, what it is like to be in this connection and how to 'surrender' and receive what is flowing
- Remembering and prayerfully 'sealing' what has been deposited
- Helping them establish intentions and daily patterns to 'live and work' as much as is humanly possible from, for, and in this quality of connection

Many people, and Christians in particular I think, have a wariness of opening up to inner experience that is unfamiliar – we don't know what we are letting in. There is a wisdom in this, which is why prayers for protection and guidance are so important. But I have always thought that this shows a limited faith in the omnipotent, omniscient, omnipresent Divine in whom we 'live and move and have our being' (Acts 17:28). John speaks directly to this and the following words are ones we can and probably must come to trust as directors: 'The gatekeeper opens the gate for him, and the sheep listen to his voice. He calls his own sheep by name and leads them out. When he has brought out all his own, he goes on ahead of them, and his sheep follow him because they know his voice. But they will never follow a stranger; in fact, they will run away from him because they do not recognise a stranger's voice' (John 10:3–5).

Our role, therefore, is to be a prayerful friend of the lonely 'gatekeeper' inside each person trying to decide what it is safe to open to. This, particularly when their egoic patterning is involved, is very difficult to do on their own – they need someone to help discern. But once the gate is open and the voice is 'known', we are no longer needed.

So, in the gathered, self-recollected state that we have been cultivating, with our awareness as awake as we can manage, we invite people to attend to their experience.

I wondered at this point whether to describe some of the many (and sometimes seemingly consistent) ways in which people I have accompanied have sensed, felt, heard, seen the Presence of God, but I will not. To do so is to invite the risk of people seeking to 'attain' the same, rather than trusting emergence, or judging whether their own experience 'measures up'. The best guidance, I believe, is to presence deeply in the impulse or 'longing' that has the person reaching out and seeking – to 'live in the question' as Rilke put it, and then to be attentive to all their inner experience – particularly their somatic experience, which is the least prone to distortion (though not wholly so).

As we help people attend to their own experience, we can also offer ourself 'as instrument' attending to the potential resonance of their experience in us. If our state is 'clean' and purely offered to the 'work', we become a 'mirror' or an 'amplifier' to help them notice – for where 'two or three are gathered, I am with you' (see Matthew 18:20). The pattern of the encounter is therefore a stream of gentle questioning, reflecting back, and silent presencing – helping people, notice, 'abide', receive, and respond.

> 'What are you noticing/aware of/sensing/feeling?'
>
> 'Where are you sensing/feeling this?'
>
> 'How are you sensing/feeling it? Does it have colour/temperature/substance/movement/weight?'
>
> 'What is happening as you give it your attention?'

'How is it flowing? Where from... to...? What happens as you follow the flow?'

'What happens if you just "allow" this... sink into it... soak it in?'

'Where/how are you sensing any invitation in this? How do you want to respond?'

'I am getting a sense of something happening in my (belly/heart/limbs)... are you aware of anything there?'

If people answer, for example, 'Just a feeling of peace,' you can simply reflect back, '"Just" peace...? What is it like just to stay with that for a few moments?' and invite them into enquiry. For example: 'What does that peace feel like? Where is it? How are you experiencing it in sensation?'

And follow the enquiry...

'What happens if you presence in it for a few moments? Where and how is it flowing?'

'Where else are you noticing this peace? What is it like in your limbs? Your head?'

'As you sense into the "substance" of this peace, is it within you or around you?'

'You may want to get curious... Where are "you" in all this? What is inside? What is outside?'

'What is happening as you are noticing all this?'

> 'What else is arising? What happens as you presence your awareness in that?'
>
> 'Are you sensing any invitation arising in this?'
>
> 'How do you want to respond?'

And, using whatever words seem most to 'fit' their experience of the Divine (e.g. the Lord, God, the Bigger Love, the greater Presence, Christ, the Holy Spirit, Divine Father/Mother...

> 'Where are you sensing the presence of *the Divine* in this?'
>
> 'How (or where) is *the Divine* Present?'
>
> 'What happens as you allow yourself to be fully with *the Divine*?'
>
> 'What is at flow between you? Is anything being communicated? Verbally or non-verbally?'
>
> 'How do you want to respond? What do you want to say?'
>
> 'How is the *the Divine* responding? Replying?'
>
> 'What is it like to wholly receive this? What is happening within you?'
>
> 'Is there anything you are being invited to let go of?
>
> 'How do you want to respond? What happens when you do?'
>
> 'What are you being invited to remember from this encounter?'

> 'What does it feel like? What is being given you, if anything, to help you remember?'

We could go on, but hopefully this is clear. Written like this, it sounds like a fearsome interrogation, but just a few of these questions could take a whole hour, with extended periods of silence to allow the directee to be wholly present in the encounter. The focus of all our 'direction' is helping them purely to attend to their inner experience and to the Presence of the One they are in encounter with.

Without us holding them in it in this way, the functional mind grabs at fragments of the experience and seeks to restore control by making sense of it, often in an excited confirming of something it feels it 'knows' or is looking for. This will always be limiting, if not distorting. So, for as long as they need, or can bear, we help people stay in their direct experience, just letting it be as it is.

As the encounter draws to a close, we can follow Merton's process with some gentle questions to help the process of 'percolating'. Here is another selection by way of an indication:

> 'Just take a few moments to notice what it feels like to be you in this here and now...'
>
> 'Maybe just take in who this "you" really is... how the world looks from this place...'
>
> 'Notice, if you can, what it is like as your more habitual patterning returns... Experiment with the awareness and recognition of moving between these states, between these versions of yourself.'
>
> 'What is it like as you gently move your body? What does your body most want to do?'
>
> 'What about your mind... what does it feel like? Let's pray, shall

> we, for any "illumination" from this experience into your usual mind – just surrendering and noticing anything it is being invited to receive or remember. Notice what it is like to allow this.'
>
> 'So, returning to some of the things you were raising at the start of our session, how do they look from here?'
>
> 'How might you be being invited to see them differently?'
>
> 'What is happening to your state as you re-engage with these things?'
>
> 'Where and how is *the Divine* present right now?'
>
> 'What do you want to retain from this as you go back to your life? How will you keep this in your awareness?'
>
> 'What do you want to say, or pray, as we close?'
>
> 'How is *the Divine* responding?'

So, every spiritual direction session in this approach *is* prayer – two people 'gathered' in the Presence of the One who is always present. If we approach it *as* prayer, we equip people also to develop their awareness of what life as prayer could and might look like.

Helping people strengthen their life and practice of prayer is one of the main fruits of direction – again, without any quest for perfection or the pursuit of particular 'results', just the simple principle of 'becoming living sacrifice'. The practices we choose to use in the direction sessions are ones we can encourage people to adopt in their own life and prayer – presencing and pausing to attend to their experience with a gentle enquiry ('Where are You, Lord..?') and a capacity and willingness to open to the Divine and let flow happen.

It is inevitably, as Christ's words about 'gathering' tell us, harder for the directee to do this on their own – distraction is omnipresent (so we do not encourage people to 'fight' distraction, just to notice it and then return). But from their experience in these direction encounters, we start to help people be with the Divine in the way the Divine is being with them – and to be constantly seeking 'The Divine Help' in all they are in.

Gradually, an expansion, in surrender and love, will occur. It is nearly always subtle. (Dramatic movements in the life of prayer are often followed by dramatic rebounds!) People will only notice after some time that the 'pattern' of their lives is being gradually transformed – a little more peace and gentleness; a touch more patience, goodness, and kindness; more faithfulness, trust, and 'self'-control; a few more moments of love and joy...

As we help people with their prayer life, we honour the same principle that underpins all this work. Their experience is their experience. It is neither right nor wrong, it just is. So, we begin there, whatever it may be. I say this because it is not uncommon, as John of the Cross and many others have explored, for us to experience 'dryness', 'absence', 'darkness', in the journey of the life of prayer (even pain, shame, and horror as we open our heart to the Divine Heart and the suffering of humanity – and our own part in this). I hope, given all we have been saying here, that it is enough to say that the Divine is present in that too. All we are being invited to do is 'stay... watch... pray.' That is enough. But of course, we all need help with this. That is the greatest joy of serving as a spiritual director.

Presencing and discernment (Chapter Ten)

Finally, we come to one of the most fundamental aspects of direction, and one which the central scripture of this book, Romans 12, points directly towards – discerning the Will of God. This may be, for example, a key decision or a sense of 'calling' or invitation to change. Our work in a presencing-based approach to this can include any of the following principles:

- Helping directees 'gather' into the recollected state; discernment can only happen when we are fully present
- Encouraging and refining their questions and attending to the energy and emotion that arises – then presencing and enquiring into this, light or dark

- Being aware of the human tendency to express an emerging change on the inside, a change in being, in terms of a change in doing. So, we encourage people to sense into the underlying energy of change, presenced in heart and body. From here they can discern between the more compulsive energy of our egoic patterning (i.e. 'driven') and the energy of our 'being' and the greater 'Being' (Will) (i.e. 'drawn'). It does not mean that the egoic energy is 'wrong', it is just being aware so they can choose
- The Ignatian teaching about not making significant decisions whilst in a state of 'desolation' is relevant here. Our process is to help the directee access and surrender to the 'consoling' Presence and to make decisions in 'percolation' from there
- In this area in particular, the constant seeking of the Divine becomes paramount – 'Where and how is God present with you/to you in this? How are you experiencing it? Where? How do you know it is the Divine? What is being communicated to you, if anything?'
- So often, particularly when people come to us with the need or desire to 'discern' their way forward in big transitions in life, the answer from the 'still small voice' of the Divine will be 'wait', 'trust Me', 'I am with you', 'You will know when you know'. As the director, you will sense the presence of the Divine in these moments of communion and can help the directee listen, receive, and trust that this is enough, and they are enough

The worrying mind is always trying to anticipate, so we encourage people to sit in their deeper knowing, presencing in belly and heart and to help sense into the 'peaceful strength' that I referenced from Merton in this chapter. Allowing this strength to arise and have its way and can be the transforming quality here. Quite often this will resolve itself into a peaceful resolution in the belly: 'This is it.' If so, it can be helpful to invite people to remember this clarity as an embodied knowing. As they proceed, they will have it as a litmus test to keep prayerfully sensing into – 'This is it, this is not it.' This is something we can hold as a thread to review in future sessions.

This brings us to the content of Chapter Eleven, sustaining presence, which I will not comment on, as I have covered this already in my suggestions for the 'in-between' work that I have been making in each of the sections above.

Suffice it to say that every spiritual direction encounter should contain some time for checking in around people's experience of their ongoing practice – their prayer, examen, and other intentions.

The Experience of The Spiritual Director

As a footnote to this chapter, we should probably recognise that our own experience as a director is of course something we can and must be present to as we accompany others. I have spoken already about the 'resonant' aspect of this – 'self as instrument'. If, through our own contemplative practice, we have learned to be attentive to the Divine Presence, then we will sense when others are 'present to the Presence'. This becomes a very important source of guidance for us while our directee is sensing into their experience. If we are not feeling and sensing it too, we should at least be curious. It is not that we have any greater wisdom, knowing, or sensitivity. It is just simply noticing when there is resonance and when not and enquiring into this.

This implies a constant attentiveness to our listening and sensing, both within ourselves and in the 'field' of presence that enfolds us and the directee. We are attentive to our own biases and blocks too, as these will inevitably surface, and allow ourselves to be drawn into ever greater surrender around these. Obviously, supervision is a very important part of this. One temptation I know too well is to think we have learned how to experience and 'know' God – we constantly have to surrender this. We may think we have questions that 'work' and as soon as we do (hopefully!), we will experience the disappointment of them 'not working'. All our knowing, inasmuch as is possible, is surrendered. Instead, we allow words and questions to arise, almost instinctively, particularly as we enter the 'presencing' phase of the encounter. If we are properly presenced, we will feel it in the 'field' when we assume too much control or direction ourselves – maybe, for example, an experience of a contraction or a narrowing and a different energy arising. We start to become much more aware of ourselves and our clumsiness (with self-acceptance, not self-judgment!). So will the directee, and we can give them full permission to say so… 'What are you doing here?'

In my experience, it is almost impossible to be in spiritual direction with someone and not be changed and opened further myself. This is part of the Grace of the Work – we are just witnesses and fellow travellers along the way. I remember only last week being in direction and a vast space opening up in which we were both astounded to be present, and I felt prompted to acknowledge as I stayed in my 'holding' of the process, 'Please don't infer from anything I am saying that I have any idea what is going on. I am following, just as much as you are.' The blind leading the blind is not necessarily a bad adage in this work!

Merton, as ever, has a straightforward wisdom around this: 'We should never presume to preach God to others as we find Him in ourselves.'

I will leave the last word to Merton in this chapter – on the sheer joy and privilege of this 'work' of witnessing.

> *It is beautiful to see God working in souls... It is beautiful to see God's grace working in a soul. The most beautiful thing about it is to see how the desires of the soul inspired by God so fit in and harmonise with grace that holy things seem natural to the soul, seem to be part of its very self... that marvellous simple spontaneity in which His life becomes perfectly ours and our life His, and it seems absolutely inborn in us to act as His children and to have His light shining in our eyes. Dear God, I love You so much. Please make Your light shine in souls.'* [4]

AFTERWORD

*Home is where one starts from. As we grow older
The world becomes stranger, the pattern more complicated
Of dead and living...
We must be still and still moving
Into another intensity
For a further union, a deeper communion
Through the dark cold and the empty desolation,
The wave cry, the wind cry, the vast waters
Of the petrel and the porpoise. In my end is my beginning.*

T.S. ELIOT[1]

Always, we begin again.

ST BENEDICT

THE CLOSING LINES from Eliot's poem above point us as only poetry can to the patterns of unfolding that I have been attempting to document in this book – the paradox, perhaps, that our greatest work is one of surrender. 'It is finished,' Christ breathes on the cross, as one body dies and another flows into life.

PRESENCING AND SPIRITUAL DIRECTION

Our preceding chapters have explored two essential qualities of the spiritual life. The first is an 'awake' attention – the capacity to see with clear eyes and an honest heart what is actually present. The second is this principle of 'active surrender' or 'living sacrifice' – presencing in the flow of 'deep calling to deep' and allowing yourself to receive and be transformed from deep within. In our end is our beginning. Daily conversion. Breath.

We have referenced James Finley's three questions, which provide a helpful guide for how we seek to live this wisdom – and support others in the same.

> 'How is it going waking up in your life and relationships?'
>
> 'How is it going surrendering to the Mystery that has intimately accessed your heart and brought you to this place so that it might transform you into itself?'
>
> 'How is it going allowing the answer to the second question to percolate up through the first?'

These summarise perfectly the process I have been expounding in this book in a way that we can, if we wish, deploy every day – and certainly in any more dedicated time of attending to our spiritual journey – possibly with the supporting presence of a spiritual director.

Home is where we start from. We begin always and in all things with a grounding and coming into our gathered state: breath and body, heart and soul and mind.

Then, we sense into our own direct experience as fully and honestly as we can, 'living the questions',[2] as Rilke puts it. The Benedictine principle of unconditional welcome is a lovely one to embody in this – letting everything be just as it is, light or dark, heavy or soft, angry or kind. I remember a spiritual mentor expressing this clearly and simply to me many years ago: 'God doesn't need us to be holy, or clever, or even good... just real.'

The only way is through. We dare to feel what is really here and let it yield its true substance to us. Beneath the pain or the buried trauma, within the loneliness or the aching care, beyond the agonising hope or unsatisfied yearning, something else is present. We realise that we are not alone, that there is a bigger force at work within us, arising, holding, healing, restoring, enlightening, inviting, softly, silently speaking: 'Let it be'; 'Let go'; 'Let Me'; 'Come'; 'Follow'.

As we yield, our attention can be drawn by the Spirit to the work that wants to be done within – this may be a freeing or healing from our old 'patterning' or it may be a new arising and expansion of being, 'transforming' or 'renewing' us, or both.

This is a precious space – a place of safety and trust that allows us to be honest, present, and vulnerable in our deepest selves, as well as with another. Likewise, the foundation for any director seeking to hold this space for others is the surrender of their ego and their availability to the Divine. So, the same work of presencing for directors is a prerequisite. This has the director make their own body 'living sacrifice', so they may almost literally be 'imprinted' by what the directee may share – and be purely with them, and God, in the holding of it.

As we have the courage to stay with our inner experience, however challenging, we find ourselves present with the Divine and to the possibility of intelligent 'receiving'. We may receive particular words, images, feelings, or sensations that have a 'rightness' to them and which have been given to us for what we find ourselves in. This is often accompanied by a feeling of peace and sometimes other 'fruits', such as love, joy, compassion, patience, and resolve. We may also even sense a deeper Will arising, a growing clarity about the music that wants to be played in the instrument of our embodied soul – 'Oh, this is what I am for...'

The result is a settling of our being and a sense of clarity about how and where the Divine is present with us in what we are in. Resisting the temptation to grasp at what is present, we allow it to 'percolate' – to quietly do what it is meant to do within us, subtly changing our seeing, thinking, choosing and doing, 'renewing the mind'. We do not even need to know what it is doing and sometimes it is better not to. We stay surrendered and allow ourselves to receive what is being 'deposited' within. The 'new self', as Paul calls it.

When the time is right, with a deep breath, we move gently and consciously back into our daily lives, noticing what it is like to put on our 'old life' again from this new place of being and begin to let it fit us, rather than us fit it.

However much we may want to cling onto the felt experience, or to re-experience it, we do not need to. We can, however, make a vow to stay awake and to re-member so that the work within us may continue and that later, when we need to, we can breathe into the place within where it lives and let it ground, centre, and re-mind us.

We may pray also for any illumination of our understanding that is needed, letting this arise into the mind, not 'reaching down' from functional head to try to 'make sense' of what has been happening.

We return to our lives with renewed intentions, and for a while allow them to flow from this place – until we forget and fall, or over-reach, again. We wake up. We return to our practice. We surrender. We begin again.

If we want to be brutally simple, this whole book can be reduced to ten words:

- Pause
- Still
- Breathe
- Ground
- Listen
- Notice
- Receive
- Trust
- Follow
- Abide

We may notice what we have been given to help us 'abide in the Vine'. One of the most obvious is the prayer Christ Himself gave us. If we take a good look at it, we can see it as a comprehensive invitation to become 'living sacrifice':

- 'Our Father in heaven' – recognising the true source of our being
- 'Hallowed be thy name' – gratitude for our existence, the Divine 'name in all the earth' (Psalm 8)
- 'Thy kingdom come' – surrender to the Greater Presence at 'Work' in all things, including us
- 'Thy will be done in earth as in heaven' – being present and available as channel of Will, Grace, Peace, Love
- 'Give us this day our daily bread' – receiving the 'food' of experience for our life, work, growth, and formation

AFTERWORD

- 'Forgive us our trespasses as we forgive those who trespass against us' – for all we do to ourselves and each other that is not in the Divine Will
- 'Do not let us be led into temptation but deliver us from evil' – asking for the Help to stay alert, and when we fail, the Grace to restore us

The first half of the prayer concerns the 'fully divine' (the first commandment) – our presence and availability to the Divine indwelling. The second half of the prayer concerns the 'fully human' (the second commandment) – our stepping vulnerably out into the world and its relationships, and our inevitable 'fall' and dependency on God.

All we are asked to do in this prayer is become present and open in heart, soul, body, mind; to notice as we do what comes up that is material within us that needs to be let go/transformed; to become fully available to receiving what is freely on offer – Life, Grace, and Will.

We could do worse than use this prayer each day as a conscious, wholly presenced work of letting go and opening ourselves to the Divine Presence at work within us. 'I will do whatever you ask in my name' (John 14:13).

Gradually, over time and in time, we find a more stable centre and learn to live from here – to 'put on the new self, created to be like God' (Ephesians 4:24). As we do so, we come to notice that something is arising within us, imperceptibly like the tide, filling us – a quiet, unstoppable, fulsome, free-flowing force, so much bigger, and gentler, than anything we could ever muster ourselves.

It is Love.
It is not a Love that we have, it is Love that has us.
In our end is our beginning.
Let's leave the last thought to Julian of Norwich:

> *If there is anywhere on earth a lover of God who is always kept safe, I know nothing of it, for it was not shown to me. But this was shown: that in falling and rising again we are always kept in that same precious Love.*[3]

Always, we begin again.

BIBLIOGRAPHY AND FURTHER READING

Books from a Christian perspective

Spiritual direction

Barry, W.A. and Connolly, W.J. *The Practice of Spiritual Direction* (Sydney: Harper Collins, 2012).

Benner, D.G. *The Gift of Being Yourself: The Sacred Call to Self-Discovery* (Downers Grove: IV Press, 2015).

Green, T.H. *When the Well Runs Dry: Prayer Beyond the Beginnings* (Notre Dame: Ave Maria, 2007).

Guenther, M. *Holy Listening: The Art of Spiritual Direction* (Plymouth: Roman and Littlefield, 1992).

Horsfall, T. *Mentoring For Spiritual Growth: Sharing the Journey of Faith* (Bible Reading Fellowship, 2008).

Marsh, R. *Imagination, Discernment and Spiritual Direction* (Oxford: Way Books, 2023).

Moon, G.W. and Benner, D.G. *Spiritual Direction and Christian Soul Care* (Illinois: Intervarsity Press, 2000).

Nouwen, H. *Spiritual Direction: Wisdom for the Long Walk of Faith* (New York: HarperCollins, 2006).

Pickering, S. *Spiritual Direction: A Practical Introduction* (Norwich: Canterbury, 2008).

Ruffing, J.K. *Spiritual Direction: Beyond the Beginnings* (New Jersey: Paulist Press, 2000).

Spiritual classics

Backhouse, H. (ed.), *The Cloud of Unknowing* (Hodder & Stoughton, 1985).

Brother Lawrence and Laubach, F., *Practising His Presence* (Christian Books, First Edition, 1973).

Brother Roger of Taizé, *Struggle and Contemplation* (New York: Seabury, 1974).

Finley, J. *Merton's Palace of Nowhere* (Notre Dame: Ave Maria, 1978).

Julian of Norwich (translated by Barry Windeatt), *Revelations of Divine Love* (Oxford: OUP, 2015).

Keating, T. *Open Mind, Open Heart* (New York: Bloomsbury, 1986).

Merton, J. *The Journals of Thomas Merton* (San Fracisco: HarperCollins, 1996–9).

Merton, T. *The Ascent to Truth* (London: Continuum, 1994).

Teresa of Avila, *The Interior Castle* (Ave Maria Press, 2007).

Thomas à Kempis, translated by Knott, *The Imitation Of Christ* (Fontana, 1963).

Contemporary spirituality

Barrett, M. *Crossing: Reclaiming the Landscape of Our Lives* (London: Darton Longman & Todd, 2001).

Bourgeault, C. *Eye Of The Heart: A Spiritual Journey into the Imaginal Realm* (Boulder: Shambhala, 2020).

Bourgeault, C. *The Heart of Centering Prayer: Nondual Christianity in Theory and Practice* (Boulder: Shambhala, 2016).

Bourgeault, C. *The Wisdom Jesus: Transforming Heart and Mind* (Boston: Shambhala, 2008).

Campbell, J. *In Search of Friendship: Lessons from a Monastic Tradition* (Farnham: Waverley Abbey Trust, 2022).

Cotter, J. *Psalms for a Pilgrim People* (Morehouse Publishing, 2008).

Cowley, I. *The Contemplative Minister: Learning to Lead from the Still Centre* (Abingdon: Bible Reading Fellowship, 2015).

Finley, J. *The Healing Path: A Memoir and An Invitation* (New York: Orbis Books, 2023).

Guite, M. *Faith, Hope and Poetry: Theology and the Poetic Imagination* (Farnham: Ashgate, 2012).

Harton, F.P. *The Elements of the Spiritual Life: A Study in Ascetical Theology* (London: SPCK, 1932).

Jameson, C. *Finding Sanctuary: Monastic Steps for Everyday Life* (London: Orion, 2006).

Jensen, R. *A Theology In Outline: Can These Bones Live* (New York: OUP, 2016).

Laird, M. *A Sunlit Absence: Silence, Awareness, and Contemplation* (New York: OUP, 2011).

Laird, M. *Into the Silent Land: The Practice of Contemplation* (New York: OUP, 2006).

Lusseyran, J. *And There Was Light: The Autobiography of a Blind Hero in the French Resistance* (Floris Books, 1985).

Nicholl, D. *Holiness* (London: Dartman Longman & Todd, 1982).

Nouwen, H. *In the Name of Jesus: Reflections on Christian Leadership* (New York: Dartman Longman & Todd, 1989).

O'Donohue, J. *Anam Cara: Spiritual Wisdom from the Celtic World* (London: Harper Collins, 2023).

Rohr, R. *Falling Upward: A Spirituality for the Two Halves of Life* (London: SPCK, 2012).

Rohr, R. *The Divine Dance: The Trinity and Your Transformation* (London: SPCK, 2016).

Rohr, R. *The Universal Christ: How a Forgotten Reality Can Change Everything We See, Hope For and Believe* (London: SPCK, 2019).

Scazzero, P. *Emotionally Healthy Spirituality* (Michigan: Zondervan, 2014).

Taylor, B. Brown, *An Altar in the World: A Geography of Faith* (HarperOne, 2009).

Books from a more general perspective

Almaas, A.H. *Facets of Unity: The Enneagram of Holy Ideas* (Boston: Shambhala, 1998).

Blakeley, C. and Blakely, K. *Leading With Love: Rehumanising the Workplace* (Routledge, 2022).

Brown, B. *Soul Without Shame: A Guide to Liberating Yourself from the Judge Within* (Boston: Shambhala, 1999).

Hawke, Red, *Self Observation: The Awakening of Conscience* (Arizona: Hohia, 2009).

Hawke, Red, *Self Remembering: The Path to Non-Judgmental Love* (Arizona: Hohia, 2015).

McGilchrist, I. *The Master and His Emissary: The Divided Brain and the Making of the Western World* (MC Escher Yale University Press, 2009).

Palmer, P.J. *Let Your Life Speak: Listening for the Voice of Vocation* (New Jersey: Jossey-Bass, 2024).

Plotkin, B. *Nature and The Human Soul: Cultivating Wholeness in a Fragmented World* (New World Library, 2008).

Psaris, J. *Hidden Blessings: Midlife Crisis as a Spiritual Awakening* (Sacred River Press, 2017).

Riso, D.R. and Hudson, R. *The Wisdom Of The Enneagram: The Complete Guide to Psychological and Spiritual Growth for the Nine Personality Types* (New York: Bantam, 1999).

Singer, M.A. *Living Untethered: Beyond the Human Predicament* (Oakland: New Harbinger, 2022).

Singer, M.A. *The Untethered Soul: The Journey Beyond Yourself* (Oakland: New Harbinger, 2007).

Welwood, J. *Journey of The Heart: Intimate Relationships and the Path of Love* (New York: Harper Collins, 1999).

Poetry

Nepo, M. *Reduced to Joy* (Berkeley: Viva Editions, 2020).

Eliot, T.S. *Collected Poems* (London: Faber & Faber, 2015).

Berry, W. *Collected Poems* (North Point Press, 1987).

ENDNOTES

Introduction
1. Wendell Berry, 'The Wild Geese.' In *The Country of Marriage*. (New York, NY: Harcourt Brace Jovanovich, 1973) p24.

Chapter One
1. See waverleyabbeycollege.ac.uk/waverley-integrative-framework

Chapter Two
1. James Joyce, *Dubliners* (Nielsen UK, 2024), p139.
2. Barbara Brown Taylor, *Leaving Church* (Canterbury Press, 2011), p64.
3. Richard Rohr, *Falling Upward: A Spirituality for the Two Halves of Life* (SPCK Publishing, 2013).
4. Rainer Maria Rilke, *Letters to A Young Poet* (Penguin Classics, 2012), p37.
5. Richard Rohr, *Falling Upward: A Spirituality for the Two Halves of Life* (SPCK Publishing, 2013), p100.

Chapter Three
1. Joshua Luke Smith, 'I am a temple', facebook.com/tearfund/videos/317012975690719/
2. Thomas Merton, *New Seeds Of Contemplation* (New Directions Books, 1949), p26.
3. *The Cloud of Unknowing and Other Works* (Penguin Classics, 2001).
4. Ibid.
5. Julian of Norwich (translated by Barry Windeatt), *Revelations of Divine Love* (Oxford: OUP, 2015), p74.

Chapter Four

1. Paul B. Badcock, 'The hierarchically mechanistic mind: A free-energy formulation of the human psyche'. discovery.ucl.ac.uk/id/eprint/10067315/5/1-s2.0-S1571064519300028-main.pdf (2019).
2. J. R. R. Tolkein, *The Lord of The Rings* (HarperCollins, 2009), p108.
3. Berrett-Koehler, *Theory U - Leading from the Future as It Emerges* (2016), p31.
4. Jacques Lusseyran, *And There Was Light: The Autobiography of a Blind Hero in the French Resistance* (Floris Books, 1985).

Chapter Six

1. Parker J. Palmer, *Let Your Life Speak: Listening for the Voice of Vocation* (Jossey-Bass, 2024).
2. Richard Rohr, *Falling Upward: A Spirituality for the Two Halves of Life* (SPCK Publishing, 2013).
3. Source unknown; widely attributed.
4. Parker J. Palmer, *Let Your Life Speak: Listening for the Voice of Vocation*, 25th-Anniversary ed. (San Francisco: Jossey-Bass/Wiley, 2024), introduction.
5. Rainer Maria Rilke, *Letters to a Young Poet*, Translated by M. D. Herter Norton, (W. W. Norton & Company, 1934).
6. Theresa of Avila, 'Christ Has No Body', stwilfridscowplain.co.uk/wp-content/uploads/2021/02/Christ-has-no-body-Teresa-of-Avila.pdf (accessed 2024).
7. Carl Jung, *Collected Works Vol. 6, Same Part II*, (Routledge & Kegan Paul London, 1971), p145.
8. *The Cloud of Unknowing and Other Works* (Penguin Classics, 2001), p37.

Chapter Seven

1. David Whyte, from 'The Sun' in *The House of Belonging* (Many Rivers Press, 1996).
2. Ram Dass, *Still Here: Embracing Aging, Changing, and Dying* (Riverhead Books, 2001), p4.
3. Jim Cotter, *Psalms for a Pilgrim People* (Morehouse Publishing, 2008).
4. Rainer Maria Rilke, 'Go to the Limits of Your Longing', from *The Book of the Hours: Love Poems to God* (Riverhead Books, 2005).
5. Mark Nepo, 'One String.' *Reduced to Joy*, 2015, pp17–18.
6. Bill Plotkin, *Nature and the Human Soul: Cultivating Wholeness and Community in a Fragmented World* (New World Library, 2008).
7. Jennifer Campbell, *In Search of Friendship: Lessons from a Monastic Tradition* (Farnham: Waverley Abbey Trust, 2022), p49.
8. Wm. Shakespeare, *Hamlet*, V.ii.

9. Daniel Ladinsky, *The Gift*, Penguin Compass (Arkana, 1999), p27.
10. Bill Plotkin, *Nature and the Human Soul* (New World Library, 2008), p383, 411.
11. Saint Benedict, (translated by T. Fry), *The Rule of St. Benedict in English (R1980)* (Liturgical Press, 1981).
12. Thomas Merton, *New Seeds of Contemplation.* (New York: New Directions, 1961).
13. Samuel Taylor Coleridge, *Biographia Literaria*, W. J. B. Owen ed. (Penguin Classics, 1996), p141.
14. Blakeley & Blakeley, *Leading with Love*, Ch.5 (Routledge, 2021).
15. Julian of Norwich (translated by Barry Windeatt), *Revelations of Divine Love* (Oxford: OUP, 2015), p74.
16. Thomas à Kempis, *The Imitation of Christ* (Ave Maria Press, 2005).
17. Barbara Brown Taylor, *An Altar in the World: A Geography of Faith* (HarperOne, 2009), pp12–13, 14, 15. Quoted on CAC blog: cac.org/daily-meditations/waking-up-to-god/ (accessed 21/3/24).

Chapter Eight

1. Ramakrishna Paramhansa, 'The Salt Doll', awakin.org/v2/read/view.php?tid=2556 (accessed 2024).
2. James Finley, *Merton's Palace of Nowhere* (Notre Dame: Ave Maria, 1978), p29.
3. Richard Rohr, CAC Blog, cac.org/daily-meditations/mirroring-the-divine-image-2018-12-24 (accessed 24/12/2018).
4. Thomas Merton, *New Seeds of Contemplation* (New Directions, 2007).
5. Jennifer Campbell, *In Search of Friendship: Lessons from a Monastic Tradition* (Farnham: Waverley Abbey Trust, 2022), p78.
6. Mark Nepo, *Reduced to Joy* (Viva Editions, 2020), p63.
7. Jennifer Campbell, *In Search of Friendship: Lessons From a Monastic Tradition* (Farnham: Waverley Abbey Trust, 2022), p17.

Chapter Nine

1. Gerard Manley Hopkins, *The Major Works* (Oxford World Classics, 2009), p39.
2. Frank C. Laubach, *Letters By a Modern Mystic* (SPCK, 2011).
3. Thomas Keating, *Intimacy with God: An Introduction to Centering Prayer* (CrossRoad Publishing, 2009).
4. Pete Greig, 24-7prayer.com/community/blog/2019/05/07/unwrapping-the-messiahs-singing-bowl (accessed 2024).
5. Thomas Merton, *A Search For Solitude* (HarperCollins, 1998).

Chapter Ten

1. Frank C. Laubach, *Letters By a Modern Mystic* (SPCK, 2011).
2. Wm. Shakespeare, *Hamlet*, V.ii.
3. Thomas Merton, *The Ascent to Truth* (Hollis and Carter, 1951), p186.
4. Julian of Norwich (translated by Barry Windeatt), *Revelations of Divine Love*, (Oxford: OUP 2015), p123.

Chapter Eleven

1. Richard Rohr, 'The Daily Meditations' (Center for Action and Contemplation, 4th March 2024).
2. Brother Lawrence, *The Practice of the Presence of God* (CreateSpace Independent Publishing Platform, 2014).
3. Gerard Manley Hopkins, The Major Works (Oxford World Classics, 2009), p39.
4. Richard Rohr, 'The Daily Meditations' (Center for Action and Contemplation, 3rd March 2024).
5. John Wimber, 'The Cross', vineyardchurches.org.uk/vineyard-vaults/the-cross (accessed 2024).
6. T.S. Eliot, *Collected Poems, Four Quartets* (London: Faber & Faber, 2015), p109.
7. Barbara Brown Taylor, Sophia Society podcast episode 58: sophiasociety.org/podcast/barbara-brown-taylor-becoming-human (accessed 2024).
8. T.S. Eliot, *Collected Poems, Four Quartets* (London: Faber & Faber, 2015), p77.

Chapter Twelve

1. William A. Barry and William J. Connolly, *The Practice of Spiritual Direction* (Bravo Ltd, 2009), p9.
2. Thomas Merton in James Finley, *Following The Mystics Through The Narrow Gate* (Center for Action and Contemplation, MP3).
3. H. Backhouse (ed.), *The Cloud of Unknowing* (Hodder & Stoughton, 1985).
4. Thomas Merton, *The Journals of Thomas Merton*, 'Entering the Silence', Entry for 9 November, 1948 (San Francisco: HarperColins, 1996), p243.

Afterword

1. T.S. Eliot, from 'East Coker' in *The Four Quartets* (Faber & Faber, 2001).
2. Rainer Maria Rilke, *Letters to A Young Poet* (Penguin Classics, 2012), p37.
3. Julian of Norwich, *Revelations of Divine Love*, (Penguin Classics 1998), p160.

APPENDIX A: COLLECTED STATE MEDITATION

Love the Lord your God with all your heart and with all your soul and with all your strength and with all your mind.

LUKE 10:27

ALWAYS BEGIN with an offering to God, e.g. 'May all my thoughts, words, actions, and intentions be directed purely to serving and glorifying You. And I ask, Holy Spirit, that You protect and guide me throughout this time of prayer.'

1. Relax the body

Sit with your feet on the floor, shoulder width apart, small of the back well supported in the chair, back upright and head level, eyes facing straight ahead. Start with a body scan relaxation. Bring your awareness out of your head and into your face. Relax cheeks, nose, jaw, neck, shoulders, arms, back, diaphragm, tummy, gut, groin, legs, feet... Just letting your awareness travel gently down your whole body. Just attending to your body, not trying to do anything except notice with an intention of relaxing and 'letting go'. Relaxing the small of the back fully into the chair and letting your arms and hands rest completely on your lap are good things to focus on. Also, as you relax your chest, free up your diaphragm, become aware of breathing from your tummy rather than your chest, just feeling your tummy rising and falling with the breath and letting breath be drawn all the way down as though it is filling your tummy and gut. Allow your body to become heavy, completely taken by gravity, so you are not doing any work yourself, just held by the chair and by the ground beneath your feet. Finish by bringing all your awareness into your feet, pressing your heels into the ground and feeling the presence/energy of the earth beneath you.

2. Come into sensation/body awareness

Hold your attention in your feet and then try to focus your awareness on the sensation in your feet – pick up the tingling of nerves in your skin, any sense of cool, warmth, the touch of your feet in your socks/shoes etc. If you can, allow that sensation to fill you upwards, gently up to your legs, into your lower body and solar plexus, then your hands and arms, up into your shoulders. Then let this awareness of sensation travel up to your face – mouth, lips, cheeks, temples, right to the crown of your head. Just hold awareness of sensation in your body for a short while, simply enjoying 'being in your skin'. Focus your awareness particularly on your hands and feet, which have so many nerve endings.

(As you get familiar with this, you should find you will be able to use this technique to quickly 'ground' yourself in the day-to-day. Simply by bringing awareness to sensation in your hands and your feet, you should find your 'centre of gravity' drop out of your head into your gut and become more aware of breath. This can still the mind, free you from worries or distracting thoughts, and enable you to recollect yourself. Softening the face can also similarly be very helpful when you are in tense or difficult conversations.)

You can pause the meditation at this point and just go to point 5 below or you can go deeper into your fuller being with points 3 and 4.

3. Come into the head

Then bring your awareness inside your head to a place just above or beyond thought. There is a place located right in the middle of the head, about level with the eyes and right between the ears, that is a 'still' place where you can just let your attention sit without being caught by your thoughts. From here you can just notice the ocean of thought ebbing and flowing around you, but do not attach to it any thoughts; just observe them and the vast expanse of mind. Enjoy the experience of being present to yourself as a thinking being – in the middle of your head. Then divide your attention, keeping half of it inside your head and returning half to your hands, feet, and face – experiencing yourself in thought and sensation.

4. Come into the heart

Then bring your awareness into the heart area, dropping down from the centre of your head through your throat and into your chest to a place right in the centre of your chest, an inch or so behind the base of your sternum. Again, just allow yourself to notice what is present in the chambers and expanse of the heart area, which stretches through the whole breadth and depth of the chest cavity, from the top of the sternum down to the solar plexus. Notice the movements of emotion and desire, lightness or darkness, emptiness or heaviness – anything present, but without attaching or entering into it in any way. Just, again, being aware of yourself as a feeling being, present in desire and emotion. Take a bit of time with your awareness right in the centre of your chest, just observing.

5. Come into the recollected/integrated state

To close the meditation, focus awareness onto your breath – in through your nose, up into the head, down into the chest/heart, pausing as you feel the air filling up your lungs, then feeling the energy in the air release through your whole body as you exhale. You can say words if you like when you breathe in/out, e.g. 'I/am' or 'I/love' or 'Be/still' as you breathe. Just breathe like this for 20 breaths or so and allow the stillness to fill you. Finally, let your awareness come back out to your body/skin, then expanding out into the room and the beyond... Let your closing thought/prayer be a simple one of gratitude to your Creator.

If you are able to practise this in the morning, it will steadily increase your ability to be present to God in your morning prayer and, during the day, to 'self-observe' and 'remember' and make more aware/positive/resourceful choices in the moment.

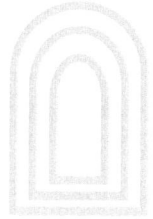

APPENDIX B: BODY SCAN

ENSURE THAT YOU will be undisturbed for the duration of your practice. Find a comfortable place to lie down, on the bed or on the floor, remembering that your intention is to foster awareness and wakefulness and not to fall asleep. Make sure that you will be warm enough and cover yourself with a blanket if necessary.

Close your eyes and focus for a while on the rising and falling of the breath in your body. This breath renews our life with every in-breath. It lets go of what is no longer needed with each out-breath. Feel the letting go as each out-breath exits the body. Feel the flowing of the entire breath throughout the body – riding the sensations like surfing a wave. Take a few moments to have a sense of your body as a whole, from head to toe, the outline of your skin, the weight of your body with the sense of gravity bearing down upon it. Notice the points where your body is in contact with the surfaces it rests upon.

Now bring your attention to the big toes of both of your feet and explore the sensations that you find here. Don't try to make anything happen – just feel what you are feeling. Gradually broaden your awareness to include your other toes, the soles of your feet, the other parts of your feet, and allow your feet to soften and relax. Imagine that your breath is moving down to your feet, and that your awareness is like a warm light, a shaft of sunlight allowing your feet to relax and be held in awareness.

Gradually broaden this light of awareness to include your ankles, calves, knees, and thighs, allowing the muscles to soften and become heavy. Imagine a sense of space in your joints and your muscles letting go of tension, falling away from the bones. Let your awareness include your buttocks and notice any holding of energy here. And again, bring the breath awareness into your legs, as if you could breathe into your legs, and broaden your awareness so you can hold the whole of your legs within it.

And gradually, in stages, allow the awareness to spread to your abdomen, lower and upper back, shoulders, rib cage and chest. Bring awareness to your spine, gently curving through your body, and the point at which it meets the skull. Have a sense of the solid frame of your body. Breathe awareness into each of these body parts – feeling the motion of the breath through the body. Bring your awareness down your arms and into your hands, fingers, fingertips. Notice the warmth and energy that is stored in the palms of your hands. Notice what the hands feel like at rest.

Gradually bring awareness to your head, neck, throat, and face, noting any tension held in the muscles around the forehead, around the eyes, the jaw, and the mouth. Notice how sensitive your face feels to the temperature of the air. Allow your face to soften with your awareness. Now bring awareness to the rest of the head: to the skull, scalp, and crown. Rest your attention at the crown for a while. Then simply scan down the body slightly more quickly than you came up and end at the base of the feet.

And now, bring your awareness back to your breathing and notice how the body tenses and relaxes as it rises and falls. Pay attention to the breath as it is felt in the body and try to maintain this awareness with an overall sense of your body – as if your whole body is breathing and held in awareness. Be aware of the quality of your experience and note any emotional tones present without judging them.

As you finish your practice, start by slowly moving the body, perhaps wriggling your toes, making sure not to jar yourself back into ordinary awareness. Turn over onto your side and gently lever yourself into a sitting position. Notice how you are feeling now. Give yourself a few minutes before you resume normal activity, remembering to carry bodily awareness forward with you into daily life as best you can.